431

D0982983

The Psychopath and Milieu Therapy
A Longitudinal Study

The Psychopath and Milieu Therapy
A Longitudinal Study

WILLIAM M. McCORD

Department of Sociology
College of the City of New York
New York, New York

With a Foreword by Milton Rokeach

ACADEMIC PRESS   1982

A Subsidiary of Harcourt Brace Jovanovich, Publishers

New York   London

Paris San Diego San Francisco São Paulo Sydney Tokyo Toronto

ACADEMIC PRESS, INC.
111 Fifth Avenue, New York, New York 10003

United Kingdom Edition published by
ACADEMIC PRESS, INC. (LONDON) LTD.
24/28 Oval Road, London NW1 7DX

Library of Congress Cataloging in Publication Data

McCord, William M.
    The psychopath and milieu therapy.

    Includes index.
    1. Antisocial personality disorders. 2. Milieu
therapy. I. Title. [DNLM: Psychopathology. 2. Milieu
therapy. 3. Longitudinal studies.   WM 100 P98933]
RC555.M29 1982   616.85'82   8218440
ISBN 0-12-482180-4

PRINTED IN THE UNITED STATES OF AMERICA

82 83 84 85   9 8 7 6 5 4 3 2 1

For my wife, Arline,
*who has put to rest some of my memories
of lonely strangers*

Contents

2
The Banality of Evil: "Normal Psychopaths" 37

II
The Detection of the Psychopath

3
From *Manie sans Délire* to Psychopathic "Life Styles": A Short History 67

Contents

IV
Changing Psychopaths

7
Treatment of Adult Psychopaths 187

8
Treatment of Child Psychopaths 207

9

The Wiltwyck–Lyman Project:
A Twenty-Five-Year Follow-Up
Study of Milieu Therapy 229

WILLIAM McCORD AND JOSÉ SANCHEZ

10

The Lonely Stranger, the Law,
and Public Policy 265

Foreword

Psychopathy is a mysterious, difficult-to-understand phenomenon because unlike other phenomena we might seek to understand—such as creativity, racism, being in love, or schizophrenia—it is well beyond the pale of our everyday intuitive or phenomenal experience. To make matters worse, we are unable to rely on psychopaths to inform us about their feelings and states because they do not possess the basic honesty, integrity, analytic ability, or insight to provide us with reliable or valid information about themselves. It is difficult to imagine a psychopath, for example, writing a book bearing the title "The Autobiography of a Psychopath" because such persons cannot conceive of themselves, or admit to themselves, that they are psychopaths. In attribution theory terms, they are incapable of taking responsibility for their own actions and, instead, attribute the causes of their behavior to external events rather than to such internal dispositions as egocentrism, lack of guilt feelings, or inability to control one's impulses.

Despite such obstacles, William McCord has succeeded in writing a comprehensive and systematic work on the nature and causes of psychopathy. He has gone to great lengths to observe psychopaths and has reviewed and assimilated the voluminous and multifaceted literature on the subject. Readers might wonder about a work on psychopathy written by one trained in sociology rather than psychology or psychiatry; the phenomenon appears at first glance to be mainly psychological or characterological in nature. But it will become increasingly clear to those who read this work that the psychopathic personality cannot be fully understood in individual terms alone, that social determinants must also be taken into careful account. Thus the literature that McCord draws on and appraises is one that spans the full array of individual and social causation, and includes not only a systematic assessment of physiological, physiognomic, genetic, neurological, and personological determinants but also of situational, environmental, cultural, and cross-cultural determinants. Moreover, McCord's "neuro-social theory of psychopathy" takes into comprehensive account the interactions between individual and social determinants.

McCord's treatment of the two sets of causes—individual and social—is, however, not altogether evenhanded. Because he is an optimist and humanist, as well as a sociologist, he proposes that the psychopathic condition is by no means hopeless or incurable, as many psychologists and psychiatrists would have us believe. McCord sees a great deal of the psychopath's behavior as arising from the emotionally deprived and impoverished conditions of early child-rearing, and, moreover, he sees it as a condition that can be overcome or at least alleviated. The data he reports in the latter part of this volume provide us with a test of the effectiveness of "milieu therapy," the treatment that McCord favors and advocates for psychopaths. In an unusual 25-year follow-up study of psychopathic youths, McCord reports that those undergoing milieu therapy (at Wiltwyck School) manifested less recidivism than a control group (at Lyman School) receiving more traditional custodial and disciplinary treatment. McCord's data are dramatic because they go against the conventional wisdom about the incorrigibility of psychopaths and therefore deserve the serious and critical attention of social scientists and practitioners.

There are several additional features in this work that I would commend to those who seek to understand psychopathy: It includes a good historical review of the concept of the psychopath as a distinct entity, an excellent analysis of the extent to which psychopathy is capable of being explained by labeling theory and critical sociology, and most interesting discussions about the role of Western society as a promotor of psychopathy, the relation between psychopathy and capitalism, and between psychopathy and Machiavellianism. Moreover, the reader will find illuminating the distinction McCord makes between the "criminal" and the "normal" psychopath, and a review of the effects of different kinds of therapy with psychopaths: individual and group psychotherapy, drugs, and positive and aversive conditioning. Finally, at another level of analysis, McCord's discussion of the effects of mandatory sentencing on recidivism is enlightening.

It is always a pleasure to recommend a book to others that is not only scholarly but also well written and free of jargon. I believe that on both counts this work stands as the definitive work on the nature and cause of psychopathy.

Milton Rokeach
Professor of Sociology and Psychology,
and Director, Unit on Human Values,
Washington State University

Acknowledgments

Gordon Allport and Ernst Papenek, both deceased, served as the mentors for this work. Wise, critical, but always sensitive to the concerns of others, Allport guided several generations of his students at Harvard into research that was both fundamental and useful to society. Papanek, at Wiltwyck, in Austria, and France, saved thousands of children from degradation by his humor, his understanding, and his compassion.

Special thanks are due to Edward Sagarin, my colleague at the City University of New York, for initiating this work and tirelessly reading the manuscript; José Sanchez, also of CUNY, who played a major role throughout the research and ably criticized the results; and to Robert McCord of Harvard who arranged for the original interviews.

Milton Rokeach of Washington State University and Arline McCord of Hunter College added their perceptive comments to the book. Among the many people who gave invaluable aid, I particularly note David Segal, research director,

Massachusetts Department of Youth Services; Dr. Bary Fireman, ex-director of Wiltwyck; Annesley K. Schmidt of the National Institute of Justice; Adam F. D'Allessandro, New York Department of Criminal Justice; Alvin M. Mesnikoff, Deputy Commissioner for Research, New York State Office of Mental Health; and Myra Gordon, Massachusetts Department of Mental Health.

The various research review boards of New York, Massachusetts, and other states ensured that our work did not invade the privacy of individuals. Their ethical and legal advice was most helpful.

People who were once on the staff of Wiltwyck—Anna Chase, Francis Sims, and Malcolm Marx—offered invaluable help during the original research. Joan Fish Silver aided in administering the tests in 1954 and in typing; the laborious job of typing this final manuscript fell to Ann Jones.

I would also like to thank the following publishers for permission to quote from their publications: W. W. Norton (Sir David Henderson, *Psychopathic States*, 1939), Alfred A. Knopf (Joseph Ullman, *A Judge Takes the Stand*, 1933), Grune and Stratton (Robert Lindner, *Rebel Without a Cause*, 1944), Philosophical Library (George Bernard Shaw, *The Crime of Imprisonment*, 1946), and the American Psychological Association (G. M. Gilbert, "Hermann Goering: Aimable Psychopath," *Journal of Abnormal and Social Psychology*, 1948, *43*, 211).

The real "heroes" of this work are, of course, the ex-inmates of Wiltwyck and Lyman Schools. Some of them, who must remain anonymous, contributed their own insights to the research. All of them, famous and infamous, had to cope with their private, childhood hells—and the majority have survived. They may now live lives of "quiet desperation" or may have emerged as lonely strangers, but most have ceased to inflict their inner torments on others.

Introduction

"Every society has its quota of trouble makers. Among the least understood, and perhaps the most destructive are the moral and emotional misfits known as 'psychopathic personalities,'" Gordon Allport once observed (Allport, in Foreword to McCord & McCord, 1956, p. iii). "Their warped natures frequently thrust them into the criminal segment of society. Even if they escape the law, they bring misery and sorrow to their fellow men far out of proportion to their numbers [p. iii]."

The psychopath—guiltless, insensitive, asocial, loveless, sometimes impulsive, or even violent—is the most dangerous of criminals, most predatory of politicians, or the most unscrupulous of businessmen (Cleckly, 1978; Harrington, 1972). At times charming and apparently bland; at other times, highly aggressive and explosive—and in still other social situations, a conspiring, patient "con man"—the psychopath has proved an enigma to medical and social science for 200 years. Some estimates suggest that there are fewer than 500,000 such people in America (Smith, 1978). Other less conservative writers suggest that the United States has 10 million psychopaths—and that they are growing in numbers (Mailer, 1958).

Statistics on Crime

Official statistics show that victims of major crimes have tripled between 1960 and 1976 (Silberman, 1978). At the same time, homicides by "strangers"—rather than so-called "crimes of passion"—have also tripled. Further, as Marvin Wolfgang's classic study (1972) of a cohort of Philadelphia youth has shown, many juveniles have been arrested for some crime or another but only a handful of chronic offenders account for more serious crimes: 19% of Philadelphia youth committed 90% of violent crimes (p. 192).

This increase in violent crimes, particularly by blacks, the poor, and the young, cannot be explained merely in terms of a growth in the number of young people (Silberman, 1978); in fact, the number of young people in the population accounts for only 25% of the increase (Silberman, 1978).

I am not maintaining that psychopaths make up all the ranks of chronic offenders, but they are surely an important segment as so many show the classic symptoms of guiltlessness and an inability to form a lasting relationship with other people. "The absence of 'affect,'" as Silberman (1978) has commented, "is the most frightening aspect of all. In the past, juveniles who exploded in violence tended to feel considerable guilt or remorse afterwards; the new criminals have been so brutalized in their own upbringing that they seem incapable of viewing their victims as fellow human beings [p. 63]." As one murderer quoted by Silberman said about his victim, "I didn't know him; why should I feel sorry about what happened to him [p. 48]?"

The Nature of Psychopaths

I met my first psychopath (or, who knows, my fiftieth?) at San Quentin prison in 1951. I did not recognize that this was my initiation into a different world. Although a counselor, I was only 20 years old at the time and had been trained in American colonial history, and I did not, of course, comprehend the nature of the man.

"Joseph Borlov"—the fictitious name of a handsome, highly intelligent person—had a record as a homosexual prostitute, forger, and thief. When I first met him in "Old Prison Segregation"—a section of San Quentin then reserved for dangerous men who could not serve their time in the "yard"—for fear of their violence—his English accent, his theatrical flairs, and his presentation of flawless credentials impressed me.

He produced a birth certificate supporting a claim to his ancestry as the illegitimate son of a Romanov prince, a batch of press clippings depicting his career on the stage, and a flow of conversation emphasizing his knowledge of criminology and his lightheartedness: "I am essentially a clown at heart—but a happy one."

Borlov said that his father, the assumed prince, helped him to escape from Russia to Paris during the Bolshevik Revolution. The father then deserted him. Visiting Americans, according to Borlov's story, kindly adopted him and launched him on a brilliant career in the Ziegfield Follies.

His descent to the lower depths of San Quentin prison, Borlov said, occurred because of an automobile accident which scarred his face, ruined his theatrical career, and forced him to forge checks out of despair. He swore that he had now reformed.

Unfortunately for society and perhaps Borlov, I naively believed him. As I was the only counselor in Old Prison Segregation, I recommended him for parole when the time came.

He blithely marched out the prison gates. Within a month, he had—without money or credit—talked I. Magnin's department store out of goods worth thousands of dollars. Within 6 weeks after his release, he had secured a gun, held up a "Mom and Pop" grocery store, and killed the man who owned it.

To my knowledge, Borlov still wanders around America.

Long-filed reports by two prison psychiatrists had described him as a psychopath, narcissistic, amoral, and potentially violent. He lied affably and without restraint. Guiltless, he had no bond with another human being. His stage career had actually culminated in female impersonations while he garnished most of his income from forgeries.

That single episode and the fact that I had helped to release a man from prison who menaced society taught me the extent of my ignorance about human nature; it led to a career as a social scientist; and convinced me of the necessity to explore this topic.

Subsequent experiences in other prisons and situations—the Norfolk prison in Massachusetts, the Wiltwyck School in New York, the Lyman School in Massachusetts, the jails of Mississippi, Houston, and New York's Riker's Island—confirmed my belief in the reality and danger of psychopaths. Exposure to other cultural areas—France,

West Africa, India, Egypt, East Africa, and Ireland—convinced me of the ubiquity of psychopaths.

Analyzing the Psychopath

In this book I address five central issues:

1. *Who is this lonely stranger?* "Labels are perilous things." Allport (1956) has written, "To call a destructive person a 'psychopath' does not, of course, prove that he belongs to a single well-defined nosological group [p. iii]."

Our first task, then, is to explicate the concept of the psychopath as a distinct entity. This task is particularly significant since, back in the 1930s, prison administrators sometimes described 94% of their inmate populations as psychopathic (Sutherland, 1950)—a ridiculously high estimate by most standards. By the 1980s, the pendulum has swung again. Some scholars deny that the psychopath existed at all (Gibbons, 1979). However, some popular writers have proclaimed that the ranks of psychopaths have grown immeasurably (Harrington, 1972).

Both groups tend to ignore the abundance of evidence—drawn from psychological, neurological, and physiological tests, clinical experience, anthropological knowledge, and the actual behavior of psychopaths—that a small but highly dangerous segment of the world's population can be legitimately and responsibly recognized as psychopaths.

By a "psychopath," I mean an asocial, emotionally and physiologically insensitive person, who feels no guilt and is unable to form emotionally affectionate relationships with other people. The core psychopath exhibits all of these characteristics. He or she is a rare type, resting at one end of a continuum that stretches to "normal," displaying all of these traits to an extreme degree and in such a manner that they constantly direct or inform his or her life.

From time to time or on given occasions, many people exhibit some of these traits. Similarly, some people may be loveless but not guiltless. Or, in extreme situations such as starvation, some generally "normal" people will exhibit a psychopathic syndrome. To conceptualize all of these people as psychopaths would not be useful because it would not isolate for study those who fit the definition. But to ignore these people entirely in a study of psychopaths would likewise be dangerous because they have a strong potential for psychopathic

4

behavior and because the study of such people can throw great light on the life pattern of the extreme cases.

In Part I, I describe the criminal psychopath—ranging from a latter-day "Billy the Kid" to mass-murderer Gary Gilmore. In addition, I examine the histories of functional or ostensibly "normal" individuals who nonetheless exhibit characteristics of the psychopath (but who have not been legally defined as criminals).

Indeed, entire groups, such as the Ik of Uganda, may consider psychopathic behavior as ordinary and commonplace (Turnbull, 1974).

2. *How can we diagnose psychopaths?* If a distinct entity exists but manifests itself in different forms, how can we locate the nature, causes, and treatment of the disorder?

In Part II, various approaches to this problem are presented. The "morally insane," as psychopaths were once known, have been recognized since 1800, when theories about witchcraft and devil possession declined. Some popular twentieth-century writers—Norman Mailer and Alan Harrington—have claimed that millions of people in industrialized societies will become psychopaths by 1982; they argued that either capitalism or technology has produced this trend (Harrington, 1972; Mailer, 1958). Diverse points of view must be reconciled in order to arrive at a more precise, nonideological definition of the psychopath.

Fortunately, various measures ranging from projective psychological tests to physiological calculations of skin conductivity offer a path out of the maze of opinions.

3. *What is the origin of the psychopath?* No one has definitively solved this mystery, but as Part III demonstrates, the combined knowledge garnered by geneticists, child psychologists, clinicians, sociologists, and physiologists offers highly suggestive clues to this ancient problem.

4. *How do we control, deter, or rehabilitate the psychopath?* Because of the psychopath's extraordinary danger to our society, he or she must be controlled. Measures extending from psychotherapy to drug conditioning, from capital punishment to early removal from destructive homes, have been advocated. Some have even suggested restructuring our entire society (Smith, 1978), or advocated that all of us, perhaps through religious experiences, should become psychopaths (Harrington, 1972; see Chapter 3, this volume).

In Part IV, I attempt to assess the validity and efficacy of these approaches as well as to present research gathered between 1952 and

1981 concerning the eventual effects of "milieu therapy" on child psychopaths.

The evidence concerning the usefulness of intensive, psychiatrically oriented treatment of delinquents is followed by a study I conducted in 1980–1981 of the later lives of boys who underwent different forms of treatment at the Wiltwyck and Lyman schools.

The results of this 1980–1981 study include a comparison with three other groups: (*a*) delinquents confined 25 years ago in a typical training school; (*b*) psychopaths who have undergone a relatively new program of de-institutionalization; and (*c*) a national sample who are of the same age, class, and ethnic groups. This study provides vital information on the behavior of both child and adult psychopaths, traced over the last quarter of a century.

5. *How should society and our legal system handle the psychopath?* In Part V, I consider the broader implications of the diagnosis, causation, and treatment of psychopaths from the point of view of general social policy and of the law. As the psychopath presents unique legal problems, particularly in determining the degree of responsibility for his or her actions and "free will," such issues present philosophical as well as legal and scientific problems. Various policies will be examined which may, in a more rational fashion than at present, reduce the cost of the psychopath to the community while still protecting the liberties of the person.

Clearly, the five issues just outlined are relevant for the consideration of criminologists, psychiatrists, psychologists, correctional personnel, social workers, sociologists, and lawyers. Their importance, however, extends far beyond parochial occupational concerns and even political or ideological boundaries.

Research reports on the psychopath have flowed in from all parts of the world—Ecuador, Japan, Nigeria, Yugoslavia. Among the most significant sources of information are Russia, the Eastern European nations, and Scandinavia.

From the point of view of "critical" or Marxist sociologists (Chambliss, 1975; Quinney, 1975), this fact poses something of a problem. In one form or another, socialist nations claim to have controlled or eliminated capitalism and to have ended poverty.

Why, then, have psychopaths attracted increasing attention in socialist nations? This can hardly be viewed as a result of Russian policy, stemming from Tsarist times, to label dissidents as "crazy," as other socialist nations report the same results. Karl Marx himself would have probably regarded the psychopath as a residue of the "lumpenproletariat." Yet, if he had found the truth, why do we discover psychopaths at all socioeconomic levels, in all classes, and in virtually every known society? The "critical" (Neo-Marxist) sociologist has only one response: A truly egalitarian, democratic society has not yet flowered. Perhaps. Yet, because the critical sociologists offer few paths to the future and no description of it, we may reasonably assume that psychopaths may be with us forever.

Conclusion

The psychopath has persisted throughout history. He or she has murdered and plundered, committed rape and stolen goods, and has even threatened the existence of particular human groups.

Together, we launch upon an enterprise to understand this elusive but ever-present lonely stranger.

References

Allport, G. In foreword to *Psychopathy and delinquency* by W. McCord and J. McCord. New York: Grune and Stratton, 1956 (3rd ed., 1970).

Chambliss, W. Toward a political economy of crime. *Theory and Society*, 1975, *2* (Summer).

Cleckly, Hervey. *The mask of sanity*. St. Louis: C. V. Mosby, 1978.

Gibbons, Don C. *The criminological enterprise*. New York: Prentice-Hall, 1978.

Hare, R. *Psychopathy*. New York: Wiley, 1970.

Harrington, A. *Psychopaths*. New York: Simon and Schuster, 1972.

Mailer, N. The White Negro. In *Voices of dissent*. New York: Grove Press, 1958.

Quinney, R. *Criminology*. Boston: Little, Brown, 1975.

Silberman, C. *Criminal justice, criminal violence*. New York: Random House, 1978.

Smith, R. J. *The psychopath in society*. New York: Academic Press, 1978.

Sutherland, Edwin, Sexual psychopath laws. *Journal of Criminal Law, Criminology and Police Science*, 1950, *4*:543– 554.

Turnbull, C. *The mountain people*. New York: Simon and Schuster, 1974.

Wolfgang, M., *et al.*, *Delinquency in a youth cohort*. Chicago: University of Chicago Press, 1972.

1

The Lonely Stranger

The Criminal Psychopath

*Psychopathy represents the most expensive
and most destructive of all forms of
deviant behavior.*
Robert Lindner
Rebel Without a Cause, 1944

I first met Salvatore Agron at the Wiltwyck
School of New York, an agency devoted to the social and psychiatric care of disordered, dangerous,
or neglected children.

A fat, short, curly-haired boy of 10, Agron
seemed to provide little threat to society. His
Caucasian biological father, hospitalized as a psychotic, had deserted him early in life. His mother,
a newly arrived Puerto Rican migrant, felt incompetent to deal with the child and had totally
neglected him, readily agreeing to a court petition
of delinquency and committing the child to
Wiltwyck. Outwardly, however, Agron seemed to
have suffered few scars from his experiences. He
was pleasant, attended school regularly, and did
not attempt to escape. In fact, he appeared to be
relieved to live away from his mother and step-
father, a strict Pentecostal minister. Nonetheless,
an interview I conducted with the boy in 1953
indicated that he simmered with aggressiveness,

felt no discernible guilt about torturing animals and depicted himself as totally alone in the world and free to inflict his anger on other human beings. After 2 years at Wiltwyck, he emerged as the leader of a group of boys. He reported no affection toward them as individuals. Rather, as fellow Puerto Ricans, they provided some base to his fragile sense of identity. He administered severe beatings to boys in his gang who displeased him.

Primarily because of his aggression toward other boys, the Wiltwyck school had no other legal choice but to release Agron to his family. A social worker in New York City visited the family occasionally but had little positive effect. The mother claimed that the boy was "born bad," that he refused to attend school, and that he frequently stayed away from home for days. Later, it was discovered that he slept under the bridges of the city. Further delinquent acts, including stabbing other children, led to his commitment to the Warwick School, a maximum security institution.

Paroled from Warwick in 1959, Agron returned to the streets of East Harlem. At that time, the antagonism among Puerto Ricans, Irishmen, and Italians had reached its height. Agron soon gained a reputation as a tough guy and, by wearing a nurse's cape, became known on the streets as the "Cape Man" and as "Dracula." He carried butcher knives under his cloak. On August 29, 1959, he used them to kill two other boys—one identified as an "Anglo" and the other of Polish descent—in an apparent attempt to assert Puerto Rican supremacy in the neighborhood. Some Puerto Rican teenagers saluted the murders as an act of braggadocio; others identified Agron to the police.

The police found him hiding under a bridge. He proudly announced that he had killed the two boys, demonstrating no remorse. His future meant nothing to him: "I don't care if I burn!" He also exhibited his disdain for his broken family: "I wouldn't care if my mother watched me." A judge sentenced him to death. An appellate court—despite psychiatric findings that Agron was a psychopath, medically if not legally insane—upheld the sentence.

Informed that New York State had never executed a 17-year-old boy, Governor Nelson Rockefeller commuted the sentence to life imprisonment in Attica. Sensationalist newspapers deplored the decision and scoffed at the governor's argument that it was the family and the institutions of society, rather than Salvatore Agron himself, which should accept the ultimate blame.

The Psychopath and Human Nature

The criminal psychopath like Agron, caught knifing two innocent boys, presents a clear challenge to the safety of all in society. The understanding of his disorder may not only serve to protect the security and serenity of each of us, a knowledge of his (or her) problems may also present us with an opportunity to elucidate certain basic philosophical issues. In what sense, for example, is a person legally responsible for his or her actions? Is the criminal psychopath—shorn of guilt, social bonds, and human contact—the essence of mankind? Certainly, Thomas Hobbes would have thought so, as do some contemporary anthropologists.

After investigating a tribe, the Ik, on the Kenya-Uganda border who all closely resemble psychopaths, anthropologist Colin Turnbull (1974) concluded that we would all be psychopaths if we had suffered similar deprivations. After spending years with the Ik, Turnbull commented: "One finds that it is oneself one is looking at and questioning: it is a voyage in quest of the basic human being and a discovery of his potential for inhumanity, a potential that lies within us all [p. 11]."

Thus, the psychopath represents a unique example of the human species. Should we, in the Western world, punish him for his actions, or treat him as if he were an interesting, pitiful, albeit dangerous, creature in a zoo? Should we attempt to transform him? These are particularly difficult questions because, despite his fearsome actions, the psychopath is a "rational man," calculating his own pleasure and pain; he exists in all ranges of intelligence; and he does not exhibit the hallucinations and delusions characteristic of the psychotic person.

The Diagnosis of Psychopaths

Such paradoxes bewilder many scholars. Some sociologists and psychiatrists would like to dismiss the psychopath from their purview altogether because of the tendency to identify the disorder with any form of antisocial behavior. As far back as 1946, psychiatrist Olof Kinberg argued, "[the concept] should be abrogated as theoretically unsatisfactory, practically misleading, and destructive to scientific thinking [p. 419]."

Labeling theorists in sociology and psychiatrists such as Thomas Szasz (1961) would like to do away with all categories for describing

mental disorders as illness. They have good reasons for fearing that
the label of psychopath could be mistakenly translated as "incurable
maniac." At one time or another, for example, 21 states in America
had "sexual psychopath" laws on their books (Sutherland, 1950).
These statutes gave judges the right to imprison sexual deviates in-
definitely or to order their castration. Such laws overlooked the fact
that the vast majority of child molesters, homosexuals, rapists, and
exhibitionists are *not* psychopaths and that castration does not necessarily tame their sexual activity. Nonetheless, during the 1920s, some
21,000 persons categorized as sexual psychopaths underwent castration in America (Sutherland, 1950) and, during the 1940s, the Nazis
used the same method to sterilize groups whom they considered depraved or dangerous to race purity (Shirer, 1960).

Even the American Psychiatric Association has exhibited ambiva-
lence. Although never relinquishing the concept, psychiatrists during
the past 30 years have altered the terms in their nosological dictionary
from "psychopath" to "sociopath" and then to "antisocial personality" (a truly grab-bag term that lumps all criminals, drunkards, and
many other deviants together; most importantly, the term ignores the
fact that the psychopath is not *anti*social but *a*social in nature). With
the current terminology, even "streakers" have been called antisocial. Perhaps, in some prudish sense they are, but I suspect that
streakers are merely exhibitionists who were part of a brief fad.

We have grave reasons, then, to mistrust the use of labels. The
label of psychopath, like that of psychotic or neurotic, should be
used with caution, based on careful research, the utmost attention to
a person's legal rights, and an assurance of his or her personal dignity.

Nonetheless, the concept of psychopathy has long historical roots
and recurs again and again in the research literature from every nation
in the world. It has been retained as an indispensable, if ever more
carefully circumscribed concept, which psychiatrists, psychologists,
social workers, and jurists have been forced to recognize as a distinct
syndrome—or ignored only at the peril of their clients or constituen-
cies. Even debunkers like Kinberg (1946) have been compelled by
their experience to recognize this clinical entity. "In the good old
times," he has written, "one exported such cases to the U.S.A. where
most of them went to the dogs or were sent back by their consulates
[p. 420]."

Much of the difficulty in defining the criminal psychopath has
emanated from ideological, often humanitarian sources, and has
been overly stressed. In practical experience, correctional administrators, prison psychologists, the police, and, indeed, few, if any,

people dealing with criminals can do their job without employing the concept of a certain syndrome of psychopathic behavior—whatever its semantic tag. Hervey Cleckly (1976), a psychiatrist who has spent years of contact with psychopaths, has commented:

> At a meeting of the American Psychiatric Association, or a staff conference at a state hospital, if a physician expresses an opinion to one of his colleagues about a psychopath, it is clearly, and at once, understood . . . that he [is speaking about] the grave character and behavior disorder so familiar to most psychiatrists as a distinct and easily recognizable entity [p. 151].

Thus, despite ideological and semantic squabbles, most social and medical scientists (Reid, 1978) agree that a common, if rare, syndrome of criminal psychopathy exists: The criminal psychopath is an asocial, insensitive, guiltless, and loveless person who has been convicted one or more times in which the commission of the crimes can be reasonably linked to his or her psychopathic character. I should emphasize again that the core criminal psychopath exhibits a configuration of these traits, and I should underline that the definition should not be confused with chronic criminal behavior, neuroses, psychoses, or certain actions that some society or another defines as "antisocial," "criminal," "eccentric," or "deviant."

Cases of Psychopaths

The lives of two men, William "Billy the Kid" Cook and Gary Gilmore, have been amply documented and concretely illustrate the concept.

Because of his exceptional crimes, Cook has received perhaps the most thorough psychological and medical examination of any single criminal psychopath (Symkal & Thorne, 1951); in addition, he wrote his autobiography.

Born in 1927 in a Missouri village, Billy Cook experienced an exceptionally deprived childhood. After probably murdering his mother, Cook's alcoholic father deserted the family when Billy was 7. Billy later described his mother's murder with a typical insensitivity: "One time my sister and me came home from playing at a yellow house and found her dead, laying on a cot. She had a large gash in the head [Symkal & Thorne, 1951, p. 314]." He did not appear to grieve or miss her.

A juvenile court judge sent Billy and his two sisters to separate foster homes. Billy was placed with a woman who abused him sexually. When he escaped from her home, police caught him and sent him to the Missouri Training School. He later said, "The training I got there was how to steal cars and pick locks [Symkal & Thorne, 1951, p. 315]."

Upon parole, Billy lived with each of his sisters, neither of whom wanted him. Now married, the sisters' husbands furthered his "education." One brother-in-law took him to brothels and showed him the finer points of burglary. The other helped him to get a job but stole his salary.

Rejected, Billy ended his young manhood in prison after one sister testified to authorities that he had violated parole.

In prison, Cook became a homosexual queen and, simultaneously, participated in many fights. Paroled again, he earned his living by theft. When the police almost apprehended him, Cook decided to hitchhike to the West.

An experienced burglar picked him up in a stolen car. Cook shot him and took the car. When the vehicle broke down, Cook again hitchhiked, this time with a family after threatening them with a pistol. "I got in the car with these people. Moser was their name. I told them what had happened and I didn't want their money or anything. All I wanted was to get away [Symkal & Thorne, 1951, p. 310]."

Cook held the family at gunpoint until they reached a gas station in New Mexico. Temporarily, he let down his guard and the husband tried to overcome him with force. He failed, and Cook forced the family back into the car. They had driven a short distance when Cook shot the father. As the mother drove, Cook turned and shot the two children. The mother screeched to a stop, and Cook killed her. He stuffed the four bodies into an old deserted mine shaft and then continued westward.

Cook got as far as the California border when police discovered the bodies of the Moser family. The police searched for the family's stolen car in six states until a sheriff apprehended Cook near San Diego. Cook, however, managed to kidnap him and stole his gun and car. He reached Tijuana, Mexico, where a squad of soldiers finally subdued him and tied him up with ropes.

He readily admitted his killings and did not appear to understand what the uproar about him was about. In his opinion, he had merely tried to avoid "trouble."

In jail, psychologists administered various projective tests: the Rorschach, the Thematic Apperception Test (T.A.T.), and a "Draw a Man" test (Symkal & Thorne, 1951). The examination revealed him as essentially isolated from other human beings, devoid of guilt (not even the murders of the Moser children disturbed him), high on aggressive tendencies, and preoccupied with his own sense of rejection.

At his trial, the new "Billy the Kid" passively accepted the judge's verdict: 300 years in Alcatraz. Three court-appointed psychiatrists had found him psychopathic—"mentally ill but not insane." The public rebelled against the judgment and called for Cook's execution. Few listened to the judge's concluding words: "Billy Cook is a symbol of society's failure [Symkal & Thorne, 1951]."

A second case illustrates the nature of a highly intelligent criminal psychopath. Gary Gilmore, brilliantly analyzed by Norman Mailer (1979) and exploited by the mass media, represents another variety of the criminal psychopath—infinitely more intelligent than Cook and hungry for death rather than life imprisonment.

Psychopaths have long exerted an appeal to the most illustrious novelists from Dostoevsky (*Crime and Punishment*) to Truman Capote (*In Cold Blood*). The preoccupation is not, I suspect, simply because of the subject's criminally bizarre behavior. One sometimes detects a grudging respect, even envy of the psychopath, on the part of some writers who themselves may have adopted a rather eccentric lifestyle. Mailer, for example, knifed one of his wives, Capote flaunts his homosexuality, and Dostoevsky kept writing because of his gambling debts. Such men are not psychopaths. There would appear, however, to be a certain affinity that will be examined later (Chapter 2).

Gary Gilmore had no claim to literary success, although some prison teachers thought he might have made a career in art, since he apparently possessed some artistic ability. Sadly, for Gilmore and his victims, fate did not decide in his favor.

In 1977, a Utah firing squad executed Gilmore, the first legal execution to take place in 10 years. They followed a court order, with the victim's agreement, but only after vociferous objections by the American Civil Liberties Union and the NAACP. Although he vainly tried to escape at the last moment, Gilmore apparently welcomed execution as a last resort. As a young, vigorous man, he hated the prospect of his only other alternative: life imprisonment.

Gary Gilmore personified the typical criminal psychopath: insensitive, devoid of self-insight (although he had a recorded IQ score of 140), guiltless, asocial, unable to understand his own or others' motives, and highly aggressive.

He had served some 19 years in reform schools and prisons. He loathed returning to one. In an unprosecuted case, he claimed to have stabbed to death a fellow inmate who, according to him was "just a nigger" (Mailer, 1979). The state paroled him, however, for he had supposedly committed only robberies and burglaries.

Various relatives sought jobs for him and offered him shelter during the brief 9 months before his final acts of violence. He eventually moved in with a teenager, Nicole Baker, who nurtured his ego.

During this period, Gilmore desperately wanted to buy a Ford Mustang and then a big, white truck. Presumably to gain the money to pay for these acquisitions, Gilmore robbed two men on successive nights. After taking pitifully small amounts of money from them, Gilmore forced his victims to lie on the floor and shot and killed them.

Captured in 1976, Gilmore never offered a motive for killing the people. Under repeated questioning, he responded to one interviewer who asked, "Why did you not just rob before you killed?"

> "Habit, I guess," said Gilmore. "My lifestyle. We're all creatures of habit. Somebody else from a different background might do it different [Mailer, 1979, p. 216]."

A detective asked, "Now, one thing. When you stopped at the gas station, did you have any intention of either robbing Jensen or killing him [Mailer, 1979, p. 216]?"

> "I had the intention of killing him," Gilmore responded.
> "When did that concept form in your mind?"
> "I can't say. It had been building all week. That night I knew I had to open a valve and let something out [Mailer, 1979, p. 799]."

Still another puzzled detective inquired, "Why did you kill the victims?" Gilmore said, "I don't know [Mailer, 1979, p. 320]."

Finally, his own lawyer wanted an answer. "Why did you go out the next night and kill Bushnell?"

> "I don't know, man," said Gilmore. "I'm impulsive. I don't think [Mailer, 1979, p. 800]."

In fact, no one—detectives, novelists, social scientists, lawyers, or journalists—could uncover a reasonable, or even conscious motive for Gilmore's unprovoked aggression. Once he had secured the money, why kill? Even Gilmore did not offer the commonsense rationale that he wanted to rid the scene of witnesses. Some clues to his impulsive hostility may be found in his background.

Gilmore's father had served time in jail and then deserted the family. His mother, whom he reportedly liked, also deserted him. She wrote him only one short letter while he awaited execution (Mailer, 1979). Shunted off to reform schools and prisons, Gilmore beat up other men and learned the bitter lessons of prison life. During the rare periods when he did not live in reform school, he sent Valentine's Day cards to all of his classmates in public school. Pathetically, no one responded. On his eleventh birthday, he invited two other boys to join him in a party. The two "friends" spent the money their parents gave them for presents for Gilmore on themselves, and then told Gilmore. As before, he felt alone in the world.

By any standard, it is safe to conclude that Gilmore was rejected by his parents and his peers. When captured on July 21, 1976, a policeman asked Gilmore if he would have gone on killing if he had not been apprehended. Coldly, Gary Gilmore replied, "probably." Lacking any emotional ties, why should he not reject the world of human beings who had treated him so shabbily?

During his short parole, Gilmore discovered a young woman who might—or might not—have satisfied his need for affection. Nicole Baker, a nubile, willing teenager, fell for Gilmore's charm. If one judged solely by the letters he later drafted from his execution block, Gilmore was able to feel affection for her.

> Nothing in my experience prepared me for the kind of honest hopeful love you gave me. I'm so used to bullshit and hostility, deceit and pettiness, evil and hatred. Those things are my natural habitat . . . should I hope that the state executes me? What do I do, rot in prison [Mailer, 1979, p. 305]?

The letter sounds full of love—a total contradiction of the psychopath's personality. Yet, if one considers other relevant facts, it is not:

- Gilmore planned to sell his letters addressed to Nicole for large amounts of money: a calculated act by a highly intelligent person, hardly redolent of love. In fact, Gilmore's estate did receive large amounts of money from publishers, journalists, newspapers, etc.
- Before his last incarceration, Gilmore could not bring the girl to sexual climax because of his own impotence.
- When living with Nicole, Gilmore molested a little girl. Nicole knew.
- During his brief interlude with Nicole, Gilmore liked her to sit naked on top of the Mustang at drive-in movies to attract attention.

Clearly, each act indicated a lack of consideration for Nicole and a definite intention to use her only to gain money, notoriety, or a reputation for sexual prowess. One could hardly call this relationship a loving one.

For her part, Nicole contributed greatly to the estrangement. During their few months together in freedom, Nicole wandered off with other men. When Gilmore was sent to prison, he suspected (rightly) that she engaged in orgies with a motorcycle club. When the firing squad executed Gilmore, Nicole went off to California to tell her life story for a great deal of money. She exhibited little, if any, remorse about his fate.

Nicole Baker, a female psychopath, had good reasons for neglecting her supposed lover. Her own parents had abandoned her when she was 15. Her uncle had seduced her when she was only 6 (Mailer, 1979). Her parents had her committed to an insane asylum at an early age because they could not handle her tantrums. At 11, she experienced sexual intercourse with another man outside her family. "No big deal," she said (p. 719).

After 15, she lived alone, entertaining any man she could capture even temporarily. Gilmore's death, which she hardly visibly mourned, offered her a lucrative opportunity to tape her memories and a chance—which her literary executors forced her to decline—to appear in pornographic magazines.

Gilmore never knew anything about Nicole's escapades. If he thought about her at all, he valued her as the recipient of his literate, potentially profitable letters and, perhaps, as a vicarious sex object. Two psychopaths had seldom been as well matched. Nicole had known about the murders, for example, but never reported them— certainly not out of loyalty to Gilmore but out of pure *sangfroid*. She felt no guilt or love.

In 1976, defense lawyers searched vainly for a legal means of excusing Gilmore's actions. No one testified that he suffered from a psychosis. Briefly, the lawyers hit on the idea that his crime had been drug-induced. In one prison, psychiatrists gave him prolixin, a very powerful tranquilizer which calmed if not paralyzed Gilmore. The lawyers gave up that defense, as one of the effects of prolixin is to decrease, not increase, aggressiveness.

Gilmore's prison psychiatrist, John Woods, knew of Gilmore's intellectual capacity, his psychopathic tendencies, his artistic abilities, and the fact that no one could consider him psychotic. Woods warned the defense lawyers that "the law wanted to keep psychopathy and psychosis apart. If the psychopath were ever accepted as legally insane, then crime, judgment, and punishment would be replaced by antisocial act, therapy, and convalescence [Mailer, 1979, p. 385]."

Gilmore's lawyers and their allies lost an appeal for clemency. They need hardly have tried. George Latimore, a Mormon who strongly believed in capital punishment—and had defended Lieutenant Calley (Calley machine-gunned Vietnamese villagers at My Lai)—headed the parole board that turned down all petitions for mercy.

Although Gilmore's execution required 3 minutes—due to bad aiming by the state-hired, volunteer riflemen—Gilmore may well have felt relief in that he had finally escaped permanent imprisonment. And Nicole? A sojourn at Malibu Beach, paid for by a journalist, apparently salved any qualms she may have felt.

Primary Characteristics of Psychopaths

What joins together Gilmore, Cook, Agron, and Borlov? They are all criminal psychopaths. Most social scientists who have actually dealt with criminal psychopaths would acknowledge that they share certain measurable, authentic traits:

THE PSYCHOPATH IS ASOCIAL

Unlike the average person, the psychopath has not been adequately socialized into the values and norms of his or her particular society—except in those rare cases where the entire group has adopted a psychopathic form of conduct (see Chapter 2). Freudian analysis would say that he or she has no conscience or superego to control or inhibit action (Bender, 1947). Generally, the individual cannot be considered a member of a deviant subculture: He or she is not like the Mafia member who swears an oath of allegiance to the "family" in order to protect comrades, or even the gang delinquent who feels an obligation to defend his turf and his comrades.

Some observers might disagree with this point of view and argue that psychopathy is the penultimate result of the socialization process offered by capitalist societies. Robert Smith (1978), for example, has argued that the psychopath's asociality is merely a product of a "market-place mentality" fostered by capitalism. Such an argument ignores two facts: (a) noncapitalistic nations report as high an incidence of psychopaths as do capitalistic nations; and (b) the actions of a Cook or a Gilmore cannot be interpreted as profit motivated. In fact, those defined as psychopaths tend to ignore economic considerations and pursue careers that even they cannot fully explain. I do not mean to deny that certain societies—the Ik, the Alorese, and perhaps even the American—encourage psychopathic behavior (Chapter 2). I would, however, deny that capitalism, in itself, cultivates psychopathy.

Although asocial, the psychopath cannot be equated with all deviant, or even all dangerous, persons (Sagarin, 1975). Child molesters, for example, pose a clear threat to the values of Western society. And yet, they are primarily a group of neurotic, inhibited, often guilt-ridden, persons who have strong inhibitions prohibiting normal adult heterosexuality (McCord & McCord, 1977). Criminal psychopaths *are* deviant, but the vast majority of deviants are not psychopaths.

Clearly, too, the definition of deviant behavior varies from culture to culture. Nicole, Gilmore's companion, might have been an honored courtesan in the entourage of Louis XIV; ancient Greece might have rewarded Borlov's homosexuality; the U.S. Army might well have given medals to Gilmore if he had committed his murders in Vietnam. Therefore, it would be a great mistake to consider any form of deviance or any type of criminality in any society as *prima facie* evidence of psychopathy.

Moreover, one cannot consider the psychopath as genuinely *anti*social. He is usually not a revolutionary seeking to overthrow the status quo in the name of some ideal. He is not, in other words, the classical wild-eyed anarchist tossing a bomb at some Tsar or a *sans culotte* screaming for the King's head. The psychopath may, of course, participate in revolutionary or genuinely antisocial activities—but he does so for his own reasons: his own profit, his own advancement, or the avoidance of punishment. He is also not the gang delinquent who deliberately flaunts his disobedience to authority, and he is not a paranoid who seeks to kill his imagined opponents.

The psychopath simply does not *care*, one way or another, about the communality of human beings known as society. Naturally, the more intelligent psychopath often recognizes social reality and takes it into account in making his calculations. He may strive to manipulate others, to avoid pain, and to maximize his own pleasure.

Many observers have noted that the psychopath can be an extremely charming person (see Chapter 2, this volume; Cleckly, 1976; Smith, 1978). At times—in their social role as politicians, con men, or businessmen—psychopaths can be brilliant conversationalists, romantic seducers, or convincing orators. Truman Capote grew to like and sympathize with two mass murderers whom he superbly described in a nonfiction novel (1965). And I very much enjoyed the charm, wit, and intelligence of Joseph Borlov.

Some psychopaths exude this charm, but they do so not out of any sympathy for other people, but rather to fulfill their particular aims. Borlov wanted me to help in arranging his parole. I did, and I never heard from him after his release from San Quentin. Gilmore wrote Nicole of his great love, expecting to reap financial rewards.

Thus, whatever conventional considerations the psychopath may extend, he does so based on the ultimate aim of achieving his own goals. He has no desire either to conform to society's moral precepts or to lead a revolution against them. As Freyhan (1951) once observed, "The psychopath . . . is unsocial rather than anti-social [p. 50]."

THE PSYCHOPATH IS INSENSITIVE

At Norfolk Prison in Massachusetts, where I was a group therapist, two young men convicted of murder approached me one day to ask a question that genuinely bewildered them. They could not comprehend why witnesses to their brutal attack appeared in court to identify and testify against them. "Why should they bother?" one man said in a bristling tone, "It was none of their business!" I tried, with no success, to talk with them about civic responsibility. Although neither lacked intelligence, they simply could not understand the concept. "Bullshit," one of the psychopaths responded, "it's each man out for himself."

Such a response is all too common among psychopaths. They apparently cannot understand the concerns of others; they feel no empathy, they lack anxiety about otherwise (normally) frightening events, and they are insensitive to the feelings of other people—unless they wish to manipulate them.

Even on a physiological level, this insensitivity has been demonstrated in a variety of ways. Since 1949, we have known that psychopaths have a very low level of anxiety (Funkenstein, Greenblatt, & Solomon, 1949). In 1955, Lykken first reported that psychopaths have a lower galvanic skin response (GSR) to lying, and a diminished GSR to classical conditioning. Moreover, psychopaths exhibit many fewer psychosomatic symptoms (often a function of anxiety and heightened sensitivity) than other people (Rotenberg, 1975). They also are subject to less heart disease. And they show less skin conductance responses than do nonpsychopaths to pictures of severe facial injuries (Mathis, 1970). However measured on tests that cannot be easily falsified, psychopaths exhibit less emotional (and physical) sensitivity than other people.

Two qualifications should be made about the psychopath's general

23

lack of sensitivity. *First,* certain chemicals can alter his condition. L. A. Lindner and his colleagues (1970) found that the injection of epinephrine increases the heart-rate response of "simple" psychopaths much more than it does for other subjects—suggesting an autonomic defect. And other scholars have noted that psychopaths learn to avoid electric shocks much more quickly when injected with adrenaline, perhaps indicating a heightened awareness of their situation (Schachter & Latane, 1964). Whether these research findings can, or should, be translated into forms of treatment remains an open question.

Second, a variety of social experiences can induce "differential insensitivity" in average people (Rotenberg, 1978). Trained parachutists exhibit little anxiety (sensitivity) prior to jumping (Epstein, 1967). Oleson and Whittaker (1968) showed that medical schools can habituate student nurses to situations that would make other people vomit or faint. Morgue attendants and doctors are similarly desensitized to grisly scenes (Becker, Geer, Hughes, & Strauss, 1961; Sudnow, 1967).

Rotenberg (1975) correctly suggested that some kinds of insensitivity may be highly functional for a society that needs doctors, soldiers, nurses, policemen, etc. Like the psychopath, they have been desensitized by their socialization to certain types of grim situations. For the criminal psychopath, however, insensitivity is often dysfunctional for the society.

Whether we should use the label of "differential sensitivity" or that of "psychopathy" remains an open issue as psychopaths, unlike others such as surgeons, have generalized their insensitivity rather than limited it to their daily occupation.

In any case, solid physiological evidence does exist demonstrating that psychopaths are unusually insensitive to other people and to threatening events. Their very lack of anxiety perhaps saves them from the psychosomatic symptoms, neuroses, and heart ailments that plague so many other people in modern societies. It also makes them more dangerous, volatile, and remorseless.

THE PSYCHOPATH IS GUILTLESS

Throughout the world, clinicians and scholars have observed that one of the greatest problems of the criminal psychopath is a lack of guilt. He can commit any action without signs of remorse or guilt; he is unfettered by a conscience. Outwardly, he can display guilt, but only if it serves his immediate purpose. It is a facade.

The moral emptiness of the psychopath, one of his crucial characteristics, has been remarked on repeatedly by psychiatrists, sociologists, and psychologists since the birth of modern social science. In America, sociologist Kirson Weinberg (1959) observed, "The psychopath can experience shame but slight guilt [p. 210]." And psychologist Robert White (1948) went further by adding that the psychopath "does not accept blame for his conduct nor feel shame about it [p. 901]." From England, Sir David Henderson (1939) reported, "They rarely if ever show any particle of remorse [p. 111]." Psychoanalyst N. Thorton (1951) concluded that "the distinguishing feature of a psychopathic personality is nothing but a conspicuously defective or else completely underdeveloped superego [conscience] [p. 419]." In France, Thomas Maeder (1979) found the same total lack of conscience in psychopaths as did Thomas Thompson (1979) in India. Psychologist Robert Hare (1970) demonstrated that the psychopath's lack of guilt serves as the prime criterion for most clinicians and that it can be independently detected by tests as diverse as the Rorschach, the Thematic Apperception Test, and Word Association Test.

In less abstract terms, the cases that I have mentioned demonstrate an extreme lack of guilt. "Billy the Kid," for example, described one of his series of murders in this fashion: "The two little kids started crying, wanting water. I gave them some and she [their mother] drove a while—and I turned around and started shooting in the back seat and then turned back and shot her. She fell over and onto the floor [Symkal & Thorne, 1951, p. 311]." He quenched their thirst and killed them: little feeling, no demonstrable guilt, and a matter of factness in his description. And Borlov told me: "There have been times when they [society] have been frantic—but I, amidst the riot I have created, remain calm and usually collected. I have always landed right side up—from the Village to the Hotel Pierre." In the world of psychopaths, these people are no exceptions. They steal, cheat, lie, or even kill without remorse. As emphasized before, they differ fundamentally from the average person, the ordinary criminal, or the mental patient in their extraordinary lack of guilt.

Some scholars have recognized a problem in this position. As Robert Smith (1978) pointed out, psychopaths can be charming, extremely nice to other people, and perceptive of others' feelings. Yet, they feel no guilt about abusing them. How can there be such a difference within the same person? The late Gordon Allport (1955) provided a theoretical base for the distinction. He argued that human beings learn in two different ways: "opportunistically" and "propriately." We all undergo opportunistic learning experiences. Through punishment and continual conditioning, we absorb certain "tribal conformities": language, wearing of certain garments or ornaments, the correct comments to make in appropriate social situations. The psychopath, too, learns these lessons and usually follows them as long as he has nothing to lose. Because of extreme deprivation in childhood, however, the typical psychopath does not develop a "proprium": in Allport's terms, a set of his own ideals, a self-identity, a coherence that is uniquely his, and, most importantly, a mature conscience. He is like one of B. F. Skinner's pigeons who can be trained ("opportunistically") to seek its food in a complicated maze. Yet, the pigeons, like the psychopath, apparently do not develop either a self-ideal or guilt about their behavior. The reasons for this lack of "propriate" learning are discussed in Chapter 6.

Certainly, a prime factor is the psychopath's alienation from human beings. Only attention from others and concern builds a stable conscience. The psychopath, because of his loveless existence, does not receive such nurturance.

Lacking compassion and comrades, the psychopath is a genuinely lonely stranger. He is unable to maintain lasting emotional relationships with anyone: his parents, his passing friends, or his spouse. He may establish temporary liaisons for purposes of lust, aggrandizement, or power, but even these do not last.

Salvatore Agron formed a gang around himself when it was useful for protection but he had no intimate friends. Borlov participated in various homosexual activities on a completely impersonal basis. "Billy the Kid" had no companions at all. Even Gary Gilmore, who trumpeted his love for Nicole in his letters, sought mainly to use her for profit. And Nicole herself flitted from man to man without concern for her supposed "lover."

Psychologist A. H. Maslow (1954) viewed the psychopath's warped capacity for affection as his central trait: "I have found it helpful in understanding psychopaths to assume that they have no love identifications with other human beings and can therefore hurt them or even kill them casually, without hate, and without pleasure, precisely as they kill animals who have come to be pests [p. 173]."

A typical psychopath, "Howard Dever," (fictitious name) whom I counseled at the Boston Psychopathic Hospital, illustrates the deep lovelessness of psychopaths. He hated his parents, alienated the people in his small Vermont town, and regarded himself as the village "scapegoat." He ran away from home at 16 to New York City where he lived on the proceeds of petty burglaries and dope peddling.

The army drafted Dever in 1941, but he felt no identification with his country or comrades. He deserted 16 times. He married in England and fathered a child. On the day of the baby's birth, he left his wife. Later, briefly reunited in America and financially supported by her, he swore complete faithfulness. Then, one day, "I met a guy in a bar, and he said he wanted to pull some jobs in Florida. Would I go along? I said O.K. but forgot to tell my wife. . . . It wasn't that I didn't like her. I just had other things to do."

He drifted to Florida where he dealt in stolen cars and fraudulent bonds, entertaining women with his new money. On a trip to Boston, police caught him impersonating an F.B.I. agent and issuing a forged check. When I met him, Dever displayed the typical lack of guilt of the psychopath: "Maybe I hurt somebody doing it, but I've had fun."

Clinicians such as Maslow believe that early deprivation has permanently stunted the psychopath's capacity to maintain emotional relationships. "In the psychopathic personality, the needs for being loved and loving have disappeared and, as far as we know today, this is a permanent loss [Maslow, 1954, p. 131]."

Certainly in animal research, experimenters have extinguished some basic drives. Analogically, many investigators regard the early rejection suffered by psychopaths as a source for totally inhibiting their own capacity for love. Other research suggests that rejection actually enhances a child's need for love, just as deprivation of food increases hunger (Sears, Maccoby, & Levin, 1956).

We do not know the definitive answer to the question, but certainly there is little doubt that the psychopath—asocial, insensitive, guiltless, and loveless—emerges as the ultimate lonely stranger. These characteristics form the core of the psychopathic syndrome. In addition, three other traits—a craving for excitement, a high degree of impulsiveness, and an explosive aggressiveness—have often been recorded among psychopaths. As these characteristics have been found in many but not all criminal psychopaths, I regard them as peripheral or secondary manifestations of psychopathy.

Secondary Characteristics of Psychopaths

THE PSYCHOPATH OFTEN CRAVES EXCITEMENT

We have all observed the insatiable craving for variety and entertainment, the "naughty" activities and desire for excitement in very small children. The great majority, however, soon learn to avoid certain types of activity because of the danger or because of parental guidance.

Many psychopaths have not learned the lesson of "normal" children, presumably because they had little to gain or lose from their parents' reactions (see Chapter 6). Most psychopaths do not seek security as a goal in itself; rather they crave constant change, whirlwind variety, and new stimuli.

Seeking Excitement: Two Cases

Ian Brady, a clerk, and Myra Hindley, a typist, in England illustrate in human terms the psychopath's craving for excitement (Williams, 1967). Confined in boring, dead-end business jobs, they experimented with alcohol, drugs, and pornographic photography as they sought even greater thrills. Myra posed as a model for their erotic pictures while Ian tried to sell them without her knowledge.

Between 1963 and 1965, they took to cruising streets looking for young boys and girls. After toying with them, they killed them and buried them in moorlands. The so-called "Moors Murders" emanated not from sexual lust, nor economic motive, nor hatred of the victims. Ian and Myra did not know their subjects at all. The murderers consciously explained their actions as simply ways to attain new levels of excitement, a new "consciousness," and a temporary escape from boredom. They giggled over their escapades, bragged indiscreetly about them to friends, and, when finally apprehended, demonstrated no guilt.

Physical Evidence

Physiologists have also provided evidence indicating the psychopath's need for excitement. Lykken (1957) discovered that psychopaths preferred even frightening experiences to boring ones. For certain psychopaths, Petrie (1967) recorded that experiencing pain might in itself serve to overcome boredom. And, in an unusually optimistic report, several therapists reported that the use of novel, exciting situations reinforced the adjustment of psychopathic offenders much more effectively than did verbal therapy (Ingram, Gerard, Quay, & Levinson, 1970).

Many people desire variety, but more important to the average person is security. We all like excitement as long as it is not inordinately dangerous. Millions of people ride rollercoasters or see horror films—but they do not participate in these activities if they think that death might actually result.

In contrast, many psychopaths seem willing to sacrifice almost anything in a search for excitement. This possibly is one reason for the psychopath's unusual impulsiveness.

When "Billy the Kid" casually turned around in the Moser car and shot two infants who could not possibly identify him, he said later that he did so merely "on impulse." Gary Gilmore could offer no reason for killing his victims after robbing them; it was just that "pressure had built up" inside him. These and other criminal psychopaths acted totally on impulse, a belief that a particular action might give them pleasure or some kind of momentary release.

Obviously, many of us act, at times, on impulse. Yet, various psychologists and psychiatrists have witnessed a qualitative and quantitative difference in criminal psychopaths. They commit crimes without planning; they move from one sexual adventure to another without thought of the consequences; they seldom conceive of a long-term plan for their lives. As Chornyak (1941) has written, psychopaths tend to gratify their immediate impulses: "the lid is off the id [p. 14]." Robert Lindner (1944) found among imprisoned psychopaths that "determined progress toward a goal—unless it is a selfish one capable of immediate realization by a sharply accented spurt of activity—the dynamic binding together of actual strands, is lacking [p. 210]." Lauretta Bender (1942), a psychiatrist who analyzed more than 800 child psychopaths, agreed with Lindner that the most distinctive trait of the children was "unpatterned, impulsive behavior [p. 418]."

However, the two psychopaths novelized by Truman Capote (1965) planned their mass murder with great detail. Before committing the crime, they carefully located their victims, cleverly forged checks to pay their expenses, traveled a great distance without incident, and purchased items that they needed such as rope with which to tie their victims. Admittedly, they lacked realistic goals as to how they would spend the fortune they expected to steal. Nonetheless, they planned the operation meticulously and cannot be accurately characterized as impulsive.

One may, of course, argue that some criminal psychopaths have great ability to control their impulses for opportunistic reasons but that more often they give way blithely to a whim of the moment. It may well depend on the degree of control the psychopath feels he has over the situation and his individual level of aggression (see Chapter 2).

THE PSYCHOPATH IS OFTEN AGGRESSIVE

Aggression is, perhaps, a universal human attribute and certainly one that every society must control or channel (Bandura & Walters, 1963). With the psychopath, however, aggression is often more impersonal, unfocused, and without purpose than with the average person.

Bender (1947) noted in her studies of child psychopaths that "frustration is reacted to immediately by temper tantrums [p. 145]." And Lindner (1944) found adult criminal psychopaths equally aggressive.

The various murderers whom I have already described often killed their victims without even knowing or caring who they were. This form of ultimate aggression seemed to provide some kind of pleasure in itself. Such aggression is unlike that of the ordinary killer who usually eliminates someone close to him (see Silberman, 1978). The brutality differs from that of some neurotics or psychotics who may act viciously but often take out their aggression on themselves or their closest relatives.

The average man, too, may have a great potentiality for inflicting injury. Milgram (1963), for example, trained college students to administer greater and greater dosages of bogus electric shocks to a victim, who was in fact Milgram's stooge. Despite some verbal disagreement, the subjects usually followed Milgram's commands. And, as concentration camp behavior tragically demonstrated, "extreme" situations may drive both perpetrators and victims to act in ways they would never have dreamed of in ordinary life (Arendt, 1963).

The criminal psychopath differs from most of us, however, in that aggression has become a "normal" ordinary occurrence in his life. His life history would seem to have trained him for it: rejected, cruelly treated, and frustrated from childhood (see Chapter 6), the psychopath considers aggression from others and blowups of his own as merely a normal part of everyday life. Perhaps, too, the psychopath has learned from his parents or others that aggression will often bring rewards (Bandura & Walters, 1963).

Oddly, as Kirson Weinberg (1959) argued, "The psychopath frequently seeks others to limit his random aggressions. . . . Actually he too is puzzled by his waywardness and unwittingly may want to put limits to his random, appetite-fulfilling and destructive behavior [p. 151]."

In my own experience, this desire for control stems partly from the psychopath's fear of retaliation and partly from his calculation of the social situation. It can disappear as easily as any other of his whims, but he can at times control his aggression to suit his purpose (see Chapter 2).

The Syndrome of the Lonely Stranger: A Summary

The psychopath is asocial, neither a revolutionary against society nor a conformist. He is, as Robert Lindner (1944) put it aptly, "a rebel without a cause." The psychopath is insensitive both emotionally and physiologically. He is capable of committing any act without the slightest show of remorse or even understanding of its consequences. And the psychopath is loveless, wandering from person to person, but never forming lasting bonds of affection. As a "lone wolf," people mean no more to him than objects such as a chair he would kick during a temper tantrum.

Many, but not all, psychopaths seem to crave excitement. Many psychopaths are impulsive; others plan their crimes carefully over a long period of time. Criminal psychopaths often demonstrate extreme aggressiveness and their violent depredations may make little sense to us; others, in contrast, may merely engage in fraud, forgeries, and fakery.

Guiltlessness and lovelessness stand out as the psychopath's most distinctive traits. These lonely strangers, exhibiting the full psychopathic syndrome, can be found in all parts of the world. Having concentrated on the American variety, two cases—one from France and the other from the Indian subcontinent—illustrate the universality of this syndrome.

Cases of Guiltlessness

In 1944, citizens of Paris' rich sixteenth *arrondissement* smelled noxious fumes in the air. Unable to detect their source, they called on police *commissaire* Georges Massu—the model for the fictional Inspector Maigret—to investigate. On March 11, the police arrived at 21 rue Le Sueur and found the cause of the odors: a basement full of pieces of human bodies and a still burning furnace that contained a female hand.

The owner of the house, bachelor Dr. Marcel Petiot, posing as his own brother, calmly explained that the bodies belonged to Germans and traitors. He announced that he headed a resistance group responsible for eliminating them. The French police, who had turned patriotic by this point in World War II, allowed Dr. Petiot to peddle away on his bicycle. He excused himself with the claim that he had to burn some documents that the Gestapo sought.

Dissatisfied with the police's acceptance of Petiot's glib assurances, *Commissaire* Massu pursued the case. He found that Dr. Petiot had a long history of erratic behavior. Rejected as a boy, Petiot often resorted to cruelty. He reportedly had dipped the paws of a kitten in boiling water and then suffocated it. He liked to spike the eyes of sparrows with needles. And he had a long history of aggressive convulsions. After an unspecified nervous disorder supposedly disabled him, he won discharge from the army. Petiot passed through medical school in 8 months, set up a flourishing practice, and dabbled in politics.

Massu collected 3 tons of evidence to demonstrate the darker side of Dr. Petoit. Preying on the panic of Jews attempting to escape from France, Dr. Petiot posed as an expert in saving lives. He charged 25,000 francs for each person with the promise that he would get that person to Spain or South America. None arrived there. The victims went to Petiot's house, carrying their remaining money and jewels. They eventually appeared in the Seine. The police recovered 13 expertly dissected bodies from the river. One family, the Knellers, fled to Petiot in 1942. Boatmen later found the dismembered bodies of the family, and policemen discovered items of clothing in Dr. Petiot's house that belonged to the family.

Dr. Petiot went undetected until 1944, as his victims, after all, wanted to disappear. Massu doggedly kept on his trail, however, and discovered more evidence of bodies. He later declared it "the greatest criminal offense of the century."

Finally brought to trial in 1946, Petiot denied any guilt; he quipped with the press, went to sleep in the witness stand, and joked about not paying taxes: "I'm a patriot. The French are notorious for tax evasion." Overwhelmed by the evidence, the court found Petiot guilty on 26 counts of murder. Although he never admitted his guilt, Petiot lost his head to the guillotine in 1946 (see Maeder, 1979).

From 1972 until 1976, across the world from France, another psychopath surfaced in such romantic places as Kabul and Katmandu, Goa and Macao. Charles Sobhraj, part Indian and Vietnamese, used many accomplices in his various enterprises but felt no affection for any of them. Essentially, he lured Western tourists with promises of sexual or monetary adventures. He would then rob and kill them. Indian police accused him of 24 murders, but a New Delhi court found him guilty of only 1. The court sentenced him to prison in 1978.

Sobhraj had been raised out of wedlock in Saigon. His beautiful mother worked in a Saigon bar where his father seduced her. He deserted the woman shortly after Sobhraj's birth in 1941.

Scrambling for a living, Sobhraj ran away from home, journeyed to Thailand and then to India. There, he hit on various schemes to entice tourists into his moneymaking, eventually deadly enterprises (Thompson, 1979). As Thompson's brilliant account of Charles Sobhraj makes clear, he represents a clear illustration of the psychopath: "the most dangerous sort of predator— intelligent, energetic, singleminded, charismatic, conscienceless [Buckley, 1979]."

"Borderline" Psychopaths

Ironically, neither Sobhraj nor Dr. Petiot had gotten into serious trouble with the law until their final apprehensions. Unlike Gary Gilmore, they could have been "part-time lunatics" (as one writer called Dr. Petiot) or "borderline psychopaths"—except that both clearly exhibited the psychopathic syndrome and neither was adjudged as officially insane.

Such borderline cases undoubtedly exist and it would be pedantic to insist on an absolute dichotomy between psychopaths and other disordered people. The true psychopath, whether his society regards him as "normal" or "depraved," rests at one end of a continuum of behavior. As Richard Jenkins (1957), commenting about diagnosing psychopaths, wrote, "If one divides the human race into persons of short stature and persons not of short stature . . . different qualified observers will find widely different numbers of short persons. . . . All observers will agree that a few extremely short persons are short [p. 100]." So it is with the psychopath.

Clearly, we should reserve the term psychopath only for those who reveal a configuration of the essential traits of asociality, insensitivity, guiltlessness, and lovelessness. By no means should society expand it to include, say, the majority of criminal offenders or deviants of any stripe. Indeed, as discussed in the next chapter, psychopaths may pass for a long time—even forever—as normal, functioning human beings. Such people may well pose an even greater threat to society than the overtly criminal psychopath.

The Incidence of Criminal Psychopathy

Because of prior confusion over diagnosis and because certain cultures have a high tolerance for psychopathic behavior, one finds it extremely difficult to estimate the exact number of psychopaths who have been labeled as criminal. Sheldon Glueck has estimated that approximately 20% of incarcerated criminals can be labeled psychopathic (Glueck, in Lindner, 1944). In Ecuador, Cruz (1939) noted that 13% of prisoners in a typical Quito prison might be termed psychopathic (1939). English psychiatrists guessed that their prisons contained 18% psychopaths (Hyland, 1942); American Naval officials put the estimate at 26% (Curran & Mallison, 1944). In our 1980 survey of institutions for juvenile delinquents, approximately 30% appeared psychopathic (see Chapter 10). Canada reported an incidence of 7% in 1971 (Reid, 1978).

In 1978, Silberman used FBI statistics to show that "hard core" criminals account for nearly 75% of all arrests in the United States; yet they composed only 9% of the officially recorded criminal population. (Obviously, one should not equate chronic offenders with the psychopathic population, although there is certainly an overlap.)

Thus, depending on the nature of the institution and the data used, reliable estimates range from a high of 30% to a low of 7%. On a rough, conservative basis, one might suppose that an average of about 10% of criminals are, on a cross-cultural basis, psychopathic.

Even this estimate overlooks the more intelligent psychopaths who may evade the net of criminal laws, and it certainly ignores those "normal" psychopaths who carry out their activities without punishment from their society.

References

Allport, G. *Becoming*. New Haven: Yale University Press, 1955.

Arendt, H. *Eichmann in Jerusalem*. New York: The Viking Press, 1963.

Bandura, A., & Walters, R. H. *Social learning and personality development*. New York: Holt, Rinehart and Winston, 1963.

Becker, H. S., Geer, B., Hughes, E., & Strauss, A. *Boys in white*. Chicago: University of Chicago Press, 1961.

Bender, L. Post-encephalitic behavior disorders in childhood. In J. B. Neal (Ed.). *Encephalitis*. New York: Grune and Stratton, 1942.

Bender, L. Psychopathic behavior disorders in children. In R. Lindner and R. Seliger (Eds.), *Handbook of correctional psychology*, New York: Philosophical Library, 1947.

Buckley, T. The friendly stranger. *New York Times,* October 21, 1979.

Capote, T. *In cold blood.* New York: Random House, 1965.

Chornyak, J. Some remarks on the diagnosis of the psychopathic delinquent. *American Journal of Psychiatry,* 1947, 97:1327–1331.

Cleckly, H. *The mask of sanity* (5th ed.). St. Louis: C. V. Mosby, 1976.

Cruz, J., Estudio de las Personalidaes Psyicopaticas en Neustra Crimnalidad. *Archives Criminalidad Neuropsychiatry,* 1939, 3:38–50.

Curran, D., & Mallison, P. Psychopathic personality. *Journal of Mental Science,* 1944, 90:266–286.

Epstein, S. M. Toward a unified theory of anxiety. In B. A. Maher (Ed.), *Progress in experimental personality research.* New York: Academic Press, 1967.

Freyhan, F. A., Psychopathology of personality functions in psychopathic personalities. *Psychiatric Quarterly,* 1951, 25:458–471.

Funkenstein, D. H., Greenblatt, M., & Solomon, H. C. Psychophysiological study of mentally ill patients. *American Journal of Psychiatry,* 1949, 106:16–28.

Hare, R. *Psychopathy.* New York: Wiley, 1970.

Henderson, Sir David. *Psychopathic states.* New York: Norton, 1939.

Hyland, H. H., & Richardson, J. C. Psychoneuroses in the Canadian Army overseas. *Canadian Medical Association Journal,* 1942, 47:432–440.

Ingram, G. L., Gerard, R. E., Quay, R. E., and Levinson, R. B. An experimental program for the psychopathic delinquent. *Journal of Research in Crime and Delinquency,* 1970, 7:24–30.

Jenkins, R. Review of psychopathy and delinquency. *American Journal of Orthopsychiatry,* 1957, 26:245.

Kinberg, O. On the concept of the psychopath. *Theoria,* 1946, 3:169–180.

Lindner, L. A., Golman, H., Dinitz, S., & Allen, H. Antisocial personality type with cardiac lability. *Archives of General Psychiatry,* 1970, 23 (September): pp. 410–411.

Lindner, R. *Rebel without a cause.* New York: Grune and Stratton, 1944.

Lykken, D. T. A study of anxiety in the sociopathic personality. Ph.D. dissertation, University of Minnesota, 1955.

Lykken, D. T. A study of anxiety in the sociopathic personality. *Journal of Abnormal and Social Psychology,* 1957, 55:6–10.

Maeder, T. *The unspeakable crimes of Dr. Petiot.* Boston: Little, Brown, 1979.

Mailer, N. *The executioner's song.* Boston: Little, Brown, 1979.

Maslow, A. H. *Motivation and personality.* New York: Harper, 1954.

Mathis, H. I. Emotional responsivity in the antisocial personality. Ph.D. dissertation, George Washington University, Washington, D.C. 1970.

McCord, W. & McCord, A. *American social problems.* St. Louis: Mosby, 1977.

Milgram, S. A behavioral study of obedience. *Journal of Abnormal and Social Psychology,* 1963, 67:371–378.

Oleson, V. L., & Whittaker, E. W. *The silent dialogue.* San Francisco: Jossey-Bass, 1968.

Petrie, A. *Individuality in pain and suffering.* Chicago: University of Chicago Press, 1967.

Reid, W. (Ed.). *The psychopath.* New York: Brunner/Mazel, 1978.

Rotenberg, M. Psychopathy, insensitivity, and sensitization. *Professional Psychology,* 1975 (August): 175–180.

Rotenberg, M. Psychopathy and differential insensitivity. In R. Hare and D. Schelling (Eds.), *Psychopathic behavior: Approaches to research.* New York: Wiley, 1978.

Sagarin, E. *Deviance and deviants.* New York: Praeger, 1975.

Sears, R., Maccoby, E., & Levin, H. *Patterns of child rearing.* Evanston, Illinois: Row, Peterson, 1956.

Schachter, S., & Latane, B. *Crime and the autonomic nervous system*. Nebraska Symposium on Motivation (Vol. 11), Lincoln: University of Nebraska Press, 1964.

Shirer, W. *The rise and fall of the third reich*. New York: Simon and Schuster, 1960.

Silberman, C. *Criminal violence, criminal justice*. New York: Random House, 1978.

Smith, R. J. *The psychopath in society*. New York: Academic Press, 1978.

Sudnow, D. *Passing on*. New York: Prentice-Hall, 1967.

Sutherland, E. Sexual psychopath laws. *Journal of Criminal Law, Criminology and Police Science*, 1950, *40*:543–554.

Symkal, A., & Thorne, F. Etiological studies of psychopathic personality. *Journal of Clinical Psychology*, 1951, *7*:299–316.

Szasz, T. Criminal responsibility and psychiatry. In H. Toch (Ed.), *Legal and criminal psychiatry*. New York: Holt, Rinehart and Winston, 1961.

Thorton, N. The relationship between crime and the psychopathic personality. *Journal of Criminal Law, Criminology and Police Science*, 1951, *42*:199–204.

Thompson, T. *Serpentine*. New York: Simon and Schuster, 1979.

Turnbull, C. *The mountain people*. New York: Simon and Schuster, 1974.

Weinberg, K. *Society and personality disorders*. New York: Prentice-Hall, 1959.

White, R. *The abnormal personality*. New York: Ronald Press, 1948.

Williams, Emylyn. *Beyond belief*. New York: Random House, 1967.

2

The Banality of Evil: "Normal" Psychopaths

As Dostoevsky knew, one can encounter psychopaths in all walks of life: from landowners to policemen, from college professors to actresses, from the ladies of "Society" to politicians. The lonely stranger need not kill or commit obvious crimes; he or she may live next door to you, maintaining an outwardly normal facade, cutting the lawn, clipping the bushes, attending church, and never coming to the attention of criminal authorities.

These "banal" psychopaths, however, have the same configuration of traits as their criminal comrades: asociality, insensitivity, a lack of guilt, and an inability to form loving relationships. Because of intelligence, the accidents of history, the cleverness of their lawyers, wealth—or many other accidents of fate—these psychopaths go largely undetected and unconvicted of crimes.

Cleckly, a psychiatrist, first noted the omnipresence of psychopaths in everyday life (1976) and the late Hannah Arendt "popularized the notion that evil in our time has become banal [Hollander,

1980]." Her analysis of Adolf Eichmann revealed him as both a psychopath and a respected bureaucrat who followed the orders of the Nazi regime (Arendt, 1963). Similarly, Alexander Solzhenitzyn's works on Russian concentration camps have demonstrated that nameless bureaucrats can commit atrocities on the grandest scale. Whether they justify their actions in the name of a "Thousand Year Reich" or Communist ideals, these banal psychopaths represent one of the greatest challenges of our age. "With a curious mixture of horror and relish," Paul Hollander (1980) astutely observed about the nameless people who ran concentration camps, "pundits and the educated public alike seemed to rejoice in the idea that potentially all of us are amoral monsters. . . . There was something morbidly fascinating about the combination of almost unimaginable moral outrages . . . and the pedestrian, mundane character of the individuals who perpetrated them [p. 499]."

Obviously, not all Nazis who turned human skin into lamp shades or all Russians who tortured dissidents were psychopaths. Equally clearly, not all members of the inner circle of these specially chosen groups would do their jobs. At the risk of death, many members of Hitler's select group, the S.S., refused to participate in the killing of Jews (Arendt, 1963).

The Case of Eichmann

And yet, some did. Adolph Eichmann one of the supreme technocrats of Nazi exterminations, accepted his task with bureaucratic determination. In 1932, Eichmann had joined the Nazi party and subsequently rose in rank as an S.S. officer. He played a key role in the exportation and killing of millions of Jews, first from Vienna and then Budapest. When Hitler's regime collapsed, he escaped across Europe and eventually found sanctuary in Argentina under an assumed name.

Israeli agents discovered him in May, 1960, kidnapped him to Jerusalem, and put him on trial in April, 1961. He faced 15 charges of crimes against the Jewish people and crimes against humanity. He stoutly pleaded not guilty to every offense. Yet, strangely, he dictated a detailed, self-justifying confession to an Israeli official in the quiet of his jail cell.

From the confines of a glass-enclosed, bullet-proof booth, Eichmann conducted his defense on peculiar grounds: He personally did not dislike Jews and he had not actually killed anyone with his own hands. Further, he maintained that any man in his position would have done his duty. A mass of evidence—which he did not attempt to contradict—showed that Eichmann had, in fact, administered the deaths of millions. The court found him guilty and he was hanged.

"He left no doubt that he would have killed his own father if he had received an order to that effect [Arendt, 1963, p. 19]." And he showed absolutely no guilt about his crimes: "Repentence," he said, "is for little children [p. 21]."

This seemingly ordinary little man emerged from a lower-middle-class environment. Much to the chagrin of his parents, he did poorly in school and was forced to earn a meager living as a vacuum cleaner salesman. Rejected by his family and society, Eichmann discovered a new home in the Nazi party. When he joined the S.S., he felt that "from a humdrum life without significance and consequence the wind had blown him into history, as he understood it; namely, into a movement that always kept moving and in which somebody like him— already a failure in the eyes of his social class, of his family, and hence in his own eyes as well—could start from scratch and still make a career [Arendt, 1963, p. 29]."

He made no close friends in the movement, and his superiors blocked his promotion to the highest S.S. ranks. Yet, at times, he rubbed elbows with the most respected men in the nation. As he repeatedly declared, execution of the Jews never bothered him as all of the highest civil servants he met approved of Hitler's "Final Solution."

In the view of Arendt, Eichmann was merely a bureaucratic child of the whole Nazi era. "Systematic mendacity constituted the general, and generally accepted, atmosphere of the Third Reich [Arendt, 1963, p. 47]." Eichmann believed that "of course . . . if he had not transported them [the Jews], they would not have been delivered to the butcher. 'What,' he asked, 'is there to admit [p. 47]?' "

Heinrich Himmler, a superior officer, had instructed Eichmann that "we realize that what we are expecting from you is 'superhuman,' to be 'superhumanly inhuman [Himmler, quoted in Arendt, 1963, p. 93].' " "I felt free of all guilt," Eichmann responded. 'Who was I to have my own thoughts in this matter [p. 101].' "

Although psychiatrists found him legally sane, Eichmann demonstrated the basic traits of psychopaths. He served the Nazi party not out of a sense of social duty or even a hatred of Jews, but because it gave him a chance to escape his lonely, insignificant life. He was "fed up with being an anonymous wanderer between the worlds [p. 42]." He felt no guilt about one of the most gigantic experiments in horror undertaken in the twentieth century.

In Arendt's view, Eichmann displayed his insensitivity in "his almost total inability even to look at anything from the other fellow's point of view [p. 43]." And, although he had married late in life, he felt no emotion about leaving his wife, having liaisons with other women (including a Jewish girl, thereby violating one of the most important of Nazi taboos), or his inability to form friendships among his peers.

If the Nazis had won the war or if Eichmann could have remained in Argentina, he would probably not have won the notoriety he craved. People would have known him, if at all, as an efficient civil servant or as a salesman.

This very banality of "normal" psychopaths makes it difficult to detect them or to stop their actions before mayhem has occurred. Unlike the criminal psychopath, the socially accepted type seldom ends up convicted by a court—unless by ill-fate, like Eichmann, he finds the entire society that encouraged his behavior in ruins around him. Lacking in anxiety or neurosis, they are most unlikely to show up on a psychiatrist's couch—although more than other students interested in psychology, they are apt to sit at the other end of the couch (that is, as clinical psychologists) (Smith, 1978). Often the mass media idolize them as the epitome of their particular time. Thus, most clinical or experimental studies of psychopaths depend on biased samples of prisoners or mental hospital inmates.

In order to examine the psychopath in all of his manifestations, we must turn to more impressionistic but not necessarily less valid portraits of the normal psychopath drawn by brilliant biographers or perceptive anthropologists.

The Normal Psychopath in Western Biographies

Three outwardly quite different people—a reclusive woman with social ambitions, a capitalistic "robber baron," and a man who almost dominated Germany—have been studied and thoroughly documented by biographers. Lizzie Borden, J. Pierpont Morgan, and Herman Goering had little in common—except their psychopathic character syndromes.

"A PRIVATE DISGRACE": LIZZIE BORDEN

On stifling hot days in summer, Lizzie Borden usually secluded herself in the "upper-crust" section of Fall River, Massachusetts (Lincoln, 1967). In August of 1892, however, the young woman picked up an axe in the basement and chopped her stepmother to pieces. An hour later, her banker father returned early from work. Lizzie dispatched him with the axe after a casual conversation. She then carefully disposed of her dress, hid the axe, and prepared to face "private disgrace" in the eyes of Fall River society.

Tried and acquitted because the defense hid critical evidence—and because the self-created orphan could bribe her maid and hire an expert lawyer for an outrageous $25,000 fee, Lizzie Borden became "Lisbeth of Maplecroft." She lived on in a bizarre, isolated atmosphere for 35 more years.

Victoria Lincoln, the gifted novelist, lived a block from Lizzie Borden, knew her well, and found the evidence that demolished the acquittal verdict (1967).

Lizzie Borden had pursued the idle interests of a rich, but parochial, young woman of the Victorian period: She played the piano, participated in church affairs, and sought discreetly but without success to find a suitable swain. All that changed in 1892: She became a legend and the subject of songs and stories about the woman who wielded an axe against her parents in a mid-morning slaughter.

Few knew that Lizzie hated her stepmother of 28 years, a bloated woman who could barely manage to navigate her way out of their house. Lizzie's miserly father, a stern man who always collected his rents and interests in person, had little time or interest to devote to her. Her only sister, whom Lizzie dominated, was a mouselike person who served her slavishly once Lizzie had inherited the family fortune.

Outwardly dignified and religious, Lizzie had one hidden problem—later diagnosed by a neurologist—which at times threw her into rages. She suffered from seizures of epilepsy in the temporal lobe (Lincoln, 1967).

Five years before the murders, an act of her father's generosity profoundly angered Lizzie. He deeded some property to Lizzie, her sister, and her stepmother. Lizzie regarded this as a grave affront as her stepmother, in her opinion a usurper, deserved no gifts. Lizzie simmered over the supposed injustice and complained openly about it to her sister and a few rare acquaintances. She went so far as to visit various local pharmacies seeking prussic acid, supposedly for cleaning clothes. The pharmacist refused her since prussic acid had no cleansing properties but could easily be used to kill another human being. (Ill-educated, Lizzie did not know that she could easily have purchased arsenic without a prescription and that it would have done the job effectively.)

Just before the murders, Lizzie learned of a further insult: Her father planned to give his wife another piece of property that Lizzie fondly remembered from childhood. Her stepmother perceived Lizzie's anger but only complained vaguely to a doctor that "someone" was poisoning her. (Probably, the doctor believed, she merely suffered from indigestion.)

In August of 1892, according to the painstaking reconstruction by Lincoln, Lizzie went to the basement and found an axe. She then chopped up her lethargic, sleeping stepmother. Her father unexpectedly came home from lunch and found her burning a bloodied dress. She sat in front of the stove on a day of intense heat. Although he must have been surprised, the father allowed Lizzie (in an unusual display of affection) to lure him into taking a nap rather than investigating the carnal scene upstairs. As he slept, she killed him with five swift slashes. She then burned the axe handle in the stove and ineffectively hid the axe blade. (Later experts testified that only that particular blade could have made the indentures on her parents' skulls.) Lizzie had the sole opportunity to kill her parents, the only motive, and was found in the house after all doors had been locked from the inside.

Yet, a jury acquitted her. Why? The remnants of her stained dress had been hidden, her lawyer performed superbly, and various groups took up her defense. Congregationalist ministers gave sermons in her defense, the Women's Christian Temperance Union (W.C.T.U.) claimed that no well-known teetotaler would commit the crime, and feminists argued that all women were innately gentle. Most importantly, a key witness to the dress burning, the maid, was bribed and soon left for Australia.

After inheriting her parents' money, Lizzie Borden lived a grand life as mistress of "Maplecroft," a mansion, while her sister and other servants catered to her needs. Her later life had its odd, but unprosecuted aspects. She sent a package of pictures of her parents' mutilated bodies to a friendly detective "as a memento of an interesting occasion." She stole art objects from a Boston firm but covered up the scandal with money. She took up various, short-lived lesbian liaisons.

Like Eichmann, she never admitted her guilt, she showed no lasting attachment to anyone, and she treated the murder of her parents with a monumental lack of sensitivity. She cared not a whit about the customs and morality of her society. She even dropped her church-going facade.

Lizzie Borden died in 1927. She was buried after an unattended service conducted by an undertaker. At her own prior orders, she was buried secretly at night.

In New York, a founder of American capitalism probably read of Lizzie Borden and may even have admired her brazen greed. Whereas J. P. Morgan shared her traits of asociality, guiltlessness, lovelessness, and insensitivity, he never personally resorted to murder. He did not need to as his well-paid underlings could be used to conduct the darker side of his operations.

THE COLOSSUS OF CAPITALISM: J. P. MORGAN

In 1901, a fierce, heavily mustached man of portly bearing marched down the halls of Windsor Castle to congratulate the new king of Great Britain and Emperor of India, Edward VII (Corey, 1930). The king–emperor looked forward to the meeting as J. P. Morgan had just formed the largest steel company in the world and had occupied himself with the buying of a British shipping trust. *The New York World* caricatured Morgan as invading England and purchasing all of the islands as well as the king (*Tribune*, 1901). "From the King down," one reporter wrote, "all concentrated their attention on Mr. Morgan and their curiosity was not unmixed with awe. . . . Maybe Mr. Morgan should take a fancy to Windsor and buy it [*Tribune*, 1901]."

The courtiers had more than a little reason to fear the American. Morgan represented the new aristocracy of money. No corporation in the world could match the economic power of his conglomerates; few if any monarchs could equal his personal fortune. Proceeding from the coronation of King Edward, Morgan allowed Kaiser Wilhelm II to dine on his yacht, "The Corsair." Later, Wilhelm called Morgan "his mascot," presented him with the order of the Red Eagle, and sent him a statue of himself. Morgan, as a giant of a new industrial power, accepted these honors as his due. Arrogant, possessed by unbounded ambition, arbitrary in temperament, known as "Pierpontifex Maximus" by the English clergy, Morgan was keenly aware that his financial power influenced global events. He felt equal—at least—to the political rulers whom he met; as he commented in regal manner about the Kaiser, "He Pleases Me [*The World*, 1913]."

By the early 1900s, Morgan had assumed an almost mystical stature. He controlled the House of Morgan, his financial instrument, with implacable will. If one of his partners disagreed with a decision, Morgan ostracized him. He dominated the board meetings of his colleagues by declaring, *"I'll* do this!" (Corey, 1930). He had "associates" but no intimates. He casually enjoyed a line of mistresses whom he cast off to colleagues who remained grateful for his generosity. He apparently felt little pity for the discarded mistresses and neither they nor their newly appointed masters ever manifested open animosity toward him. He appeared, as well as behaved, imperially: a jutting jaw, glowering eyebrows, fierce eyes, and a huge nose characterized his face. He brutally crushed his competitors and faced the world with a truculent, overbearing, and merciless facade (Corey, 1930).

Morgan as a Child

Morgan began his life as a fragile child and suffered from an undiagnosed lung disease. Doctors coddled him until he entered the English High School in Boston at the age of 14. The other pupils disliked him. He was a poor student, except in mathematics. Silent and alone, he apparently suffered an unhappy adolescence (Corey, 1930). He was born to a wealthy family, headed by Junius Morgan, who controlled an international banking firm. His father, worried about his son's apparent lack of talent, was known to ask visitors: "What shall I do with him? [Corey, 1930, p. 130] "

At age 22, J. P. Morgan vowed never to enter into a serious romance or marriage. Timidly trained and financed by his father, he went into the world of banking. Women or friends were never to figure prominently in his life.

J. P. Morgan immersed himself in his work. He did not abandon it even for such relatively minor affairs as the American Civil War. Instead, like many financiers of his time, he bought a substitute who fought in his place for $300.

Never actually fighting in a war, Morgan seldom failed to realize profits as other men shed their blood. In 1870, during the Franco–German War, Morgan and his father issued bonds to France that cleared more than $5 million in profits immediately before the Prussian victory. In 1889, Morgan and his father successfully intervened on Britain's side to make sure that Argentina paid her foreign debts. Argentina paid back Britain (and the Morgans) by raising taxes on the poor. In 1900, J. P. Morgan loaned Great Britain $43 million and in 1901, another $180 million to aid her during the Boer War. As usual, he cleared a very nice profit.

While reaping a good part of his fortune from abroad, J. P. Morgan did not ignore opportunities at home. He and his associates amassed a fortune in America by amalgamating properties and repressing labor discord.

Among his first domestic endeavors, Morgan enlisted in the wars over control of railroads. He took over the Susquehanna railroad after the board that he controlled issued him 3000 shares of "watered" stock. This enraged James Fisk, Morgan's opponent, for it meant direct competition with Fisk's own lines. In a series of complicated maneuvers, Fisk ordered the Tammany machine (which he controlled, and, in turn, had appointed the judiciary) to declare Morgan's stock invalid. The compliant judge did so and appointed one of Fisk's men as a receiver of the railroad. Morgan hired his own judge in another jurisdiction and had one of his men appointed as the "true" receiver. The legal machinations deteriorated into a physical battle. Morgan's men, masquerading as policemen, "arrested" Fisk. Fisk retaliated by ordering an Erie locomotive to ram one of Morgan's locomotives. Morgan's mercenaries then tore up tracks and severed telegraph lines.

Morgan won control of the railroad by having one of his judges pass the final decision. He proceeded to acquire the Philadelphia and Reading, the West Short Line, the Great Northern, and other railroads, as well as their coal mining fields. By 1900, Morgan and his interests controlled 67,183 miles of railroads; Harriman came in second with a mere 20,245 miles; and the Gould–Fisk system had only 16,074.

By the late 1890s Morgan proceeded to consolidate the steel industry. He formed the National Tube Co., the Federal Steel Co., and the American Bridge Co. out of 39 competing firms. Together, they claimed a virtual monopoly over some 1000 items of finished steel products. Merely in return for their services, Morgan and his associates got $4,450,000 in profits from Federal Steel in one year and another $37,500,000 from the other steel companies for "promotional" activities.

Few, except Morgan himself, could trace the intricacies of his business interests. Congressional committees met with strange lapses of memory when they asked Morgan to outline his activities. "No man was brighter," one of his associates said, "and no man could suffer from aphasia so conveniently as Morgan [Don McCord, 1950]."

Many of the ministers and moralists of the day looked on the House of Morgan as engaging in God's work. Great preachers condemned

Morgan's enemies, the trade unions. Henry Ward Beecher, who organized his church as a profit-making organization, and paid himself an annual salary of $20,000 a year, announced from the pulpit,

> "Is the great working class oppressed? Yes, undoubtedly it is. God has intended the great to be great and the little to be little." He added, "I do not say that a dollar a day is enough to support a workingman. But it is enough to support a man! . . . The man who cannot live on bread and water is not fit to live [Hibbins, 1927, p. 326]."

Many in the organized labor movement could not reconcile Morgan's actions with the teachings of the carpenter from Nazareth. At times, such as the coal strike, Morgan had used violence to force laborers into submission. At other times, he subtly coerced dissident workers into cooperation. In 1908, for example, he convinced United States Steel workers to avoid unionization with a vague promise of some kind of profit sharing. Actually, only about 4% of U.S. Steel's 168,000 workers received any extra money (Congressional Report, 1908).

By such methods, Morgan achieved secure financial control over much of the nation's wealth. During the gold panic of 1907, even his old opponent, Teddy Roosevelt, requested Morgan's aid in saving the nation's currency. The government deposited $42 million in Morgan's banks to spend as he wished. Morgan buoyed up the stock exchange by placing $25 million in investments. The panic subsided.

Morgan died peacefully on March 31, 1913, while on his customary trip to Europe. His one-time bitter enemy, William Jennings Bryan, had assumed the role of secretary of state. In deference to Morgan's "services" to the nation, Bryan ordered a special entourage to convey J. P. Morgan's body from Italy to the United States.

He had successfully won the game of his time without ever betraying a sense of guilt or insensitivity about the men he defeated. Unlike Carnegie and Rockefeller, he never wasted money on charities, as he believed only the strong won in the end.

In 1913, no one dared call him a psychopath. He had acted within the social norms of his day—more or less—and reaped the rewards.

THE "AMIABLE PSYCHOPATH": HERMANN GOERING

Like J. P. Morgan, Hermann Goering—head of the *Luftwaffe* in World War II, minister of production, President of the Reichstag, and heir apparent to Hitler—operated well within the twisted standards of morality of his own era. Only the debatable, post facto Nuremberg

trials conducted by his enemies led to his conviction as a war criminal. If the Nazis had won, their historians might well have portrayed him as a great man who ruled a vast empire.

G. M. Gilbert, chief psychologist at the Nuremberg trials, thoroughly examined Goering and described him as an "amiable psychopath." Even in defeat, Goering maintained a facade of charm, humor, and good spirits. Underneath this cover, however, Gilbert detected total guiltlessness, complete insensitivity to his victims, brutality, and a devotion to himself—rather than Hitler's cause—as his prime traits (Gilbert, 1948).

Goering's Background

Raised in a Prussian military atmosphere, Goering lived in a rigid, loveless environment. His father, a Prussian official, ignored him. His mother distrusted and disliked him. When Gilbert asked Goering what his first memory was, Goering replied that he recalled "bashing his mother in the face with both fists when she came to embrace him after a prolonged absence [1948, p. 11]."

Unable to control his impulsive brutality and attacks on his sisters, his parents moved Goering from one boarding school to another. He enjoyed the flashy uniforms of a military school more than anything else. "Hermann will either be a great man," his mother prophesized, "or a great criminal [Gilbert, 1948, p. 14]."

Luckily for him, World War I exploded when he was a youth. His military background, his aggressiveness, and his greed "found its most desirable expression in the military prerogatives of his culture [Gilbert, 1948, p. 45]." Second only to Richtoven, Goering emerged from the war as a crack air ace. He enjoyed the excitement of war but hardly the discipline of the German army: He took leaves when he wanted, established a fake quartermaster company, and reaped in the profits when he was not flying. His reckless bravery in the air saved him from prosecution.

Defeat and peace bored him. He married a Swedish countess who lavished riches on him. Yet, he remained distant from her. In the early 1920s, he met members of the Nazi movement. Its symbols, promise of glory, and paramilitary panache appealed to him—and Goering's war record added luster to the Nazi party.

As the Nazi party gained power, Goering moved with it. He was not just an obedient slave, as were many of Hitler's people, or a faceless bureaucrat like Eichmann. Goering wanted power and was perfectly willing to sacrifice Hitler's interest—when the war came to an end—by trying to save himself.

Goering cannot be depicted as a sadistic monster. He, together with Himmler, saw to it that men with a record of criminal brutality would not be admitted to the S.S. or serve as actual executioners in concentration camps (Gilbert, 1948). Goering wished rather to enlist men who would do his will without question and without "irrational" sadistic pleasure.

Goering was not, however, above the use of blustering threats. As president of the Reichstag, he despoiled Germany's young parliamentary tradition in an effective maneuver to get rid of possible opponents. As Goering once announced to the Reichstag, "I am not here to exercise justice, but to wipe out and exterminate! [Gilbert, 1948, p. 218]"

As Hitler's hegemony eroded, Goering tried vainly to take over the rule of Germany. Hitler learned of his plans and reduced him to a powerless position. Goering retired to his castle, presided over orgies, and adorned himself in lipstick and fingernail polish.

During the Nuremberg trials, Gilbert noted an air of total insensitivity and insouciance about Goering as the prosecutors documented his atrocities. Goering watched films of gaunt concentration camp victims, for example, but said, "It was such a good afternoon, too, until they showed the film . . . everybody was laughing with me . . . but the film spoiled it all [Gilbert, 1948, p. 288]." When convicted, Goering took poison to escape the hangman. Just before his death, he snapped, "You can take your morality and your repentance and your democracy and stick it up! [Gilbert, 1948, p. 228]"

His guiltlessness, insensitivity, and isolation from other human beings marked him as a prototypical psychopath. And yet, his abilities and position, like Morgan, almost allowed him to run an entire nation according to his impulsive whims. Goering's history, as Robert Lindner (1944) warned, suggests that "the psychopath is the embryonic storm trooper [p. 79]."

The Psychopath and Society

Clearly, the proper social, economic, and historical conditions can place psychopaths like Goering and Morgan in control of a nation's destiny, while less flamboyant people like Eichmann follow in their path.

This vital connection between personality and social structure has often been ignored. American sociologists have been primarily guilty of this omission. Edwin Sutherland and Donald Cressey (1974), two of

the most famous American criminologists, for example, have virtually denied any connection between psychopathy and crime. They have, however, admitted that "social interaction"—which can only mean the interaction between particular personalities in a particular social situation—is crucial. Sutherland also highlighted the importance of "white collar," largely unpunished crimes. Yet, he failed to make any connection between the kinds of people who commit such crimes and the society—such as America in the nineteenth century or Germany in the 1930s—which encouraged and even rewarded them. This antipsychological, ahistorical nature of (American) sociology has greatly hindered the exploration of psychopathy.

In quite different ways, Don C. Gibbons, Walter Reckless, as well as Marxist critics have made some efforts to correct this myopia (see Gibbons, 1979). Alex Inkeles has developed the most impressive prevailing arguments in favor of uniting sociological, historical, and psychological perspectives (1968). Rightly, Inkeles (1968) argued that sociology must consider psychological factors as certain qualities draw people to play particular social roles in their historical context and, in turn, the needs and desires of individuals affect the nature of their social structure. Naturally, too, psychiatrists and psychologists must understand the social and historical forces that allow psychopathy to flower.

Anthropologists have made perhaps the greatest contribution to an empirical understanding of the interaction between personality and social structure. Specifically, they have produced evidence that certain societies—perhaps one would be wiser to call them "conglomerations" or "collections" of people—create a "normal" pattern of psychopathy. In such groups, the psychopath represents an expected, often ideal type while the scorned, ridiculed "abnormal" person demonstrates love, trust, moral accountability, and sociability.

The "Normal" Psychopathic Group in Anthropology

THE IK OF UGANDA

When Colin Turnbull (1972), the distinguished anthropologist, first stumbled upon the Ik in the mountains of Uganda, he reported it as "my first taste of real loneliness [p. 3]." He had experienced the wilds of Africa before, but had always met with hospitality and kindness from groups such as the pygmies. The Ik—scattered in fortresslike huts in the borderland between Uganda and Kenya—proved quite

49

different and established, for Turnbull, some basic judgments about the nature of man.

He had recruited two Ik boys from a missionary settlement as his translators. Dressed in proper Western attire (unlike their relatives who ran naked), the boys seemed friendly enough. Yet, in their first confrontation with the real Ik, Turnbull heard a weak old man's voice coming from a hut: "Give me cigarettes." One of the mission boys shrugged and said, "There's no one there!" Turnbull threw cigarettes in the hut. The old man could not reach them. "You see," the mission boy said triumphantly, "You should not have wasted cigarettes in that way." The old man's wife had died and he clearly was on the verge of death. The boys did not wish to bury them. Utterly hopeless and helpless, Turnbull tossed a bag of food into the stockade, much to the amusement of his child translators (p. 53). His later experience over a 2-year period merely confirmed his first impression of Ik cruelty.

The Ik never directly harmed Turnbull since he bought them off with food and cigarettes. Yet their everyday life throbbed with brutality and an almost complete insensitivity. They hated the old and the infirm. Children stole food from the mouths of the elderly or their own parents. They kicked dead people into ravines. Upon the death of a "loved one," the elders, children, and others fought with each other over any food or baubles left on the body. The adults laughed as infants burned in fires. One "mad" child tried to cuddle her arms around adults. Her mother and grandmother jumped up and down on her back, laughing at her absurdity.

The Ik had no families: The only use of a wife was to earn money as a whore from soldiers at a nearby army post. The Ik earned their livings by guiding—and then betraying—various other tribes who stole cattle. The Ik had no system of ethics as we know it: the word *good* meant simply *food*. Once, they had believed in some sort of God, but He had long ago withdrawn into mystery. Children were intolerable "mistakes." Turnbull learned of only three births among some 2000 people during the time he lived there. Sex, too, was burdensome because it took so much energy, but adultery (in the Western sense) was universal as it might bring in some profits in food.

When not betraying their neighbors or each other, the Ik had little to do. They sat on perches and watched vultures gather; they kicked cripples who scrambled for food; they laughed at children who tried to find something to eat. The children shuttled off into gangs at age 3 to fend for themselves. They beat up the old and crippled. The strongest children survived and went off on their own. If one stayed alive, the best age for males was between 15 and 19 when they were strongest. After that, old age soon set in. A very old man survived until 30. An extremely ancient, clever one might live on to 50.

Although devoid of a code of ethics as others would recognize it, the Ik still took pride in certain activities. They often formed a bond of "brotherhood" (*nyot*) with other tribesmen or people from distant villages. This allowed them to take anything they wished from their "brother" upon demand. The greatest feat of all, of course, was to trick your "brother" out of something he valued or merely steal it from him. The cardinal maxim for the Ik was never to show sympathy, care, or love to anyone.

As for food, women foraged for berries, men caught animals and ate them in solitary fashion off in the bush, and children "learned from the baboons"—a practice which Turnbull confessed he never quite understood. At times, elders would brag when their sons caught an antelope, devoured it themselves, and came home covered with blood.

The Ik and Psychopathy

"These people," Turnbull concluded, "did not suffer from some new form of sin [p. 190]." He learned that this dark, sinister tribe—which will undoubtedly die off by killing itself—was once a prosperous, religious, kindly group of hunters and gatherers. In 1934, however, the creation of a game preserve deprived them of the main source of their livelihood: the animals they hunted. They could not adjust and, within three generations, had turned into a group of cold, relatively isolated, selfish psychopaths.

Turnbull's eloquent summation of these food-starved people sounds very much like a description of psychopaths in Western society: "The lack of any sense of moral responsibility toward each other, the lack of any sense of teaming up, needing or wanting each other, showed up daily [p. 218]."

Because of his generosity with food, Turnbull fell under suspicion by the Ik. Perhaps, they thought, he served as a government agent seeking to convert them from betraying their fellow tribes in cattle stealing. One crucial confrontation—exhibiting the total lack of sensitivity or of a social bond between the Ik and others—revealed to them that he was merely a "fool." The tribal elders kept laughing at Turnbull for his kindness to them and accused him of ulterior motives. Turnbull asked Atum (perhaps his closest associate in the tribe) the reason for the derision. Atum said that "I had helped them a lot and what had I got out of that? When I said 'nothing,' the group just split its sides. 'That,' said Atum, 'is what we are laughing at.' And his clear blue eyes sparkled with pleasure [p. 111]."

Turnbull himself soon found that he had absorbed much of the Ik's insensitivity and lack of remorse. After hiding his remaining food, he departed to a Uganda army post where he pleaded, uselessly, for the plight of the Ik. The experience may well have altered Turnbull permanently—even as it would for those of us who are not experienced anthropologists (p. 295).

Deviance among the Ik

Turnbull found only two "deviants" who tried to escape this particularly fearful economic situation. One was a little girl named Adupa who sought love from others: the rest of the Ik thought her crazy. They beat and isolated her.

> Adupa cried, not because the others would beat her, but because of the pain she felt at that great, vast empty wasteland where love should have been. It was *that* that killed her. She demanded that her parents love her. She kept going back to their compound [p. 133].

> The parents of Adupa locked her in the compound and left her tight behind them. Ten days later, she died: "Her parents picked up what was left of her and threw it out, as one does the riper garbage, a good distance away [p. 133]."

Another woman, Nangoli, decided quite rationally to move her family to an area where food was more bountiful. Turnbull reasoned that, "under conditions of plenty, surely, the Ik would be a different people [p. 267]." He followed the small group to a lush valley where they had all the food they needed. Alas, the new environment did not fulfill his expectations. The people ate all of the available food immediately and hid the rest. Three generations of "socialization" as psychopaths proved too much. "The main problem was that there was too much and although each person had all he could eat, he was still unwilling to see others eat what he could not [p. 267]."

Nangoli went mad; she hallucinated, and soon committed herself to jail. She refused Turnbull's help in releasing her from jail. Turnbull concluded: "Nangoli, I think, was the last Ik who was human [p. 268]."

THE ALORESE IN PARADISE

A lack of food may well drive a group of people into a pervasive psychopathic pattern. Yet, as Turnbull showed, an abundance of food cannot revive patterns of trust that once existed. A tribe that lived far away in space and time from the Ik underlines this point.

The Alorese live on one of the agriculturally abundant islands of the Indonesian archipelego. When Cora DuBois (1944) studied them, they did not suffer from a lack of food as they implemented both agricultural and fishing techniques that kept them fully supplied.

Yet, they had developed a social organization that deprived and isolated children at birth. In Alor, women carried the main burdens of work. Two weeks after birth, the mother left her baby and returned to the field to work. No one had particular responsibility for nurturing the child. The baby was shifted from house to house in an inconsistent, sometimes rejecting chaos. At times, the maternal uncle took charge of the baby; at other times, older children guided his socialization. As the Alorese did not value children, the parents themselves seldom dealt with the babies. When they did, they teased and ridiculed the children, and sometimes tortured them. The typical child seldom experienced a lasting, continuous relationship with an adult.

The result, as DuBois viewed them, was the creation of a suspicious, guiltless, self-centered people. The Alorese commonly explored in anger; they sought power for its own sake, and competed ruthlessly against each other. They possessed only a vague self-image and treated each other with lightly veiled hostility. In other words, the neglected Alorese child grew up to become a psychopath, yet one considered normal in that society.

A particularly important aspect of DuBois' research was that she administered Rorshach tests to the Alorese. She dispatched the results, without comment on her expectations, to an expert analyst in New York. Without knowing anything about the people or their society, the analyst blindly interpreted them and came to a conclusion identical with that of DuBois: the subjects were guiltless, hostile, suspicious, competitive, and had an ambivalent self-image. Thus, for the first time, a combination of anthropological fieldwork and psychological analysis independently revealed the existence of an entire group of psychopaths.

Psychopathy in Simple Societies

The situation of both the Alorese and the Ik strongly suggests that severe deprivation in childhood—whether caused by the economic disintegration of a once secure society or by a long-standing tradition of childrearing—contributes to the production of "normal" psychopaths. Both of these studies, of course, dealt with relatively unsophisticated, technologically backward societies. What happens if supposedly "civilized" people are thrown into a situation of severe deprivation as adults?

THE URUGUAYAN CANNIBALS: "CIVILIZED" PSYCHOPATHS?

Under certain extreme, rare circumstances, people from technologically advanced societies have been placed in situations of terrible deprivation that one might predict would produce psychopathy.

A dramatic illustration of this situation occurred in 1972. An Uruguayan air force plane destined for Chile crashed in the high Andes mountains. The plane carried a rugby team from an elite public school, some of their parents, and a few of their supporters. All people on the aircraft came from a rich, privileged, and Catholic background; none had criminal records and few, if any, could be called psychopaths. They looked forward to a championship match with an equivalent Chilean school (Read, 1974).

Somehow, the plane veered into an impenetrable, barren mountain range and crash-landed. Some of the passengers were killed, and their bodies were thrown onto the snow. The survivors staggered out of the plane and prayed for rescue. Their prayers went unanswered, and they soon ate the last morsels of food they had brought with them. They discovered—as had the Ik for generations—that such mountains produced no vegetation or game.

As their hunger grew and rescue planes failed to sight them, the survivors faced a grim alternative: to starve, or to eat the bodies of their dead comrades. They debated the morality of their decision but—with the exception of one man who refused to eat his wife—decided to chop up the bodies and consume them. At first, they divided the flesh equally after stripping and "cooking" it on the plane's wing.

Then, even the flesh began to dwindle in quantity and people developed a taste for certain parts—the liver, the thigh bone, etc. Pilfering began. The strong stole from the weak. The people who cut up the bodies gulped an extra sliver or two when they went unobserved. "The burden fell on those who either could not or would not work [Read, 1974, p. 125]." Faced with starvation, many of these highly moral survivors lapsed into a state of selfish guiltlessness.

As their situation deteriorated and rescue parties failed to arrive, the survivors chose the four strongest men to form a team charged with the task of climbing over the mountains into Chile. A new moral code evolved since the survival of the entire group depended on the success of this expedition. The group awarded extra meat to the four men, gave them rest, and excused them from "housekeeping" duties around the plane. "Once the four expeditionaries had been chosen," Read observed, "they became a warrior class whose special obligations entitled them to special privileges [p. 135]."

Although the expeditionary team became an elite, they allowed two factors to curtail their privileges. First, a group of three cousins who had been on the plane emerged as a form of judiciary that arbitrated disputes between the four chosen expeditionaries and the others. Second, the elite group encouraged those who worked at cutting up the bodies to receive more nourishment than the injured.

Eventually, after great hardships, the four men marched across the mountains to Chile. They sent rescue planes to pick up the other survivors.

Adult Trauma and Psychopathy

The cannibals had not turned into psychopaths but instead developed a rough code of justice that, admittedly, scorned the weak. As Catholics, the survivors justified eating their fellow men by comparing their actions to the symbolism of the Catholic mass where one "eats" the flesh of Christ. Read, the biographer of this group, has suggested that this rationale was developed while the people starved. Another source, however, says that the survivors thought up this moral justification as they returned, healthy and fat, on a plane from Chile to Uruguay (private communication, 1979).

In any case, the survivors went back to their ordinary lives in Uruguay. Deprivation had not transformed them into psychopaths, presumably because of their early socialization, just as abundance did not change the psychopathic behavior of the handful of Iks who moved to a land of plenty. Apparently, in the matter of psychopathy, early experiences have more power in shaping the personality than do adult traumas or triumphs.

These anthropological findings suggest that certain human groups under particular historical circumstances either create psychopathic personalities or allow psychopathic tendencies a broad range of expression, if not approval. The reverse also holds true. Early socialization experiences, as with the survivors, make them relatively immune to the corrosive effects of temporary deprivation. Studies of concentration camp victims, who obviously suffered from the most severe forms of deprivation and brutality, also showed that they did not—as a group—emerge as psychopaths. Indeed, certain societies seem virtually free of psychopathy.

THE HUTTERITES: AN "ANTIPSYCHOPATHIC" SOCIETY

The Hutterites, an Anabaptist group of some 9000 people, escaped from Germany to America because of religious persecution. They chose to live a life of rural isolation, cut off as far as possible from contacts with modern America. Their original prophet laid down strict rules which enjoined pacifism, a form of religious socialism, and simple living. He tried to order the life of his followers down to the most minute details: their form of dress, the meals eaten on each day (always duck on Sundays), and the exact social roles that every man, woman, and child is expected to perform.

Joseph Eaton and Robert Weil (1955) examined this isolated, rigidly controlled sect with the hope of measuring their level of "mental health." They found virtually no deviance within the group: there were no cases of divorce, murder, arson, physical assault, or sex crimes. The community maintained a jail, but even the oldest member could not remember when anyone had been incarcerated there. Eaton and Weil, using projective tests, found that the Hutterites had some aggressive tendencies but effectively suppressed them. Most importantly, for our purposes, they noted that "no individual warranted the diagnosis of psychopath [p. 235]."

The religious context of the community, its complete harmony, and its prescription that every individual follow an exact, specifically outlined social role from birth until death effectively inhibited the growth of psychopathy. As the most extreme penalty for the slightest deviation from the rules, the Hutterites exiled the offender. (To some degree, this might also explain the complete absence of psychopaths among those who remained in the community.)

The Hutterites, of course, have paid a price for their rigidly controlled society: a total lack of creativity. One woman, for example, received permission to outside of the community and gain training as a midwife nurse. When she returned, she attempted to establish a clinic and to teach expectant mothers some elementary rules of hygiene. Even these minor deviations proved too much for the elders and they banished her from the commune. Thus, it would appear that the complete suppression of any form of slight deviance, let alone psychopathy, may also require a totalitarian control over all forms of behavior.

Psychopathy and Culture

The Hutterites are a rare exception to the rule. As we view the full panoply of societies, it is clear that psychopathy was often praised or considered normal within a culture. Although possessing the same character structures as criminal psychopaths, members of such a culture do not behave in the wrong way, at the wrong place, and at the wrong time. How, then, can we detect the actual incidence of "normal" psychopaths in different societies?

The Prevalence of "Normal" Psychopaths in Different Societies

Because of different cultural milieus, different diagnoses, and different ways of gathering statistics, we will probably never know the exact incidence of those characterized by psychopathy but remaining within the bounds of acceptable behavior for particular groups around the world. Several suggestive studies do, however, offer a tentative insight into the problem. In general, these studies suggest (*a*) that the incidence of "normal" psychopaths is considerably higher than one would expect; (*b*) that in some countries, "normal" psychopaths outnumber more ordinary people suffering from a psychiatric disorder, such as neurotics; and (*c*) that certain populations exhibit a high, if unfulfilled, potential for psychopathic behavior.

THE OFFICIAL INCIDENCE OF "NORMAL" PSYCHOPATHS

The most superficial review of Western societies suggests that psychopathy permeates every level of society but can go largely unpunished. Consider just a few people who have risen into the public limelight:

• John Mitchell, once an American attorney general and a staunch upholder of law and order, supervised the Watergate burglaries, lied shamelessly, and spent a brief time in a "country club" jail for perjury. As described by the reporters who eventually uncovered his activities, he had distinctive psychopathic characteristics but had never been caught for a crime before (see Bernstein and Woodward, 1974).

• Andy Warhol, the king of pop sensitivity in the 1960s, has blatantly but graphically described his own psychopathy (Warhol & Hackett, 1979). As an artist and blue movie director, he enjoyed watching people destroy themselves. One victim of his attractions got drugs from her psychiatrist by allowing him to listen in on her dirty phone calls; another woman played at being Warhol's twin and when he tired of her, she disappeared into the drug world. Amusing, clever, lurid, and handsome, Warhol attracted the eccentrics from New York to California. He wanted them around him to sustain his creativity which resulted in his greatest triumph: an exact replica of a Campbell's soup can. He discarded his ties to people frivolously and readily admitted to his own amorality. "I don't think of myself as evil," he claimed, ". . . just realistic [p. 159]." One of his female companions shot him, but he recovered and continued on his own blithe path.

• Lieutenant William Calley murdered hundreds of villagers during the Vietnam War. He justified his massacre of women and children on grounds that he merely followed higher orders—a familiar refrain from the days of Nazism. The U.S. Army, however, disagreed and court-martialed him to a light penalty of house arrest in a pleasant cottage.

MENTAL HEALTH STATISTICS

These apparently "normal" psychopaths have received a great deal of public attention in America. They are undoubtedly merely the tip of an iceberg.

Most estimates of the number of socially functioning psychopaths have to be based on cases that come to the attention of mental health authorities (excluding criminal justice officials). Since psychopaths, unless forced, see little reason for presenting themselves to therapists for treatment, official figures probably deflate the actual incidence. As a minimal baseline, however, cross-national studies suggest that psychopathy hovers between 2 and 5% of the population as labeled by psychiatrists, psychologists, and social workers.

In the United States, Saenger (1968) found that 3.3% of patients in New York state mental clinics were psychopaths. In a classic study of New Haven, Hollingshead and Redlich (1958) found approximately 2% of the population had psychopathic symptoms. Dutch clinics report 4.3% psychopaths (Saenger, 1968). In a comprehensive estimate, Smith (1978) noted that Canada in 1972 had approximately 9% of mental inmates diagnosed as psychopaths; Finland reported 4% of inmates. Lebanese investigators found an incidence of 1.85% of the general population in 1973 (Katchadourian & Churchill, 1973).

In studies that have examined the relationship, scholars have found psychopathy more prevalent among the lower classes than among those who are more economically privileged (Hollingshead & Redlich, 1958; Katchadourian & Churchill, 1973). Most studies indicate that men predominate in the ranks of psychopaths, but some nations such as West Germany report about equal proportions of females as males (Smith, 1978).

Such estimates are necessarily rough and perhaps unduly conservative. Clearly, any compilation of prevalence data would benefit from the use of national, random samples diagnosed on the basis of behavior and symptoms, rather than labels. The most outstanding study that approximates this standard was done by Gabriel Mercuri (1977).

PSYCHOPATHY IN ITALY

Mercuri examined a general, nonclinic population in Italy. Between 1971 and 1974, Mercuri reviewed the case histories of all males who had been recruited to the Italian army and then refused service for psychiatric reasons. Using standards that conformed to our definition of the psychopath, Mercuri found a high proportion of psychopaths among this large and varied sample of Italians. In fact, many more men were found to be psychopathic than neurotic—a surprising conclusion since most social scientists believe that neuroses are far more rampant in Western societies, like Italy, than is psychopathy.

Despite Mercuri's excellent study, we still do not have an exact estimate of the incidence of psychopathy in different societies. As Robert Smith (1978) reasonably concluded, "More definitive cross-cultural comparisons await more definitive cross-cultural practices [p. 150]." Some indirect research strongly suggests that the actual incidence of psychopathic attitudes among a general population may well exceed most psychiatric estimates.

SOME INDIRECT MEASURES OF THE INCIDENCE OF PSYCHOPATHY

Two social psychologists, Richard Christie and Urie Bronfenbrenner, have developed intriguing, if indirect measures of the pseudo-psychopathic nature of some normal people in a variety of social situations. Neither researcher claims to have measured the true incidence of psychopathy in their populations (largely composed of students), but both have shed light on the possible nature of the "normal" psychopath and the environment that produces him or her. Drawing his inspiration from the writings of Niccolo Machiavelli,

Richard Christie and his associates (1970) developed a simple questionnaire that accurately delineates "Machiavellians" from others.

The Machiavellian person, according to Christie and Geis (1970), bears a striking resemblance to the psychopath: He or she has little affective interest in other people and manipulates them as objects; is unconcerned with conventional morality; is rational and lacks any gross signs of neurosis or psychosis; and the person lacks any ideological or idealistic goals. Machiavellian subjects (as would psychopaths, if they thought it expedient to tell the truth) agree with such statements on Christie's questionnaire as "the best way to handle people is to tell them what they want to hear" and to disagree with assertions such as "honesty is the best policy in all cases."

The so-called "Mach" scale has proved to be a highly discriminating instrument when used on outwardly normal people. The results of the use of the "Mach" scale indicate that:

- High "Machs" gain more money by manipulating people in experiments than low "Machs" (Christie & Geis, 1970).
- Machiavellians feel less trust in others and feel less altruistic than low "Machs" (Christie & Geis, 1970).
- The Machiavellian "does not enter into relationships that produce mutual solutions to problems." In artificial experimental situations, "He is psychologically 'stand-offish' [Smith, 1978; p. 160]," although he may solve problems more effectively than people who consider the feelings of others.
- The Machiavellian does not, as one would expect, score high on measures of neurosis or psychosis. Yet, a high score on the psychopathic deviant scale of the Minnesota Multiphasic Personality Inventory, a well-standardized test which differentiates psychopaths from others (Rosen, 1958), correlates .25 with Machiavellianism (Smith & Griffith, 1978).
- Measures of anomie (a state of normlessness) correlate significantly with the Mach test (Smith & Griffith, 1978).

One must remember that all of these tests concerned American or Canadian college students—presumably "normal" representatives of their generation. One should also keep in mind that virtually all American males and about 85% of American females will admit anonymously to minor crimes (McCord & McCord, 1977). Obviously, too, it should be emphasized that measures of Machiavellianism concerned only expressed beliefs. (A mature, intelligent psychopath might easily fake the results.) Thus, Machiavellianism cannot be equated with actual psychopathy.

Nonetheless, the extent of confessed Machiavellianism in modern American society is stunning. At the minimum, it indicates a high degree of mistrust, deceit, and cynicism in young, normal American populations.

AN INCREASE IN MACHIAVELLIANISM?

Moreover, as Christie and Geis showed, the degree of Machiavellianism has apparently increased over the years both in contemporary America and in other urbanizing cultures. Christie and Geis have produced definitive evidence of such an increase in America between 1955 and 1964, long before the revelations of Watergate and "Abscam."

Urbanization and bureaucratization, in themselves, seem to promote Machiavellian attitudes:

- In the United States, Gutterman (1970) found that urbanization, with its emphasis on anonymity, correlated with scores on the Machiavellian test among white-collar workers.
- Milbrun noted a similar tendency among young American girls (Christie & Geis, 1970).
- de Miguel found an extremely high correlation (.89) between industrialization and "Mach" scores among Spanish students (de Miguel, in Smith, 1978).

In essence, therefore, Machiavellians seem well adjusted to urbanized, industrialized, bureaucratic societies. This possibility, as Robert Smith (1978) pointed out, holds an ominous portent: "It is the manipulator who is in tune, and not those who officially deplore him. Like it or not, all world governments seem to be moving inexorably in the direction of top-heavy bureaucracies [p. 95]."

INDIVIDUALISM IN AMERICA

Urie Bronfenbrenner (1972) produced a number of comparative studies of children's attitudes that suggest that America, in particular, is more likely to produce psychopathic-like characteristics than are other nations. Bronfenbrenner studied American and European schools that tend to promote individual competition, as well as Russian schools that try to engender a sense of collective responsibility. In general, he found that Russian children more often express attitudes of mutual concern for others than children from American or West European schools. The latter emphasize higher regard for individualism and lower regard for social responsibility.

2. The Banality of Evil: "Normal" Psychopaths

As one example, Bronfenbrenner presented Swiss and Russian children with a series of "moral dilemmas" where they had various choices concerning what they would do about some violation committed by another student. They could ignore their comrade's actions, report it to an authority, correct the friend directly, etc. Twenty percent of the Swiss children as opposed to only 1% of the Russians said that they would "do nothing since it doesn't concern me [p. 113]."

In a similar comparison of American and Russian children, Bronfenbrenner found that the Americans were more willing to engage in some form of antisocial behavior and were more responsive to peer pressure in that direction than the Russian children. (Naturally, one must be slightly cautious about such results since Russian authorities may have conditioned the parents and, in turn, the children, to hide what they might really do.)

Such evidence is not meant to indicate that there are fewer psychopaths—or even "unconcerned" people—in Russia as opposed to Western, capitalistic societies. After all, such studies are based on questionnaires, not actual behavior, and deal with minor infractions of the rules. Some interpreters, however, believe that a "marketplace" mentality fosters such individualistic responses in America (Smith, 1978); others deduce that the actual incidence of psychopathy has been alarmingly increasing (Harrington, 1972). Whereas both Christie's and Bronfenbrenner's work suggests that some, perhaps as many as 20% of Westerners, harbor values and attitudes congruent with psychopathy, biographers and anthropologists have estimated that only about 2% (or as much as 5%) actually exhibit psychopathic behavior (Mercuri, 1977).

Even the smallest figure of prevalence—including as it does bureaucrats and businessmen, manipulative women and Machiavellian students, soldiers who "obey orders" or daughters who axe their parents—should frighten any civilized society.

Psychiatric reports, psychological tests, anthropological studies, and perceptive biographies must convince the reasonable observer that socially functioning psychopaths can be found in virtually every human group.

References

Arendt, H. *Eichmann in Jerusalem.* New York: Viking Press, 1963.
Bernstein, C., & Woodward, B. *All the president's men.* New York: Simon and Schuster, 1974.

Bronfenbrenner, U. *Zwei, welten: kinder in USA und UdSSR.* Stuttgart: Deutsche Verlag-Anstalt, GmbH, 1972.

Christie, R., & Geis, F. *Studies in Machiavellianism.* New York: Academic Press, 1970.

Cleckly, H. *The mask of sanity* (5th ed.). St. Louis: C. V. Mosby, 1976.

Congressional Report of Steel Corporations, 20 and 113, 1901.

Corey, L. *The House of Morgan.* New York: G. Howard Watt, 1930.

DuBois, C. *The people of Alor.* Minneapolis: University of Minnesota Press, 1944.

Eaton, J. W., & Weil, R. J. The mental health of the Hutterites. In A. M. Rose (Ed.), *Mental health and mental disorder.* New York: Norton, 1955.

Gibbons, D. C. *The criminological enterprise.* Englewood Cliffs, New Jersey: Prentice-Hall, 1979.

Gilbert, G.M., Hermann Goering: Amiable psychopath. *Journal of Abnormal and Social Psychology,* 1948, *43:*211.

Gutterman, S. S. *The Machiavellians.* Lincoln, Nebraska: University of Nebraska Press, 1970.

Harrington, A. *Psychopaths.* New York: Simon and Schuster, 1972.

Hibbens, P. *Henry Ward Beecher.* New York: Harpers, 1927.

Hollander, P. How banal is evil? *Contemporary Sociology,* 1980, *9:*497–501.

Hollingshead, A. B., & Redlich, F. C. *Social class and mental illness.* New York: Wiley, 1958.

Inkeles, A. Personality and social structure. In P. Talcott (Ed.), *American sociology.* New York: Basic Books, 1968.

Katchadourian, H. A., & Churchill, C. W. Components in prevalence of mental illness and social class in urban Lebanon. *Social Psychiatry,* 1973, *8:*145–151.

Lincoln, V. *A private disgrace.* New York: Putnam, 1967.

Lindner, R. *Rebel without a cause.* New York: Grune and Stratton, 1944.

McCord, D. C., private conversation, 1950.

McCord, W., & McCord, A. *American Social Problems.* St. Louis: Mosby, 1977.

Mercuri, G. The concept of psychopathic personality. *Lavoro Neuropsichiatrico,* 1977, *10:*217–219.

New York Journal, October 31, 1896, p. 1.

New York Tribune, June 2, 1901, p. 1.

New York World, April 1, 1913, p. 1.

Read, P. P. *Alive.* New York: Avon, 1974.

Rosen, A. Differentiation of diagnosis groups. *Journal of Consulting Psychology,* 1958, *15:*213–222.

Saenger, G. Psychiatric outpatients in America and the Netherlands. *Social Psychiatry,* 1968, *4:*149–164.

Smith, R. *The Psychopath in society.* New York: Academic Press, 1978.

Smith, R. J., & Griffith, J. E. Psychopathy, Machiavellianism and Anomie. *Psychological Reports,* 1978, *42:*258.

Solzhenitsyn, A. *The Gulag Archipelago—Three.* New York: Harper and Row, 1978.

Sutherland, E. H., & Cressey, D. R. *Criminology* (9th ed.). Philadelphia: Lippincott, 1974.

Turnbull, C. *The mountain people.* New York: Simon and Schuster, 1972.

Warhol, A., & Hackett, P. *PoPism: The Warhol '60's.* New York: Harcourt Brace Jovanovich, 1979.

11

The Detection of
the Psychopath

3

From *Manie sans Délire* to Psychopathic "Life-Styles": A Short History

> [The concept] *is an attempt to return to belief in demon possession.*
>
> J. Ordronaux, 1873, preacher
> "Moral Insanity," *American Journal of Insanity*

> *The psychopath may indeed be the perverted and dangerous frontrunner of a new kind of personality which could become the central expression of human nature before the twentieth century is over.*
>
> Norman Mailer, 1958, novelist
> "The White Negro," *Voices of Dissent*

For some 200 years, social scientists and psychiatrists have debated the nature of the psychopath. Some, like Joseph Ordronaux, a minister in the last century, viewed the introduction of the concept of psychopathy as part of a vast plot to undermine moral responsibility. Others, like Mailer, consider psychopathy as a new "hipster" life-style and view its growth with a high degree of tolerance, if not benevolence.

This continuing controversy about the nature of psychopaths began about 1800. From the Middle Ages until the Enlightenment, psychopathic behavior—or indeed any form of deviance—was viewed as the result of sin or devil possession (Rothman, 1971). As mankind was inherently sinful, society should not concern itself with eliminating endemic evils. All that could be done was, in sheer retribution, to punish them severely. In the eighteenth century, stocks, whips, and pillories were commonly used. Some criminals suffered branding. Others went to their deaths for even the most minor offenses, such as pickpocketing (Empey, 1978).

Children were not exempt since, until the end of the seventeenth century, the concept of childhood hardly existed. Adults allowed (or forced) children to drink in taverns, to engage in sexual activity, to carry and use weapons—in short, to behave as small adults (Ariès, 1962). By the eighteenth century, childhood became recognized in some circles as a distinct phase. Protestant adults enjoined strict obedience in their children and warned them of an early destruction if they deviated: "Appetites and passions unrestricted become furious in youth," one authority intoned, "and ensure *dishonor, disease*, and an *untimely death* [cf. Rothman, 1971, p. 17]."

With the decline of religion and the advent of the Enlightenment—with its beliefs in reason, human perfectibility, the progress of society—public attention became focused less on the sinful soul of the offender and more on the environment that produced him. Hopes rose that new institutions might actually cure or prevent crime. Hand in hand with the decline of simplistic theories of evil, psychiatrists and social reformers turned their attention to the differing nature of various types of criminals.

The First Students of Psychopathy

Phillipe Pinel, the French psychiatrist, stood out among those who tried to understand the nature of crime, mental disorder, and psychopathy. Pinel was a true son of the Enlightenment and of the French Revolution. He upheld the rights of all men, including hospital inmates, and despised what he called the cruel and inhuman treatment of mental disorders in his time. In its place, he advocated treating the mentally ill with a kind and compassionate firmness, a form of therapy that he labeled the "moral side of treatment" (Maughs, 1941, p. 329). Appointed to the famous Bicêtre mental asylum in Paris in 1792, he effected a number of dramatic cures.

Pinel first recognized psychopathy as a specific type of mental disorder, calling for its own particular treatment. (I do not mean, of course, to assert that psychopaths appeared only at this time: descriptions of "rebellious sons" in the Old Testament, of Lucretia Borgia, of Nero and Genghis Khan seriously undermine any such belief.) Pinel described individuals at the Bicêtre who were apparently normal but subject to strange attacks of rage, unaccompanied by guilt. Pinel first used the label *manie sans délire* (mania without delirium) and *emportement maniaque sans délire* (crazy behavior without delirium) to describe a French aristocrat in 1801.

This aristocrat enjoyed all of the privileges of his birth and usually managed his affairs in a competent fashion. He could not tolerate, however, any restraint upon his self-indulgent desires. When he disliked a dog, he kicked it to death, and a recalcitrant horse met with a similar fate with a whip. After he "became enraged at a woman who had used offensive language to him, he precipitated her into a well [Kavka, 1949]." Pinel interviewed the aristocrat at the Bicêtre. The case puzzled him for the man appeared so rational and outwardly sane (Rotenberg and Diamond, 1971). He did not suffer from any obvious symptoms, except his guiltless anger, and he did not come from a socially deprived background that Pinel found common among his other patients.

Pinel wrote an article about this case, categorizing the man with other disorders he had encountered from paranoids to neurotic hysterics. Despite the crudeness of this first diagnostic approach, Pinel successfully brought public attention to the fact that some outwardly normal people may suffer from psychopathic symptoms. Medical people throughout the world recognized the pattern and contributed their own observations. A new literature on the psychopath was created.

BECCARIA AND PUNISHMENT

In addition, Pinel's description of the psychopath set off a debate among the "hedonists," the "constitutionalists," and the "environmentalists." All the groups wanted to reform the brutal correctional practices of their time and to humanize them, but differed in the basic assumptions they made about the nature of men.

The hedonists included in their ranks Locke, Hume, Bentham, and Mill. They believed that mankind acted rationally on the basis of a calculation of pleasure and pain involved in a particular action. Cesare Beccaria emerged as perhaps the most influential criminologist of this school of thought. As early as 1764, Beccaria, an Italian nobleman, had sought to reform the brutal practices of his time and to establish a standard of justice that would apply to all peoples.

He reasoned that "pleasure and pain are the only springs of action in beings endowed with sensibility [Beccaria, 1770, p. 10]." Therefore, the one sure way to stop criminal actions was to inflict pain on the evil-doer in a completely equal fashion for the same crime: "If an equal punishment be ordained for two crimes that injure society in different degrees, there is nothing to deter men from committing the greater as often as it is attended with greater advantage [1770, p. 11]." Laudably, Beccaria tried to reduce favoritism and paternalism in the administration of criminal justice. His system did not fully account, however, for the psychopath whose actions may stem not so much from a rational calculation of risks, but more commonly from an impulse and reasoning that he will not be caught.

RUSH AND FREE WILL

In America, the most distinguished psychiatrist, Benjamin Rush, became intrigued with Pinel's ideas concerning the psychopath. In 1812, Rush agreed with Pinel that certain people suffered from a specific defect in their moral capacities. After dealing with such cases, Rush presented a dilemma that still faces the courts of the world:

> How far the persons whose diseases have been mentioned should be considered as responsible to human or divine laws for their actions, and where the line should be drawn that divides free agency from necessity, and vice from disease, I am unable to determine [quoted in Henderson, 1939, p. 13].

Rush, unlike Pinel or Beccaria, attributed the moral insensitivity of his cases to some unknown congenital defect. Thereby, he founded a school of theorists who continue even today to seek a constitutional basis for psychopathy.

PRITCHARD AND MORAL INSANITY

In England, J. C. Pritchard may be regarded as the forerunner of the environmentalist school of thought. He, too, recognized psychopaths among his clients and labeled them "morally insane" in 1835. Pritchard, however, attributed the disorder to a "bad" environment, separation from the family, and an unsettled condition of life precipitated by industrialization. He defined the "morally insane" as people who suffered from "little or no injury to their intellectual functions. . . . In cases of this sort, the moral or active principles of the mind are strongly perverted or depraved . . . the individual is found to be incapable, not of talking or reasoning upon any subject proposed to him, but of conducting himself with decency and propriety in the business of life [Pritchard, 1835]." Although Pritchard included under his definition many disorders that have more recently been recognized as psychoses, he did much to further attempts to change the psychopath through environmental measures.

REFORMATORIES

Adherents of the environmentalist school of thought believed that all criminals, not just psychopaths, might well be changed if placed in a proper environment. Thus, the nineteenth century witnessed the growth of prisons for adults and public reformatories. The first of the juvenile reformatories, the Lyman Training School, opened in Massachusetts in 1846. Hopes were high for it and similar institutions that later opened. "In the institution, we are able to control absolutely the child's environment. We can select his school teacher . . . we can bring to bear upon him the most helpful and elevating influences. . . . Under these circumstances, why should we not be able to produce satisfactory results? [Hart, 1910, p. 10]." Alas, Lyman and most of the reformatories did not match these high ideals. "Many of the juvenile reformatories were . . . in reality, juvenile prisons, with prison bars, prison cells, prison garb, prison labor, prison punishments, and prison discipline [Hart, 1910, p. 11]."

We found these prisonlike conditions in modified form to prevail at the Lyman School more than 100 years after its founding (see Chapter 9), and Massachusetts' authorities permanently closed the institution in the 1970s. Thus ended a noble but unsuccessful experiment, the first in America, whose long-term results are evaluated in Chapter 10.

In the late nineteenth century, however, the environmentalist point of view about reformation had won full sway over the minds of those who actually had to deal with criminals. Perhaps due to the optimistic idealism of America and its expanding frontiers, social reformers ardently embraced the idea of rehabilitation. In 1870, members of the Cincinnati Prison Congress adopted a set of principles in which they affirmed their faith in "hope and love" as "regenerative forces." The correctional officials proclaimed their faith in rehabilitation rather than punishment, the use of indeterminate sentences, education, prevention, and the treatment of criminals rather than crimes (Henderson, 1910). The reformers of 1870 were far ahead of their time in recognizing that differences between various types of offenders required a flexible approach to their reformation:

> The treatment of criminals by society is for the protection of society. But since such treatment is directed to the criminal rather than to the crime, its great object should be his moral regeneration. Hence the supreme aim of prison discipline is the reformation of criminals, not the infliction of vindictive suffering [Henderson, 1910, p. 39].

GOUSTER

As a logical result of trying to treat crime and not criminals, psychiatrists attempted to refine the unique concept of moral insanity. By 1878, M. Gouster was able to present a portrait of the "morally insane" with which many of the psychiatrists of his era agreed: the "morally insane" person suffered from "moral perversion," excitability, insensitivity, and "enfeebled judgment." To his eventual embarrassment, Gouster also advanced the argument that the "morally insane" exhibited certain physical abnormalities. His work depended heavily on the opinions of Caesar Lombroso, an Italian doctor.

LOMBROSO

On the basis of various physical measurements, Lombroso (1876) argued that some criminals were atavistic throwbacks to a more primitive stage of mankind. Criminals were described as having a large jaw, strange facial features, unusual ears, etc. His theories of causation, inspired by Darwin, found short shrift at the hands of other criminologists. By 1913, Charles Goring demolished Lombroso's position by comparing 3000 English convicts to a large number of the noncriminal population. He found no differences in physical features between the two groups.

Despite the hash they made of his causal theories, most social scientists recognized that Lombroso made two major contributions: First, he insisted that criminology should be "positive"—that is, based on empirical evidence. "Lombroso did establish a world-wide reputation during his lifetime," Gresham Sykes (1978) observed. "[He] attempted to place the explanation of crime on a scientific footing—even though his theories later proved to be in error [p. 12]."

Second, in his typology of criminals, Lombroso clearly separated the person whom we know as the psychopath from other criminals. Such individuals, he maintained, were guiltless, "moral imbeciles," insensitive to pain or pleasure, impulsive, and immune to the society that might criticize them. In this definition, he further refined the older categories of *"manie sans délire"* and *"moral insanity."* Unfortunately, however, he described this type of person as a "born criminal"—a term repulsive to many because of its genetic implications.

THE NINETEENTH-CENTURY DEBATE

Attempts by Lombroso, Bush, Gouster, and Pinel to understand the psychopath met with the stoutest opposition from lawyers and preachers. Many lawyers felt that their work erased the thin line between insanity and criminality. For most of the nineteenth century, criminals could be excused from their actions only because of the grossest of psychotic behavior. A person had to be viewed as "raving mad" or a complete imbecile before the courts would consider him (or her) as "irresponsible."

Similarly, religious people believed that use of the concept might destroy the foundations for morality and the concept of "free will." If, after all, one could not blame a person's actions on his or her freely chosen decision, how could they be held responsible? "The only disease to which the moral nature is subject," wrote Professor Ordronaux (1873, p. 12), "is sin." Ordronaux believed that the concept, as used by Rush, represented an attempt to return to a belief in witches and devil possession. One Dr. Elwell supported Ordronaux by claiming that foreigners were spreading the idea of "moral insanity," specifically, "a class of modern German pagans who are trying with what help they can get in America to break down all the safeguards of our Christian civilization, by destroying, if possible, all grounds for human responsibility [quoted in Maughs, 1941, p. 356]."

In America, the dispute became a great public issue with the assassination of President Garfield. Guiteau, Garfield's confessed murderer, went to trial in 1881. Defense psychiatrists testified that he suffered from moral insanity. The prosecution countered with its own witnesses who held that Guiteau knew "the difference between right and wrong" and should, therefore, suffer execution. The prosecution won and Guiteau went to his death. Although widely publicized at the time, the trial hardly settled the perennial issue of moral responsibility.

Psychiatrists continued to argue about the nature of psychopathy throughout the end of the nineteenth century. In 1888, J. L. Koch tried to replace the term "moral insanity" with "psychopathic inferiority," implying a constitutional cause to the disorder; in 1912, Meyer succeeded in excluding neurotics from the definition of psychopathy; in 1913, C. Mercier won official recognition in Britain that psychopathy was a unique form of mental disorder; and K. Birnbaum, in 1914, successfully distinguished between habitual criminal behavior and psychopathy (see Maughs, 1941). He also demonstrated that psychopaths were not necessarily victims of mental retardation (see Maughs, 1941). Despite theoretical differences, the evidence from all over the world accumulated that a distinct syndrome existed.

Studies of the Psychopath in the Twentieth Century

By the early twentieth century, investigators turned their attention to other behavioral correlates of psychopathy. In America, Bernard Glueck (1918) examined 608 Sing Sing convicts, of whom 18.9% presented the classical psychopathic syndrome. In contrast to other convicted criminals, psychopaths, he maintained, had begun their asocial behavior at the earliest age, were most resistant to any form of therapy, and had the highest rate of recidivism. In 1922, John Visher examined the character and motives of psychopaths in a veteran's hospital (see Hunt, 1944). In contrast to other mental patients, psychopaths, Visher found, were impulsive, egotistic, guiltless, and almost totally uninhibited. As in Glueck's study, Visher found the psychopaths resistant to any variation of mental hospital treatment.

FREUDIANISM

By the late 1920s and the 1930s, two conflicting schools of thought—Freudianism and a renewed "constitutionalism"—battled over the origins of psychopathy.

Traditional Freudian views of the psychopath did not easily encompass the disorder. Freud himself seems never to have analyzed a psychopath. As Freud considered all aberrant behavior a result of inner conflicts, it was difficult indeed to understand the psychopath who seemed remarkably devoid of inner conflicts, guilt, anxiety, and neuroses.

As Richard Jenkins (1960), one of the more perceptive observers of psychopaths, later commented about the attempt of some psychiatrists to depict all mental disorder as the result of internal conflict, "The realization that morbid conditions may be due primarily to a *lack* of conflict within the personality represents a readjustment of thinking which is apparently beyond the flexibility of many professionals [p. 320]."

Some American sociologists of the time also preferred to ignore the psychopath altogether and, indeed, continue to do so (see Sykes, 1978). They, of course, reason from different premises: The concept of the psychopath had dangerous connotations that criminality was somehow innate, just at the time when sociologists wished to demonstrate that crime had an entirely social origin. Further, the concept remained unappealing as it seemed to imply a denial of the process of socialization and to suggest that certain psychological factors might be of equal importance as social facts in the understanding of a particular phenomenon. Concerned with preserving their own domain, sociologists have tended to reject both the constitutional and Freudian concepts of the psychopath.

Freud did, however, postulate a "superego" (an internalized conscience), as did George Herbert Mead with his idea of "the generalized other." Some people of the Freudian persuasion described the psychopaths they encountered as suffering from an underdeveloped superego caused by various frustrations in childhood. In a variety of ways, Freud's followers attempted to formulate a conception of the psychopath that fit the theoretical scheme of psychoanalysis: I. H. Coriat depicted the psychopath as an immature child who had never resolved the Oedipus complex (Partridge, 1928); F. Wittels (1937) thought of the psychopath as fixated at an early phallic stage; G. E. Partridge (1928) portrayed him as fixated at the oral stage of development, forever seeking immediate gratification. They described various family situations that would produce psychopaths as ranging from the impact on the child of a highly indulgent mother to that of a rejecting mother (see Buss, 1966). The Freudians did not view the psychopath as constitutionally different from other people but as psychologically maladjusted from childhood. They agreed on his central trait: "The psychopath is alone in his tendency to treat others as objects rather than as fellow beings [Buss, 1966, p. 431]."

Among Freud's immediate followers, Franz Alexander had probably the greatest impact. In 1930, he described the "neurotic character" who, in some ways, seemed akin to the psychopath. Such people gave impulsive sway to their immediate desires, hated their fathers, and "acted out" their conflicts by trying to change their environments (sometimes in a destructive fashion). Alexander attributed this maladjustment to some deficiency in the person's ego. Subsequent research suggests that Alexander's cases more closely resembled "acting-out neurotics" rather than psychopaths (see Chapter 4).

The psychoanalytic treatment of psychopaths has been notably unsuccessful, partially because psychopaths lacked the necessary anxiety to seek or desire treatment and partially because many psychoanalysts attempted to loosen the strength of the superego— precisely the obverse of what the psychopath requires (Smith, 1978). Whatever its shortcomings, the Freudian approach did focus attention upon psychopathy as one form of mental illness produced—at least partially—by the person's early environment.

CONSTITUTIONALISM

During the 1930s, a revitalized school of "constitutionalists" grew up in direct contrast to the Freudians. In 1924, D. Volsi discovered that encephalitis could, at times, result in psychopathic symptoms. Some medical men hailed this finding as a first step in discovering a true organic basis for psychopathy. A variety of neurological studies did, in fact, support the position that the psychopath might suffer from some defect in his neural system (see Chapter 5).

Particularly in Germany, medical writers attempted to revive Lombrosian ideas with new approaches to understanding the "physical" nature of psychopaths. In 1931, for example, Eugene Kahn categorized a variety of clinical symptoms and labeled it psychopathy. Among other symptoms, Kahn threw in anxiety, sensitivity, hyperthymia, and "cold autism." Only his "cold autists," a perversion of the term, even vaguely resembled what other investigators of the time regarded as psychopaths: "They suffer from a moral feeble-mindedness," Kahn said, "they know as a rule what right and wrong is but they do not feel it [p. 348]." Kahn ascribed the disorder to different body builds, governed by an undefined *anlagen*. His research, in turn, led to William M. Sheldon's (1949) later attempt to classify varieties of delinquents. Sheldon found that "mesomorphic" body builds (relatively tall, muscular types) more often become psychopaths (as well as athletes and military men).

CLARIFICATION OF THE CONCEPT

The continuing disputes led some social scientists to throw up their hands in dismay. "The term psychopathic personality, as commonly understood, is useless in psychiatric research," J. M. Hunt wrote in 1944, and added with justification, "It serves as a scrapbasket to which is relegated a group of otherwise unclassified personality disorders and problems [1944, p. 933]."

During the 1940s, most psychiatrists and psychologists found, however, that the exigencies of dealing with real-life psychopaths did not allow them to dispense with the concept. A number of distinguished practitioners—Sir David Henderson, Hervey Cleckly, Benjamin Karpman, and Robert Lindner—set out to isolate psychopathy as a distinct disorder.

In 1939, Sir David Henderson clarified the distinction between an "epileptoid personality" and the psychopath. He concentrated on the psychopath's central traits of asociality and guiltlessness. He asserted that some psychopaths could be highly creative individuals.

This last contention stirred some controversy as Henderson labeled individuals such as "Lawrence of Arabia" as creative psychopaths. Admittedly, Lawrence (one of the architects of British victory in the Middle East during World War I) seemed impulsive, subject to mood swings, and overly devoted to the more bloody aspects of war. Henderson, however, neglected to mention some other aspects of the man: his masochism, his conflict between shyness and a desire for fame, his self-effacing behavior, and his high level of guilt. As Lawrence wrote, "The craving to be famous, and the horror of being known to like being known, disturbed me; I was standing court-martial on myself [quoted in Henderson, 1939, p. 111]." Lawrence may well have experienced personality problems but can hardly be accused of being psychopathic.

German theorists picked up Henderson's belief in creative psychopaths and greatly extended the category to include Rousseau, Shelley, Nietzsche, Flaubert, Carlyle, and Schiller (Lange-Eichbaum, 1956).

Only by the wildest stretch of the imagination could one label the activities of creative individuals as psychopathic. In fact, mental disorder of any type seems to inhibit creativity. Some investigations have shown, for example, that Nietzsche probably died of general paresis—a psychosis caused by syphilis which drastically curbed his creative productivity. A very few creative individuals, such as Rousseau, *might* possibly be labeled as psychopathic. And some of the "normal" psychopaths whom we have discussed might, by the standards of their particular culture, be called "creative." J. P. Morgan certainly developed the art of finance to a high level; and Goering superbly understood how to manipulate the political system of Germany. As one could consider their activities as equally destructive and "creative," one must be extremely cautious in drawing any connection at all between creativity and psychopathy.

In America during the 1940s, Hervey Cleckly, a psychiatrist who dealt with both criminal and "normal" psychopaths, outlined a lasting portrait of the psychopath (1941; 5th edition, 1976). In this classic book, *The Mask of Sanity*, Cleckly emphasized the psychopath's traits of lack of remorse, incapacity for love, asocial behavior, etc. As he apparently encountered mostly "normal" psychopaths, Cleckly particularly noted their superficial charm, their absence of nervousness or psychotic or neurotic manifestations, and their ability to think rationally. As Smith (1978) later commented about the psychopath's positive traits, a person displaying such an orientation would seem mentally healthy and would, indeed, approach Maslow's "self-actualizing" level or Jung's "self realization." Unhappily, the psychopath combines his superficial charm with his more base characteristics of asociability, insensitivity, lack of guilt, and an inability to form close relationships.

Cleckly attempted to label the disorder "semantic dementia" (i.e.,

77

a dissociation between one's words and one's actions). Clearly, as Cleckly pointed out, the psychopath can understand the rules and customs of his society. He can often play the game of obeying them very well and, depending on his society, he may be highly rewarded. Yet, he acts in his own asocial realm.

Benjamin Karpman, a psychotherapist at St. Elizabeth's hospital, investigated a variety of psychopaths during the 1940s. He attempted to draw a distinction between "ideopathic" and "symptomatic" psychopaths. In his opinion, the "ideopathic" psychopath exhibited the basic traits, which we have previously described, and was immune to treatment (Karpman, 1941). In contrast, the "symptomatic" psychopath was actually, in Alexander's terms, a "neurotic character." Following such reasoning, Karpman believed the symptomatic psychopath could be treated by tracing the psychogenic reasons for his disorder (Karpman, 1946). In actuality, Karpman had made a distinction between true psychopaths and "acting-out neurotics" (see Chapter 4).

In a series of articles and in his classic *Rebel Without a Cause*, Robert Lindner examined some of the physical characteristics of psychopaths (1943), various experiments in delineating the psychopath, the psychological problems of the psychopath (1948), and new methods of treatment (1944). Lindner, rejecting Karpman's belief that certain psychopaths would not respond to any therapy, found that some psychopaths—when put under deep hypnosis—could recall events that had irrevocably shaped their personalities (1944).

Lindner also pioneered in the use of the Rorschach test as a means for identifying psychopaths. Lindner showed that this projective diagnostic instrument established well-defined differences between psychopathic criminals and other criminals (1943). He administered the test to 40 psychopathic criminals, diagnosed independently by a prison psychiatric staff, and 40 nonpsychopathic criminals. The psychopaths were found to be more explosive, impulsive, asocial, and generally superficial in their relationships with other people than nonpsychopathic criminals (1943).

During the 1940s, other investigators using the Rorschach found similar characteristics. In 1946, K. D. Heuser noted emotional isolation and violent tendencies as characteristic of psychopathic soldiers. In 1947, D. E. Bowlus and A. Shotwell found a similar pattern among psychopathic girls who lacked inner controls and expressed their desires impulsively.

A beginning had been made in diagnosing the psychopath as an independent entity. By nature, of course, the Rorschach is an impressionistic, "projective" test. Yet, analyzed by objective, trained people experienced with the testing process, the Rorschach does produce reliable interpretations. Indeed, even experts in diagnosing the Rorschach, unlike experts on the so-called "lie detector test," cannot find means to falsify their results. Thus, the original results of Lindner and others substantiated the claim that, indeed, psychopathy could be identified through psychological tests and differentiated from both criminal and noncriminal samples.

WORLD WAR II AND PSYCHOPATHS

The advent of the second World War in the 1940s necessarily brought the psychopath to the attention of the world. First, all of the armed services had to deal with such individuals in one fashion or another because of conscription. The American army generally segregated psychopaths in prisons or sent them on suicidal missions, which demanded courage and guiltlessness (Caldwell, 1941). At times, the psychopath proved a very useful instrument of destruction, assuming that he obeyed orders. "We need one psychopath in each squad," General Douglas MacArthur told his personal secretary, "any more than that would destroy morale. One is sufficient to do the killing [private communication, 1980]."

Second, as we have noted, the coming of Nazism, with its program of mass killings, gave the psychopath unprecedented publicity. From Goering, to Eichmann, to Colonel Hoess (chief of Auschwitz), "normal" psychopaths assumed power in Germany. Their prominence led to a variety of investigations of the nature of psychopaths. As a result of the war, numerous researchers produced evidence concerning the psychopath's neurology, family history, and behavior.

During and after the war, few psychiatrists or psychologists demurred from the fact that the psychopath differed markedly from the normal criminal, the neurotic, or the psychotic. From those who had to deal with thousands of cases, thrust to their notice by universal drafts, the judgment seemed virtually unanimous that psychopathy was a dangerous, distinct entity. In America, J. Chornyak (1941) wrote, "Those of us who work in psychiatric clinics and in courts . . . continuously have to deal with this type of abnormal personality [p. 1327]." An English psychiatrist, E.T.O. Slater (1948), commented, "If we were to drop the term altogether, we should be obliged to invent an equivalent or to overlook a whole series of clinically very important phenomena [p. 277]." By 1951, the editors of the influential *British Journal of Delinquency* declared, "Psychopathy has now emerged as the most important of the great transitional groups of mental disorders. . . . It is no longer possible to maintain without fear of brisk contradiction that the concept of psychopathy is a psychiatric fiction covering inadequacies in clinical classification [p. i]."

Psychopathy in the 1950s

During the 1950s, many philosophers turned to existentialism and some of the more brilliant portrayed the psychopath as a rebel against "reason." In a fundamentally absurd world, some philosophers such as Albert Camus in *The Stranger* (1960) pictured the psychopath as the ultimate "anti-hero." And, in the German tradition, H. Haefner (1961) viewed the psychopath as a person unable to attain true *Dasein* (Being).

The 1950s also marked a period when various medical and social scientists turned their attention to the problems of treating the psychopath. They rejected the assumption of the "constitutionalists" that psychopathy was incurable. Physicians experimented with many different drugs from Dilantin Sodium to barbiturates to tranquilizers, attempting to change adult psychopaths. Each therapy enjoyed a fashionable vogue in its own time. Surgeons did lobotomies, other medical men used shock treatment, and some psychologists utilized hypnosis in abortive attempts to "cure" the psychopath (see Chapter 7).

Inspired by the original work of August Aichhorn, other psychiatrists and social workers such as Bruno Bettelheim, Fritz Redl, and Ernest Papanek wanted to stop psychopathy early in life by treating children (usually in a residential setting). Although their experiments won initial success, financial difficulties and a general ignorance of their work by scholars hampered the efforts of these innovators (see Chapter 8).

Indeed, by the 1960s, two movements within sociology—the emergence of "labeling" theory and of "critical" sociology—threatened to undermine any theoretical base for treating either adult or child psychopaths. Implicitly or explicitly, and with the same ardor as nineteenth-century preachers, adherents of both groups claimed that psychopaths did not really exist except as fictions of society's biased imagination.

Labeling Theory and "Critical" Criminology

Launched in the 1950s, *labeling theory*, in its crudest form, implied that society creates criminals (including psychopaths) by labeling them as such. In its original manifestations, labeling theory exhibited a rabid antipsychological and antibiological position. As Gywnn Nettler (1978) pointed out, labeling theory "denies . . . the causal importance and explanatory value of personality variables. In fact, labeling theorists regard as futile the search for personality differences that might distinguish categories of more or less criminal persons [p. 109]." The theory appealed strongly to those who opposed the institutional structure of modern society and supported the civil liberties of individuals.

In 1951, Edwin Lemert played a prominent role in launching labeling theory in America—a movement he later partially repudiated. Lemert located the cause of all criminal behavior in society's response to the first criminal action ("primary deviance") of the person. He believed that individuals begin to "react symbolically to their own behavior aberrations and fix them in their social-psychological patterns [1951, p. 75]." Thus, after a boy first steals a car and is caught, society labels him as delinquent, and the child incorporates this image of himself. He then proceeds to further deviation and society imposes ever more severe penalties. Finally, the person comes to accept the label attached to him—say, that of a psychopath—and to behave in a fashion that others expected of him.

Thus, as Gresham Sykes (1978) commented, "Society was very apt to worsen the ill rather than improve it [p. 295]" as occurred, for example, in the temporary effort to impose Prohibition. Further, "If one identified with the poor and the oppressed who were blamed by society for the conduct that society itself produced, then a scientific analysis of those who did the blaming was far more attractive than a dissection of those who were blamed [1978, p. 299]."

According to advocates of the theory, the labeling process occurred because of the personal bias of corrections officials or judges. Social class and ethnic differences also led officials to attach an opprobrious label (and sentence) to the person. Aaron Cicourel (1968) further argued that even the physical appearance of juveniles, the expressions on their faces, and their manner of dress could critically affect the person's future. Thus, Kai Erikson argued that "deviance is not a property *inherent* in certain forms of behavior; it is a property *conferred* upon these forms by authorities which directly or indirectly witness them [Erikson, 1964, p. 11]."

This position had some obvious merit for describing crime in general. Obviously, as we have noted, cultures differ in their standards. Clearly, too, once a person is labeled a "bad boy," he may have difficulty in escaping from the image associated with the description. Even with the best of intentions, for example, many convicts have trouble in finding legitimate work after they go on parole merely because they have been labeled criminal.

CRITICISMS OF LABELING THEORY

Labeling theory, however, did not withstand the test of time when applied to psychopaths for a variety of reasons:

1. The theory could not explain why the first act of deviance occurred.
2. It could not account for the fact that the vast majority of delinquents—once arrested and labeled—*stop* their delinquency.
3. The theory ignored the "normal" psychopath who is *not* labeled as deviant.
4. The theory overlooked the accumulating social, psychological, and biological evidence that indicates the eventual onset of psychopathic behavior long *before* anyone has publicly labeled the person (see Chapter 12).
5. Psychopathic behavior patterns did not disappear merely because society ignored them or "labeled" them in a certain way.

After reviewing a variety of studies, David Mechanic (1969) reasonably concluded that there is "little evidence that such labeling processes are sufficiently powerful to be major influences in producing chronic mental illness [p. 311]."

CRITICAL THEORY

"Critical" or Marxist criminologists in the 1960s and 1970s bore some resemblance to labeling theorists. They, too, wished to blame all social ills on the society itself, and they rejected the belief that any quality of a particular individual led to criminal activity. The critical criminologists gained prominence during the social turbulence of the 1960s when both the civil rights movement and opposition to the Vietnamese War dominated the news. For them, psychopaths did not exist—or, at least, would not exist in an ideal socialist society. The critical sociologists blamed all problems on the nature of capitalistic society. Crime, including psychopathic behavior, should be viewed as one result of the exploitative class system of America (and, implicitly, any other capitalistic nation). From the point of view of William Chambliss (1976) and other critical sociologists, class conflicts produced crime. In turn, the ruling class (capitalists) defined the nature of law and therefore of crime. The sole purpose of criminal law was to promote the property interests of the wealthy. As Barry Krisberg argued,

> The concept of private ownership is based upon a form of wealth that depends upon the theft of labor power. Criminal laws and systems of law enforcement exist to promote and protect a system based upon this conception of property, and these laws and systems of organized violence or coercion are thus linked intimately with those persons who possess the most private property [in Chambliss, 1976, p. 219].

From this point of view, all crime is political crime (a protest against the capitalistic system). The police and all other branches of criminal justice are merely agents of the rulers of the status quo. Thus, as Richard Quinney (1974) asserted, "The national government—an instrument of the ruling classes—is now building a comprehensive, coordinated system of repression [p. 109]." The contradictions within capitalistic society force the state to adopt measures of oppression: "To protect the system from its own victims, a war on crime is being raged [p. 175]."

Overlooking rhetorical flourishes, such arguments contain a grain of truth. Obviously, the ruling classes of any society define the nature of crime to a large extent: Crimes against private property are perhaps more directly punished in America than in socialist societies, just as crimes against "state property" in the Soviet Union entail capital punishment. Certainly, victims of poverty, racism, and other forms of discrimination commit more crimes and are more severely punished than are others. (They also happen to be victims of the crimes far more often than the more privileged.)

Does this mean that the conversion of capitalist societies into socialist ones will end crime or psychopathy? This hardly seems believable. Like labeling theorists, the critical sociologists ignored the social, psychological, and biological evidence that psychopaths appear in virtually every society and that their prevalence can be predicted in childhood. They also closed their eyes to the brutal, repressive practices of the police in socialist countries and the continuing reports from such nations of the existence of psychopaths. They blinded themselves to all evidence that linked psychopathy and crime in general to urbanization and industrialization (Christie & Geis,

1970) rather than to the particular political ideology of a nation. And, they refused to recognize that some societies have certain ethical systems (such as canons of truth in science) that can hardly be interpreted as dictated by the ruling class. Finally, they did not acknowledge that virtually every society has standards that prohibit certain actions such as murder, incest, and rape. The critical sociologists answered all criticisms by conjuring up a nonexistent democratic, decentralized, participatory socialism that has yet to be created.

As a citizen, one has the choice of hoping for such a utopia. As social scientists, such a vision should not prevent us from examining psychopathy as it presently exists. As Gresham Sykes (1978) concluded in summarizing "critical criminology," "It is difficult to assess the validity of such theoretical viewpoints, for they are often presented as self-evident truths without empirical support [p. 401]."

1960 to the 1980s: Some Psychological and Psychiatric Studies

Although both labeling theorists and critical criminologists remained oblivious to the facts, revolutionary new discoveries about the psychological and physical nature of the psychopath proceeded at a fast pace during the 1960s and the 1970s.

Working at a tangent from many sociologists, psychiatrists and psychologists during the 1960s and 1970s proceeded to refine and measure the concept of psychopathy. Their studies—particularly concerning the physical insensitivity of psychopaths—have produced some startling findings. Yet many sociologists seemed oblivious to the new findings, even when they could have—with some difficulty—been fitted into the frameworks of labeling theorists or critical criminologists.

Among some of the more significant diagnostic findings made between 1960 and the 1980s (see Chapter 4), one might list the following advances:

- Using a factor analysis of case history data, Richard Jenkins and his associates (1964, 1966) have repeatedly demonstrated that chronic delinquents fall into three different clinical types: the *psychopathic* (unsocialized, aggressive, guiltless person); the *neurotic* (overanxious, seclusive, sensitive); and the *socialized delinquent* (an essentially normal person who adheres to the mores of his subgroup, such as a gang). Also using factor analysis, H. C. Quay (1964) found that psychopathy could be isolated as a specific factor.

• A large number of studies extensively reviewed by Robert Hare (1970) indicate that psychopaths perform equally well as other subjects on the Wechsler–Bellevue intelligence test. Indeed, as most of the subjects in such tests have come from prison or mental hospital situations, the possibility is strong that the normal psychopath—undetected and unpunished for his transgressions—is actually *more* intelligent than his comrades in prison. "If so," as Hare (1970) noted, "it would probably mean that the *total* population of psychopaths is, on the average, more intelligent than the general population [p. 14]."

• Various types of self-report tests have significantly distinguished between the psychopath, other criminals, and nonpsychopaths. The MMPI, for example, indicates that psychopaths score high on the "Pd" scale (when answering such questions as "I am sure I get a raw deal from life") and on the "Ma" scale (when responding to items like "When I get bored I like to stir up some excitement") (Hare, 1970, p. 180). Similarly, in self-reports of anxiety, psychopaths consistently reported fewer symptoms of anxiety (Van Evra & Rosenberg, 1963). Thus, the psychopath could not be considered a neurotic person.

On the semantic differential test, subjects have been asked to rate themselves and their parents on a variety of characteristics. One of the more interesting studies contrasted psychopathic girls and normal girls of the same age, education, and social class. The experimenter asked the girls to rate their parents in terms of such dimensions as trust, love, "mother as I would like her to be," etc. The investigator found great differences between what the psychopathic patients would have liked and how they perceived their parents as actually behaving, suggesting a pathological family environment. The nonpsychopathic subjects closely identified with their parents (Maas, 1966).

• EEG studies of the psychopath's neurological activity (generally measuring rhythmic patterns in the brain) have definitely established certain cortical patterns that are typical of psychopaths (see Chapter 5). Such a finding does not necessarily mean that the psychopath's behavior is caused by neurological abnormalities; it does, however, provide one more diagnostic tool. Specifically, extremely high proportions of psychopaths suffer from "slow-wave" activity in many parts of the brain (Arthurs & Cahoon, 1966). Some investigators found slow-wave activity among psychopaths to exist particularly in the temporal lobes of the cerebral hemisphere; this particular abnormality is associated with aggressive behavior (Bay-Rakal, 1965). "Positive spike" activity also occurs frequently among psychopaths (Kurland, Yeager, & Arthur, 1963). Positive spikes come in "attacks" and are characterized by extreme aggression and impulsivity. After a destructive act, the individual expresses no guilt or anxiety. Such positive-spike activity occurs among 40 to 45% of psychopaths—far higher than in the normal population (Kurland, Yeager, & Arthur, 1963).

With measurable success, physiologists and psychologists also attempted to diagnose the psychopath's physical responses:

• As previously noted, Lykken found that psychopaths do not respond to shock conditioning as much as neurotics or normal subjects in trials of solving a mental maze. The psychopaths, however, as did others, responded to positive rewards. Lykken interpreted this finding as suggesting a very low level of anxiety—and thus, an indifference to "avoidance learning" among psychopaths (1957).

• Schachter also found a low level of physical sensitivity among psychopaths in 1971. Using a similar set of groups as Lykken, Schachter administered adrenaline and placebos to his experimental and control groups. When injected with adrenaline, psychopaths avoided shock significantly more often than previously. Placebos effected no differences between the groups. Schachter believed that this discrepancy was due to the autonomic nervous system arousal properties of adrenaline. As in Lykken's experiment, all groups reacted similarly to positive rewards rather than to punishment.

Schachter and Bibb Latané (1964) concluded that "the effects of adrenaline . . . are dramatic and almost startling. . . . This astonishing relationship . . . would certainly seem to indicate that adrenaline sensitivity appears to be a remedy, but a remedy for what [1964, p. 96]?" They suggested that psychopaths appear to be more responsive than others to virtually every titillating event; whether only mildly provoking or dangerously threatening.

As Alan Harrington later contended, adrenaline may possibly

> boost the psychopathic subjects out of their usual state of random and diffuse searching for excitement to a level of not being bored. The shots substitute for adrenaline-raising explosions, crises, and aggressive action disruptive to others. . . . He even worries a little, pays closer attention to electric shock games. . . . So we achieve the restoration of anxiety, temporarily socializing the outlaw [1972, p. 97].

Quay (1965) agreed with these basic findings but argued that psychopaths may have a lower basal reactivity and therefore a greater need for exciting stimuli. An intolerance of boredom could easily be translated into an interminable seeking after excitement— whatever the results in terms of punishment.

• In support of Quay, Emmons and Webb (1974) found that subjective measures (scores on the MMPI and Lykken's Activity Preference Questionnaire) indicated that psychopaths were "pathological stimulation seekers." This occurred among the ranks of psychopaths to a much higher degree than among neurotics or normal subjects.

• Borkovec (1970) supplemented previous studies by noting that psychopathic delinquents had lower skin conductance response than did neurotic or normal delinquents to punishment. The underreactivity of the psychopaths—and thus, one would assume, their relative indifference to punishing stimuli—emerged from a lack of sensitivity. At first, Borkovec used sound as a stimulus. The psychopaths showed no response. When, however, he flashed pictures of nude females on a screen, the skin conductivity responses of the psychopaths assumed the same pattern as others. Robert J. Smith (1978) observed that many experimental stimuli must seem "irrelevant, silly, and boring" to the male psychopath. Nude women are not.

• In a somewhat similar study, Schmauk (1970) reported that psychopaths could learn to avoid punishment as well as a normal control group but only when a loss of money rather than the administration of an artificial noxious stimulus was used.

• Reid and his associates (1978) noted a distinction between episodic psychopaths (those who suddenly explode in aggression) and the core psychopath (who chronically exhibits the full range of psychopathic symptoms). They found that pharmacological treatment could temporarily calm the "episodic" psychopath but had no effect on the true psychopath.

• Siddle (1977) also noted that psychopaths show greater decreases in electrodermal activity in monotonous situations and less of an increase than others when presented with noxious stimulation (1977).

All of these studies suggest that the core psychopath is relatively insensitive to punishment, to tranquilizing drugs, and to boring stimuli, but that he will certainly respond to stimuli—such as pictures of naked women or the loss of money—which are of greater intrinsic importance to him.

Such discoveries have placed in our hands some objective means for diagnosing the psychopathic personality. Despite the changes

87

3. From *Manie sans Délire* to Psychopathic "Life-Styles": A Short History

in labeling from *"manie sans délire"* to "moral insanity" to "psychopath," and then onward to "sociopathy" (American Psychiatric Association, 1952), and the World Health Association definition of "antisocial personality" (WHO, 1972), the clinical concept of such individuals, now reinforced by objective measures, can hardly be refuted by the history of the last two centuries.

THE CLINICAL JUDGMENT OF PSYCHOPATHS

Despite changes in terminology, the clinical portrait of the psychopath—now supplemented by physical measurements—has not basically changed over the years. A questionnaire directed to virtually all Canadian psychiatrists indicated that more than 89% regarded the concept as indispensable (Gray & Hutchinson, 1964). In various ways, this large sample of Western psychiatrists mentioned a lack of a sense of responsibility, inability to form meaningful relationships, impulsivity, and antisocial behavior as the primary traits of psychopaths whom they had encountered. Some 14% thought that psychopathy had constitutional causes; 38% believed that it emerged from environmental origins; and about 44% were convinced that it was a mixture of both factors. Seventy-eight and one-half percent believed that a diagnosis could be made before the age of 18.

As Robert Hare has noted, psychiatric diagnoses can be highly unreliable. Yet, when the criteria are made quite explicit and the diagnosticians have access to biographical and psychological data on the subject, the reliability of diagnoses appreciably increases— *particularly* for psychopaths (Hare, 1970; also see Spitzer, Cohen, Fleiss, & Endicott, 1967).

Buttressed by a near unanimity in clinical judgment, by psychometric data, and by physiological measures, one would have thought that social scientists had resolved the problem of the diagnosis of psychopathy by the 1980s. They had not. Some sociologists continue to deny all of the evidence and claim that psychopathy does not exist. In contrast, other writers—notably Norman Mailer, Michael Glenn, Alan Harrington, and Robert Smith—have gone to another extreme by vastly expanding the definition of psychopathy and suggesting that it has become the "life-style" of millions of people in the Western world. Indeed, as Mailer did, some prophesized that virtually all of us would become psychopaths by the year 2000. In a short history of the concept, such theories deserve consideration.

Psychopathy as a "Life-Style"

MAILER ON PSYCHOPATHS

In 1958, in his provocative essay on "The White Negro," Norman Mailer suggested that many artists, politicians, and businessmen were psychopathic. Mailer asserted that more than 10 million Americans were already psychopathic in the clinical sense, and that, by the end of the century, psychopaths would become "the central expression of human nature [1958, p. 203]." Mailer argued that the style of life of "hipsters"—exemplified by rock musicians, some politicians, and entertainers—might well become the model for most Americans.

He argued that an increasing rate of violence, the rapid change of industrialized societies, greater urbanization, and the influence of the mass media would aid in spreading the phenomenon. Mailer viewed American society as caught in a series of contradictions between an idolization of violence and the Protestant work ethic; a glorification of impulsive sexuality and a Puritan demand for repression; a compulsion to be "successful" and a belief that the good man should be humble. Such contradictions, Mailer believed, could produce a new generation of psychopaths as "the psychopath is better adapted to dominate those mutually contradictory inhibitions upon violence and love which civilization has exacted of us [1958, p. 203]."

Mailer wrote that psychopathy is an "extreme case" on some continuum of human personality. Yet, he maintained that psychopaths exert a predominant influence over publicity and the mass media: "The condition of psychopathy is present in a host of people including many politicians, professional soldiers, newspaper columnists, many entertainers, artists, jazz musicians, call-girls, and half of the executives of Hollywood, television, and advertising [1958, p. 203]." Addicted to hyperbole, Mailer may well have exaggerated the influence of what I have called "normal" psychopaths. Yet, there can be no doubt that some psychopaths "already exhibit considerable cultural influence [1958, p. 203]."

Following Mailer, some writers—including psychiatrists such as Michael L. Glenn—have gone further and wrote paeans to the psychopath (1967).

GLENN ON PSYCHOPATHS

"The hero of our age is—the psychopath [p. 198]," Glenn argued. "Free from responsibility, free from guilt, free from anxiety, he pursues his goals. Corporation presidents, statesmen, educator, physician: his calling is irrelevant; his features are everywhere the same [p. 198]." Successful or "normal" psychopaths are "glorified week after week on the covers of *Time, Life,* and *Newsweek.* Moreover, every level of our society seems unwittingly bent on imitating this behavior [p. 198]."

Like Mailer, Glenn argued that the lonely stranger is best "able to deal coldly with reality, is best fitted for our culture [p. 197]." He believed that

> after all, we all operate in a social labyrinth of roles and rules, talking and giving cues to one another as we seek the easiest route to our goals. . . . An adaptive and essentially psychopathic response is to feel the mask as mask . . . a curious sanity rests at the heart of true psychopathy . . . if one realizes that social interaction is role playing and appearance, one can play the game without getting lost in it [p. 198].

HARRINGTON ON PSYCHOPATHS

In his highly provocative book, *Psychopaths,* Alan Harrington (1972) picked up a similar theme. Harrington has argued that we may have a plague of psychopaths—criminal, "normal," and mere imitators who claim that they are heralds of a revolution in consciousness. "From now on," says Harrington, "perhaps the race will require a new nervous system in order to survive. In a godless universe, the anxiety-free psychopathic style may be the antidote to mass suicide [p. 30]." Harrington posed a particularly legitimate question:

> Why do supposedly normal people so frequently find themselves bowing down to widely differing kinds of psychopaths? . . . We may discover that we bow down to the psychopath because in times of little faith, seeming to care about the fearful child, he comforts the child in each of us. With the old gods gone, *he* has no doubts, betrays no fear, gives a meaning and authority to life, no matter how twisted, wild, or mysterious it may be [p. 35].

Harrington admitted that "to deny psychopathy as an aberration . . . would be foolish. But today psychopathic behavior can no longer be described *only* in terms of a disease. . . . The psychopathic style has become endemic around the country [p. 196]." Harrington predicted that psychopathy might well become the norm of American society: "A host of rebel souls, some clinically psychopathic, others not, run loose around the country untreated—and they have begun en masse defying and invading the citadels of those who traditionally sit in judgment of them [p. 797]."

Quite rightly, Harrington has drawn attention to "normal," successful psychopaths, but his book ended on a utopian note, advocating the establishment of a new religion uniting psychopaths and nonpsychopaths for their mutual enlightenment.

Harrington hoped for the birth of a church that would teach psychopaths the ethics of "the bourgeois" and inform nonpsychopaths about the values of living in an anxiety-free, guiltless universe. This "Church or Temple of Rebirth" would use drugs or any other means to teach psychopaths and nonpsychopaths "to lie down and live with one another. . . . The Spiritual Circus put on by such a faith would celebrate and give sacred authority to every form of the death–rebirth trip [p. 283]." Its leaders would use ritualistic violence, orgies "bringing sex and religion back together where they belong," encounter sessions, fasting, asceticism, yoga, "mystical calisthenics," etc. "Carnival is the secret, but not as farewell to the flesh. In simulation, carnival of dying with resurrection only a few hours away [p. 283]." Harrington argued that such "spiritual circuses would be designed to provoke therapeutic hallucinations, keep (in the head) all the colored lights going, and pinwheels and crystalline explosions [p. 284]."

Perhaps this fantastic vision of the future may come true. And perhaps it might be of benefit to psychopaths, although existing evidence leads to some skepticism (see Part IV).

SMITH ON PSYCHOPATHS

Robert Smith (1978)—although agreeing that the psychopath is an apotheosis of American individualism and of the "market place mentality"—has strongly rejected Harrington's implicit pleas that we all become uninhibited hedonists. Smith quite rightly regarded the lonely stranger as a "harbinger of distress" and, perhaps, as a growing phenomenon in American society. He also recognized that the "normal" psychopath may be better adopted to the fierce competition of American life than others.

Smith, however, criticized Harrington for lumping together a variety of mental disorders with psychopathy and rejected his opinion that psychopathy represents "the new health." In contrast, Smith has argued that the psychopath should be regarded "as the logical extreme, or the fantastic exaggeration perhaps, of what our Western societies not only tolerate, but virtually demand of us if we want to win fame and fortune [1978, p. x]." What is required, then, is a transformation of our institutions and values to promote a more "humanistic," socialized human being—a person imbued with the cooperative, group-oriented values of a more collective society than present-day capitalistic ones. Smith apparently believed that certain movements in Eastern Europe and the emergence of a "counter-culture" in America might well presage a change to less materialistic values.

Conclusions

Smith—as did Mailer and, to some degree, Harrington—shifted focus to the very nature of Western society as the promoter of psychopathic values and away from the view of the psychopath as "unsocialized." Certainly, this view has merit in uniting sociology, psychology, and social philosophy. Clearly, as we have argued, certain societies such as the Ik reward the psychopathic syndrome and actively cultivate it. Whether the nations of the West should be placed in a similar category remains in doubt and, if one believes they should be so regarded, few writers can suggest practical ways of altering the values of the West.

In the history of psychopathy, we should welcome the global approach of those who emphasize culture as the prime force in encouraging psychopathic behavior. Yet, this new focus should not blind us to the fact that a psychopathic syndrome does exist in almost every culture and that over the centuries—sometimes at an agonizingly slow pace—evidence has accumulated about its nature. Since 1800, the study of psychopathy has marked a series of extremely important advances:

• In 1800, due to the efforts of Pinel, the concept of *"manie sans délire"* first challenged earlier beliefs in witchcraft and devil possession.

• By the early 1800s, Rush had raised disturbing (and continuing) questions about the "free will" of "morally insane" persons, while Pritchard first suggested environmental theories of causation.

• In Italy, Caesar Lombroso identified "born criminals," although he unfortunately attributed their disorder to an atavistic regression.

• By the late 1920s, Freudians turned their attention to psychopaths and identified some of the familial constellations that produced them.

• The 1930s marked a period when "constitutionalists" attempted to assert that psychopathy was a physically caused condition and sociologists tried to dismiss the concept as scientifically backward.

As evidence that the psychopathic syndrome existed and had social roots rapidly accumulated, neither movement succeeded .

• In the 1940s, Henderson, Cleckly, Karpman, Lindner and various army psychiatrists throughout the world further refined and identified the crucial characteristics of the psychopath.

• By the 1950s, psychiatrists had reached fundamental agreement about the nature of the psychopath and various innovators—Bettelheim, Redl, and Papanek—tried to cure child psychopaths.

• During the 1950s and 1960s, labeling theorists and critical sociologists attempted to focus attention on the nature of society and its agents as instruments in defining some psychopaths as "criminal" while they allowed others to run free and do what they wished.

• In the 1960s and 1970s, a variety of psychologists and psychiatrists—Jenkins, Hare, Lykken, Schachter, Quay, and many others—succeeded in isolating certain specific characteristics of the psychopath by physiological measures. They were able to pinpoint the psychopathic syndrome through such various measures as the E.E.G., skin conductivity responses, and immunity to shock.

• By the 1970s, despite changes in terminology which made cross-cultural comparisons difficult, social and physical scientists had established a definitive portrait of the psychopath.

• Some writers—Mailer, Harrington, Smith—attributed the prevalence of psychopathy to contradictions in Western culture, to the demands of Western society, or to the basic values of America. While controversial in their portrayals of "capitalistic" society and their prescriptions for a solution, such writers succeeded in bringing the question of the psychopath to wide public attention. Idolized or condemned, the lonely stranger became a hallmark of cultural criticism.

• By 1982, no investigator of the psychopathic personality has ventured on virgin ground. Research had demonstrated the existence of a psychopathic syndrome, even though interpreters viewed the disorder in a variety of ways: Carl Frankenstein, in 1959, described this disorder in primarily Jungian terms (1959); Harold Palmer attributed the aberration to constitutional defects (1958); and Robert Smith (1978) and Alan Harrington (1972) maintained that capitalistic American culture was at fault.

Clearly, even after centuries of exploration, we do not fully understand the causation of psychopathy, the nature of the psychopath's mind, or the differences between him or her and other human beings. Even today, the structure of the psychopathic personality calls for further scientific observation.

References

Alexander, F. The neurotic character. *International Journal of Psychoanalysis*, 1930, *11:*292–313.

American Psychiatric Association, *Diagnostic and statistical manual of mental disturbance*, 1952.

Ariès, P. *Centuries of childhood*. New York: Knopf, 1962.

Arthurs, R. G. S., & Cahoon, E. G. A clinical and electroencephalographic survey of psychopathic personality. *American Journal of Psychiatry*, 1964, *120:*875–882.

Bay-Rakal, S. The significance of EEG abnormality in behavior problem children. *Canadian Psychological Association Journal*, 1965, *10:*387–391.

Beccaria, C. *An essay on crimes and punishments*. London: Newburry, 1770.

Borkovec, T. D. Autonomic reactivity to sensory stimulation in psychopathic, neurotic, and normal juvenile delinquents. *Journal of Consulting and Clinical Psychology*, 1970, *35:*217–222.

Bowlus, D. E., & Shotwell, A. A Rorschach study of psychopathic delinquents. *American Journal of Mental Deficiency*, 1947, *52:*23–30.

British Journal of Delinquency (editors), 1951, *2:*77.

Buss, A. H. *Psychopathology*. New York: Wiley, 1966.

Caldwell, J. M., The constitutional psychopathic state. *Journal of Criminal Psychopathology*, 1941, *3:*171–179.

Camus, A. *The stranger*. New York: Knopf, 1960.

Chambliss, W. The state and the criminal law. In W. Chambliss and M. Mankoff (Eds.), *Whose law? What order?* New York: Wiley, 1976.

Chornyak, J. Some remarks on the diagnosis of the psychopathic delinquent. *American Journal of Psychiatry*, 1941, *97:*1327–1331.

Christie, R., & Geis, F. *Studies in Machiavellianism*. New York: Academic Press, 1970.

Cicourel, A. *The social organization of juvenile justice*. New York: Wiley, 1968.

Cleckly, H. *The mask of sanity* (1st ed.), St. Louis: Mosby, 1941.

Emmons, T. D., & Webb, W. W. Subjective correlates of conditioned responsivity and stimulation seeking in psychopaths, normals, and acting-out neurotics. *Journal of Consulting and Clinical Psychology*, 1974, *42:*620, 1974.

Empey, LaMar T. *American delinquency*. Homewood, Illinois: Dorsey Press, 1978.

Erikson, K. T. Notes on the sociology of deviance. In H. S. Becker (Ed.), *The other side*, New York: The Free Press, 1964.

Frankenstein, C. *Psychopathy*. New York: Grune and Stratton, 1959.

Glenn, M. L., Press of freedom. *Village Voice*, September 14, 1967.

Glueck, B. A study of 608 admissions to Sing Sing prison. *Mental Hygiene*, 1918, *II:*85–151.

Goring, C. *The English convict*. London: His Majesty's Stationary Office, 1913.

Gouster, M. Moral insanity. *Revue Des Sciences Medical*, 1878, *5:*181–182.

Gray, K. C., & Hutchinson, H. C. The psychopathic personality. *Canadian Psychiatric Association Journal* 1964, *9:*452–456.

Haefner, H. *Psychopathen: daseinanaltische untersuchungen zur struktur und verlaufsgestalt von psychopathien*. Berlin: Springer-Verlag, 1961.

Hare, R. D. *Psychopathy*. New York: Wiley, 1970.

Harrington, A. *Psychopaths*. New York: Simon and Schuster, 1972.

Hart, H. *Preventive treatment of neglected children*. New York: Charities Publication Committee, 1910.

Henderson, C. R. (Ed.). *Prison reform and criminal law.* New York: Charities Publication Committee, 1910.

Henderson, Sir David. *Psychopathic states.* New York: Norton, 1939.

Heuser, K. D. The psychopathic personality:Rorschach patterns of 28 cases. *American Journal of Psychiatry,* 1946, *103*:105–112.

Hunt, J. M. *Personality and the behavior disorders* (Vol. II). Boston: Ronald Press, 1944.

Jenkins, R. The psychopathic or anti-social personality. *The Journal of Nervous and Mental Disease,* 1960, *131*:318–334.

Jenkins, R. L. Diagnoses, dynamics, and treatment in child psychiatry. *Psychiatric Research Reports,* 1964, *18*:91–120.

Jenkins, R. L. Psychiatric syndromes in children and their relation to family background. *American Journal of Orthopsychiatry,* 1966, *36*:450–457.

Kahn, E. *Psychopathic personalities.* New Haven: Yale University Press, 1931.

Karpman, B. On the need of separating psychopathy into two distinct clinical types: The symptomatic and the ideopathic. *Journal of Criminal Psychopathology,* 1941, *3*:137.

Karpman, B. Seven psychopaths. *Journal of Clinical Psychopathology and Psychotherapy,* 1944, *6*:299.

Karpman, B. Psychopathy in the scheme of human typology. *Journal of Nervous and Mental Disease,* 1945, *103*:276–288.

Karpman, B. Autobiography of a bandit. *Journal of Criminal Law, Criminology and Police Science,* 1946, *3*:305–332.

Karpman, B. The sexual psychopath. *Journal of Criminal Law, Criminology, and Police Science,* 1951, *42*:184–198.

Kavka, J. Pinel's conception of the psychopathic state: An historical critique. *Bulletin of the History of Medicine,* 1949, *23*:461–468.

Kurland, D. H., Yeager, C. T., & Arthur, R. J., Psychophysiologic aspects of severe behavior disorders. *Archives of General Psychiatry,* 1963, *8*:599–604.

Lange-Eichbaum, W. *Genie, Irrism, und Ruhm.* Munich: E. Reinhardt, 1956.

Lindner, R. Experimental studies in constitutional psychopathic inferiority. Part I. *Journal of Criminal Psychopathology,* 1943, *3*:252–276.

Lindner, R. *Rebel without a cause.* New York: Grune and Stratton, 1944.

Lindner, R. Psychopathic personality and the concept of homeostatis. *Journal of Clinical Psychopathology and Psychotherapy,* 1945, *6*:511.

Lindner, R. Psychopathy as a psychological problem. *Encyclopedia of Psychology.* New York: Philosophical Library, 1948.

Lemert, E. *Social pathology.* New York: McGraw-Hill, 1951.

Lombroso, C. *Delinquent man.* Rome: 1876.

Lykken, D. T. A study of anxiety in the sociopathic personality. *Journal of Abnormal and Social Psychology,* 1957, *55*:6–10.

Maas, J. P. Cathexes toward significant others by sociopathic women. *Archives of General Psychiatry,* 1966, *15*:516–522.

Mailer, N. The white Negro. In *Voices of Dissent.* New York: Grove Press, 1958.

Maughs, S. G. A concept of psychopathy. *Journal of Criminal Psychopathology,* 1941, *2*:329–356.

Mechanic, D. *Mental health and social policy.* Englewood Cliffs, New Jersey: Prentice-Hall, 1969.

Nettler, G. *Explaining crime.* New York: McGraw-Hill, 1978.

Ordronaux, J. Moral insanity. *American Journal of Insanity,* 1878, *29*:313.

Palmer, H. *Psychopathic personalities.* London: Peter Owen, 1958.

Partridge, G. E. A study of 50 cases of psychopathic personality. *American Journal of Psychiatry*, 1928, *7:*953–973.

Pritchard, J. A. *A treatise on insanity.* Philadelphia: Haswell, Barrington, and Haswell, 1835.

Quay, H. C. Personality dimensions in delinquent males as inferred from the factor analysis of behavior ratings. *Child Development*, 1964, *1:*33–37.

Quay, H. C. Dimensions of personality in delinquent boys as inferred from the factor analysis of case history data. *Child Development*, 1964, *35:*479–484.

Quay, H. C. Psychopathic personality as pathological stimulation seeking. *American Journal of Psychiatry*, 1965, *122:*180–183, 1965.

Quinney, R. *Critique of legal order.* Boston: Little, Brown, 1974.

Reid, W. H. (Ed.). *The psychopath: A comprehensive study of antisocial disorders and behaviors.* New York: Brunner/Mazel, 1978.

Rotenberg, M., & Diamond, B. L. The Biblical conception of psychopathy. *Journal of the History of the Behavioral Sciences*, 1971, *7:*29–38.

Rothman, D. J. *The discovery of the asylum.* Boston: Little, Brown, 1971.

Schachter, S. *Emotion, obesity, and crime.* New York: Academic Press, 1971.

Schachter, S., & Latané, B. Crime, cognition and the autonomic nervous system. Nebraska Symposium on Motivation, 1964, Lincoln, Nebraska.

Schmauk, F. J. Punishment, arousal and avoidance learning in sociopaths. *Journal of Abnormal Psychology*, 1970, *76:*325–335.

Sheldon, W. H. *Varieties of delinquent youth.* Boston: Ronald Press, 1949.

Siddle, D. Electrodermal activity and psychopathy. In S. Melnick and K. O. Christiansen (Eds.), *Biosocial bases of criminal behavior.* New York: Gardner Press, 1977.

Slater, E. T. O. Psychopathic personality as a genetical concept. *Journal of Mental Science*, 1948, *94:*277.

Smith, R. *The psychopath in society.* New York: Academic Press, 1978.

Spitzer, R., Cohen, J., Fleiss, J., & Endicott, J. On quantification of agreement in psychiatric diagnosis. *Archives of General Psychiatry*, 1967, *17:*83–87.

Sykes, G. *Criminology.* New York: Harcourt Brace Jovanovich, 1978.

Van Erva, J. P., & Rosenberg, B. G. Ego strength and ego dysfunction in primary and secondary psychopaths. *Journal of Clinical Psychology*, 1963, *19:*61–63.

Wittelg, F. The criminal psychopath in the psychoanalytic system. *Psychoanalytic Review*, 1937, *24:*276–291.

World Health Organization. *International classification of diseases.* Geneva: 1972.

4 The Problem of Identification

One might think of a person outside on a cold snowy night, looking through a window into a warm room, seeing a family, sensing happiness, almost able to feel the warmth but realizing that he can never be inside.
William Reid, *On the sadness of the psychopath.* (Reid, 1978, p. 1)

Although the past 200 years have brought about much greater precision in diagnosing psychopathy, confusion about the concept still lingers on.

In 1950, as Edwin Sutherland pointed out, estimates of the number of psychopaths varied wildly: in one midwestern prison, officials labeled 98% of inmates as "psychopaths"; a similar prison found that only 5% of its population could be called psychopathic. (The definition of "sexual psychopaths"—a term tagged solely on sexual deviance that has fortunately dropped out of fashion—fluctuated erratically.) Within the same city, New York court psychiatrists believed that only 15% of their patients fitted the category whereas New York's Bellevue Hospital claimed that 52% of similar patients could be so named (Sutherland, 1950). Such confusion led to the demise of laws directed specifically at the so-called sexual psychopath.

Yet, as late as the 1970s, reputable sociologists, psychiatrists, and clinical psychologists issued statements that confused an American public already deeply frightened about the threat of crime. Some sociologists still refused to recognize the existence of psychopaths while others issued clarion calls to "incapacitate" all convicts as no other approach worked.

"Nothing Works"

The late Robert Martinson (1974) popularized the phrase "nothing works" as a description of all attempts to change criminals or psychopaths. As a "freedom rider" during the civil rights movement, Martinson himself had spent time in Mississippi's Parchmont Prison. Quite naturally, he opposed attempts to "rehabilitate" criminals that one subgroup—such as Southern whites—labeled antisocial. Martinson contributed to a prevailing mood of the time: that society should lock up all criminals and "throw away the key." He changed his mind before his premature death in 1979, but his new views had not achieved as wide publicity as his earlier, pessimistic conclusions (see Sanchez, 1980).

And, in the late 1970s, Stanton Samenow and the late Samuel Yochelson received enormous publicity with their work, *The Criminal Personality* (1976, 1977). The book revived Lombrosian views that criminals are born, not made. The authors asserted that *all* criminals are psychopaths. On the basis of 240 cases, they said that "criminal children" rejected their parents (rather than that the parents rejected the children). They stated that all criminals suffered from 52 "errors in thinking"; they argued that female criminals were the same as male criminals (although they had only males in their sample and not even a male control group). Further they contended that their new methods of treatment had—after 16 years—"cured" 13 of the original 240 forensic patients.

Many practitioners with wider experience of criminal behavior, most notably Theodore Sarbin and O. J. Keller, attacked the unscientific nature of the book; its sweeping often contradictory generalizations, and its meaningless statements such as "the criminal child operates alone, with an accomplice or in a group [Keller, 1980]." Even Keller's destruction of the book's premises, pretensions, and conclusions did not prevent prominent newspapers from publishing such headlines as "You Can Stop Feeling Sorry For Criminals" and "Criminals Are Born, Not Made."

Progress in Diagnosis

Devastating as these statements might be to a scientific understanding of crime, less spectacular but more solid research on identifying the criminal psychopath quietly progressed. By 1982, advances in measuring psychopathic tendencies made possible both more accurate diagnoses and equally importantly a greater understanding of the interaction of sociological, psychological, and physiological forces in contributing to the development of a psychopathic pattern. Progress occurred on three fronts:

1. *Physiological* researchers have explored the autonomic nervous system and neural patterns of psychopaths. Such research makes it feasible, as one illustration, to investigate the interrelationship of autonomic nervous system patterns, family backgrounds, and social-class status in the identification of psychopathy.

2. *Social–psychological* researchers have identified the cluster of traits that distinguish psychopaths from others and have made possible truly differential approaches to the treatment of the problem.

3. Greater sophistication in *clinical judgment* by psychiatrists, psychologists, social workers, and correctional administrators has eliminated much of the confusion that existed in their assumption that psychotics, neurotics, psychopaths, and other criminals all suffered from a similar mental disorder.

Unraveling the riddle of the psychopath has required the combined efforts of sociologists, clinicians, psychologists, physiologists, and many other specialists. Only such an accumulation of interdisciplinary information can provide clues to solving the puzzle of psychopathy.

Physiological Approaches to Identifying the Psychopath

Sarnoff Mednick, the late Karøl O. Christiansen, and their colleagues (1977) have led the way in Scandinavia to a greater understanding of psychopaths. They postulated that biological and social factors interact in the identification and perhaps the creation of psychopaths. These investigators conducted much of their research in Denmark because of that nation's excellent criminal records and the government's ability, because of its issuance of "internal passports" to all citizens, to follow the history of twins.

Among their many findings, these researchers have confirmed (or discovered) certain basic characteristics of psychopaths in Scandinavia.

• Original studies of psychopaths—measured by physiological standards of differences between adopted versus nonadopted children in criminal and noncriminal families—suggested that social factors have overwhelming importance among the lower social classes in producing psychopaths. In contrast, possibly genetic factors have greater importance than social influences (such as being raised by a criminal father) in the Danish upper classes.

• Confirming prior studies, Mednick and Christiansen (1977) found definite differences in the autonomic nervous system of psychopaths and nonpsychopaths. Specifically, psychopaths in the higher social classes (versus the lower social classes) evinced less fearful responses to experimental punishments than did nonpsychopaths.

• Measured in terms of electrodermal activity, the researchers found that the recovery rate after a punishing stimulus is slower among psychopaths than among other maximum security prisoners or college students (Mednick & Christiansen, 1977). Hare (1975) independently noted a similar pattern in the United States.

Why should psychopaths exhibit signs of slower autonomic nervous system responses to punishment? Why should psychopaths from an upper-class environment have an even lower rate of physiological recovery from fear than lower-class psychopaths who, in turn, recover from fear more slowly than nonpsychopaths? Why should adopted psychopaths raised by criminal fathers have a slower rate of recovery from fear than children raised by noncriminal fathers (Mednick & Christiansen, 1977)? These questions become even more difficult to answer when one makes certain basic assumptions:

The *faster* the rate of autonomic nervous system recovery indicates a faster rate of the dissipation of fear. As psychopaths are, by all clinical reports, less fearful, less anxious, and more impulsive than nonpsychopaths, why should their physiological signs indicate a pattern that, on the surface, seems in absolute contrast?

Mednick, Hare, and others have suggested a very simple, biosocial model that seems a persuasive way of explaining such anomalies.

A BIOSOCIAL THEORY OF PSYCHOPATHY

Following Mednick and Christiansen (1977), one may reasonably posit the following common sequence of events:

A child or an adult wishes to act aggressively (or illegally) toward someone else;

Previous punishment from family, peers, or authorities creates fear that is reflected in electrodermal activity;

Possibly, the effectiveness of this punishment is enhanced by the person's biological endowment;

Because of the fear of future consequences, a normal person stops the action.

The person's fears then (monitored by measures of the autonomic nervous system) should dissipate.

One should add that the speed with which fear dissipates is positively correlated with the effectiveness of the operation of a person's inhibitions or conscience.

Accepting, for the moment, the validity of this model, one would expect that:

Psychopaths have not undergone a series of experiences (or possibly lack the neural characteristics) effectively inhibiting behavior that their society deems as harmful;

When psychopathic children or adults entertain ideas of aggressive (or illegal, asocial, or merely unpopular) actions, such impulses do not arouse as much fear as in nonpsychopathic persons.

This relative lack of fear does not trigger a major inhibitory response from the autonomic nervous system.

Thus, the psychopath either undertakes the socially disapproved action, or

The psychopath's relatively low level of fear temporarily inhibits the action.

In either case, one would expect few physiological responses among psychopaths (particularly among lower social classes where "illegal" actions may be tolerated), less recovery from fear among children raised by criminal fathers (who may actually applaud the subject's action), and a slower rate of autonomic nervous system recovery in the dissipation of fear as the original level of fear is lower and the need to dissipate fear is less intense. These expectations would fit exactly what Mednick, Christiansen, Hare, and their associates found in their physiological discoveries.

Diagnosis and Causation

Although the search for the basis of psychopathy has led some researchers to develop biophysiological indicators, the acceptance of these does not preclude other factors. Using such indicators for identifying the psychopath does not entail affirming either a physiological or a sociological explanation for the psychopath's actual behavior. These measures do, however, provide objective ways for identifying psychopaths.

Indeed, they can be applied in childhood. Sarnoff Mednick and colleagues (1977) measured the autonomic nervous system responses of children *before* they committed a delinquent act. Thus, they eliminated the possibility that differences in electrodermal activity might have been a result of registration for asocial actions. The pre-delinquents responded with less electrodermal activity and recovered at a slower rate from noxious stimuli (a loud noise) than did other children. Although this finding is consistent with previous studies of criminal psychopaths, it should be noted that the pre-delinquents in the sample had committed only mild offenses by the time they developed a criminal record. Some among them may have been psychopaths but we do not know.

I should stress that Mednick and his colleagues' results are of particular interest as Denmark is a relatively homogeneous nation culturally, ethnically, and economically (approximately 90% of the population earns an income that is within a narrow range). Thus, the researchers have more or less eliminated the possibly contaminating influence of ethnic and economic discrimination from their studies.

OTHER MEASURES OF PSYCHOPATHS' PHYSIOLOGICAL RESPONSES

Various scholars have confirmed the Scandinavian research. In Britain, John Hinton and Michael O'Neil (1978) found that psychopaths as compared to nonpsychopathic inmates of a maximum security hospital had a reduced rate of spontaneous fluctuations on skin resistance patterns and, in addition, lower heart rate variability. In general, the psychopaths seemed calmer and less anxious than nonpsychopaths—a response compatible with both clinical and other physiological results. In 1979, Aniskiewicz found similar results when giving subjects an electric shock: "primary" (more criminal) psychopaths exhibited less anticipatory electrodermal activity than others.

In England, Wadsworth traced all the males born in England, Scotland, and Wales during a particular period in March 1946. The pulse rate of these children had been taken prior to a mildly threatening event (a school medical examination) in 1957. A slow pulse rate indicating less fear accurately predicted serious delinquencies of the boys (not necessarily psychopathy) by the time they were 21 years of age (1977).

The entire infant population of Mauritius has been tested physiologically in an on-going longitudinal study. Preliminary reports indicate that infants with the slowest electrodermal recovery rate were those who cried least, showed less anxiety about testing, and were relatively unfrightened (Mednick, in Bittner & Messinger, 1980). Whether these measures on infants actually correlate with adult psychopathy remains to be seen.

These studies done in various parts of the world and utilizing diverse methods have produced a portrait of the psychopath (or potential psychopath) as relatively immune to punitive conditioning, and as calmer and less anxious than other people.

The Psychopath and the Lie Detector

Interesting, if controversial, tests have been made of the psychopaths' responses to lying. In the usual experimental situation, one would expect the less anxious psychopath to evince fewer signs of nervousness on the polygraph than would the normal individual when lying. The first results of the psychopath's response to lie detector tests supported this assumption: Tests of psychopaths when they lied did not differ from when they told the truth (Lykken, 1955).

In 1978, however, Raskin and Hare found that no differences could be detected between psychopaths and nonpsychopaths' responses on the polygraph in a "mock crime" situation. When the subjects had supposedly stolen $20 (or not stolen it), their physiological responses were the same: the polygraph detected 96% of both groups (Raskin & Hare, 1978).

Lykken (1978) suggested that perhaps psychopaths can "beat" the lie detector. Lykken had previously noted that psychopaths in prison became slightly excited, but not anxious, about lie detector tests. They regarded this test as a minor challenge to their abilities. One psychopath revealed that he had "beaten" the polygraph by digging one thumbnail under another to produce proper physical responses at the right time. In contrast, as we have seen, Raskin (1978) challenged the ability of psychopaths to mask their deception.

The dispute remains unresolved, although few clinicians question the ability of psychopaths to lie in actual situations. The difference between what the psychopath perceives as a "real" challenge as opposed to an artificial situation may account for much of his physiological reactions to stress.

A Need for Novelty?

A number of studies have suggested that psychopaths seek new situations and novel challenges. Physiologically unresponsive to the more common forms of punishment, the psychopath may well seek ever more exciting situations.

Quay (1965) originally argued that psychopaths are perennially bored and, therefore, cannot reflect the autonomic nervous system response of other people. If true, this would explain the low level of skin conductivity response in typical experimental situations. Psychopaths cannot tolerate monotony, so the theory goes, and restlessly seek after action. Thus, minor punishments fail to deter them. In a somewhat similar fashion, Hans Eysenck (1964) argued that psychopaths were unstable extraverts—labile in emotion, unanxious, and uninhibited.

Emmons and Webb (1974) found some support for the view that psychopaths were "pathological stimulation seekers" in comparison to acting out neurotics and "normal" people.

In several quite different experiments, other scholars provided additional supporting evidence for the hypothesis that psychopaths seek novel situations more than other people. Gul'dan and Ivannikov (1974) examined the motor time reactions of psychopaths in applying past experience to solving problems. As one might suspect, psychopaths did not appear to profit from their past experience as much as other people. Rather, psychopaths invented completely new solutions to "puzzles," even if this entailed punishment, rather than following similar paths. Perhaps, then, psychopaths are relatively deficient in learning or they are more intelligent.

Comparison of psychopaths and neurotic delinquents indicated that psychopaths preferred novel, presumably more stimulating situations than did neurotics (Skrzypek, 1969). In general, psychopaths showed less anxiety than neurotic delinquents and a greater desire for novelty. Perceptual isolation further increased the psychopath's desire for complexity. Hare (1970) interpreted these results as indicating that the psychopathic delinquent is in a state of cortical underarousal and sensory deprivation. Other evidence suggests that psychopaths preferred frightening to nonfrightening experiences, even though both were unpleasant, than did neurotic criminals or noncriminals (Lykken, 1955).

In addition, Hare (1970) found that psychopaths' heart deceleration rates responded less to noise stimulation (once they had been habituated to a repetitive stimulation) than nonpsychopaths'. Hare interpreted this finding as again indicating that psychopaths have a greater need for cortical excitement than others. One should also recall that psychopaths may simply have been bored by the experiment.

In real life, psychopaths may exhibit the same need for unconventional stimulation. On October 28, 1980, for example, a young female psychopath approached a man on a Manhattan subway. The girl, Kathy Rios, poured lighter fluid over his hair and face. She then set fire to him. She apparently selected her victim at random from other passengers. The girl said she "torched" the man simply because "she felt like it." The girl had no apparent motive and did not rob him. Later, when apprehended, she boasted of her action (*New York Times*, October 29, 1980).

Thus, the preponderance of evidence suggests that psychopaths have a greater need for new situations to excite or arouse them than do others. One may attribute this physiological response to the psychopath's lower level of cortical arousal or merely to his or her relative lack of anxiety.

Greater Ability to Respond to Real Stress?

Although psychopaths do not show physiological signs of responding to minor artificial punishments, such as loud noises, and apparently seek greater stimulation regardless of punishment, the possibility remains that they react more effectively than do others to real-life stress. The evidence on this problem is still cloudy.

In Sweden, Lidberg and his associates (1976) measured hormonal differences of psychopaths and nonpsychopaths by their urinary output. They ran both groups through a mock criminal trial and also measured the two groups before their actual trials. Before their real trial, psychopaths excreted more adrenalin (presumably helping them to cope with stress) than did nonpsychopaths. Similarly, a psychopath who escaped from prison immediately after being measured had shown a great increase in adrenalin. Lidberg suggested that efficient coping behavior during real stress, such as the actual trial or an escape, may be associated with a high level of adrenalin and with a capacity to cope with actual dangers.

Yet, the same investigators reported 3 years later (1979) that psychopaths did not increase their secretion of adrenalin (a correlate of anxiety) or noradrenalin (a correlate of aggression) before an actual trial, while nonpsychopaths did (1979). The differences in results may perhaps be due to the fact that subjects in the first test were measured behaviorally while those in the second were chosen on the basis of questionnaires such as the Eysenck Personality Inventory.

Hare and others (1978) independently demonstrated that psychopaths have more "effective" physiological responses to threats than do nonpsychopaths. During a countdown of a highly noxious tone, psychopaths increased their heart rate (a "normal" physiological response) but showed less electrodermal activity (also a "normal" response). Hare had argued that this finding indicates that psychopaths developed more effective physiological mechanisms for coping with threats than did nonpsychopaths.

There is also evidence that psychopaths have a high concentration of noradrenalin in their bodies and that they recover more quickly from stressful situations than do others (Hare, 1970). Since noradrenalin is negatively correlated with anxiety, psychopaths may respond to stressful situations with less anxiety than others. The high level of noradrenalin may be responsible for the psychopath's proclivity to violence.

Because of the paucity of evidence, I would tentatively conclude that psychopaths are relatively more effective in dealing with real-life stress than are other people. Even this "efficiency" and their reasonable level of intelligence may, however, be marred by their tendency to react to stress in an aggressive, impulsive manner.

Greater Aggressiveness?

Many clinicians have described the criminal psychopath as highly aggressive although, as I have noted, the "normal" psychopath usually seems able to curb his or her aggressive impulses. Physiological evidence, based mainly on criminal populations, suggests that there may well be reasons for the criminal psychopath's destructive impulsivity.

Kaplan (1960) administered mecholyl to both psychopaths and neurotic criminals. Mecholyl generally produces a drop in blood pressure when used for medical purposes. Nonetheless, people respond quite differently to the drug. Psychopaths have shown a slow drop in blood pressure, as do other people, but a rapid return to their original autonomic status. More importantly, they tended to become more aggressive. When given depressants such as sodium amytal, they became even more aggressive. This finding coincides with the opinion of clinicians that alcohol produces a lessening of inhibitions and a consequently greater increase in aggression among psychopaths as it does for other people (Cleckly, 1976). As alcohol is readily accessible to psychopaths as well as other people, this drug may well serve to increase their aggressive responses.

Tunk and Dema (1977) demonstrated that psychopaths may suffer from a "dyscontrol syndrome" due to abnormal sensitization of the limbic system. This dysfunction, in turn, shows up in EEG abnormalities and a tendency toward violence. Psychotrophic drugs may cure this problem but psychopaths seldom take such drugs.

Inconclusive evidence suggests that increased glucose activity in the right temporal lobe may be associated with manic, aggressive attacks (Newsweek, 1980). Such a finding would indicate abnormal metabolism in the psychopath's brain.

With some caution, then, one may speculate that criminal psychopaths have a greater tendency toward violence. In addition to a higher physiological potential for aggression, psychopaths may also have a greater tendency to seek immediate pleasure—at least to the extent that such "short-run hedonism" can be measured physiologically.

A Search for Immediate Pleasure?

Many observers have recorded the psychopath's tendency to seek immediate gratification (Cleckly, 1976). As I have mentioned, criminal psychopaths are highly impulsive and seek pleasure wherever they can find it, although "normal" psychopaths seem capable of delaying gratification. Physiological studies of criminal psychopaths support the belief that they are "short-run hedonists."

Hare (1970) recorded that psychopaths seek pleasure immediately without contemplating the eventual effects of their action. In situations where the psychopath believes that he or she is about to receive an electric shock, the threat of future discomfort does not interfere with his or her choice of immediate pleasure. In general, psychopathic delinquents have much less fear about eventual punishment than do anxious, neurotic delinquents (Schalling & Levander, 1967).

As psychopaths come from emotionally deprived, rejecting backgrounds (see Chapter 6), Arieti (1967) reasonably hypothesized that "no benevolent mother was there to help the child to make the transition from immediate gratification to postponement. He did not learn to expect approval and tenderness, to experience hope and to anticipate the fulfillment of a promise [p. 306]."

A "Maturational Lag"?

A variety of studies have indicated that psychopaths suffer from various abnormalities, particularly in the limbic system, including the medial frontal cortex, temporal lobes, and the hypothalamus (Morrison, 1978). Specifically, the EEG abnormalities appear in bilateral rhythmic slow-wave activity that, in turn, correlates with slow cortical maturation (Morrison, 1978). This is significant as bilateral theta activity often occurs in young children but disappears normally between the ages of 10 and 20. Adult psychopaths, however, continue to exhibit the "childlike" pattern until they reach middle age (Elliott, 1978).

Hare and Cox (1978) suggested several interpretations of this fact. Perhaps the slow-wave activity indicates delayed cortical maturation or some underlying cortical dysfunction. It would be consistent with other evidence to expect that the slow-wave activity reflects the psychopath's low cortical arousal and his or her need for excitement. Conceivably, the adult psychopath's EEG pattern—with its similarity to that of normal children and its gradual disappearance—suggests that adult psychopaths more often remain at a "childish" level of cortical development. Such a hypothesis fits well with other evidence. Clinicians have often found that psychopaths "burn out" around age 35 (Reid, 1978). They tend to lose much of their aggressiveness, impulsivity, as well as their seeking of immediate pleasure.

Obviously, many factors—changes in their social situation, repeated punishment, or the effects of treatment—could account for such a change. We should not rule out, however, the possibility that the eventual disappearance of slow-wave activity indicates that the psychopath has finally physiologically matured.

Physiological Indicators of Psychopathy

Psychology, psychiatry, and physiology have fortunately advanced far beyond the times of Pinel, Pritchard, and Lombroso. It is now possible to measure physiologically the traits which many practitioners have denoted as typical of criminal psychopaths.

We must, however, proceed with caution as (a) noncriminal psychopaths have usually not been included in the physiological studies; (b) some criminal psychopaths do not exhibit the physiological signs that the experimenters predicted; and (c) some criminal psychopaths can manage to fake their responses to such physiological measures as the lie detector.

Nonetheless, with these qualifications in mind, we can tentatively suggest that psychopaths differ from other people in a number of physiological ways:

- Psychopaths evince less anticipatory fear of punishment than do nonpsychopaths. This relative lack of fear differs by social class and family background.
- Psychopaths' electrodermal activity reverts to a normal pattern after punishment more slowly than that of other people, perhaps

indicating a lower degree of inhibition and less fear of the consequences of their actions.

- Psychopaths differ significantly in pulse and heart rates from others.
- By all physiological measures, psychopaths appear less fearful than other people.
- In times of real-life stress, psychopaths may respond on a physiological level more efficiently and recover more quickly from stress than other people.
- Measured by the EEG and the amount of noradrenalin they secrete, psychopaths demonstrate a greater propensity for violence than do other human beings.
- The psychopath's typically "childlike" EEG pattern may indicate a maturational lag.

Again, I should emphasize that these physiological measures—while of great significance—are merely indicators of the psychopath's nature. Such tests are useful for diagnosis. They do not, however, resolve any issues concerning causation. Is the psychopath physiologically less responsive, less anxious, and more pleasure seeking because of heredity? Or, in contrast, does he or she exhibit such physical signs because of being "trained" to act insensitively, to ignore fear, and to get immediate gratification when he or she can? Psychological tests have not yet provided us with definitive answers. Social and clinical psychologists have, however, delineated the psychopath's character with even greater clarity.

Social–Psychological Approaches to Identifying the Psychopath

Psychologists—using projective tests, questionnaires, experiments, and other techniques—have generally produced a picture of the psychopath that corresponds with the physiological evidence. Their research has been particularly fruitful in differentiating psychopaths from other types of offenders.

THE PSYCHOPATH AND OTHER CRIMINALS

Since the 1940s, psychologists and psychiatrists have reliably demonstrated that three basic types of offenders exist: the psychopathic, the neurotic, and the socialized criminal. The *psychopath* exhibits the behavior and symptoms that we have noted, the *neurotic criminal* responds to anxiety and inner compulsions, and the *socialized criminal* reacts to the demands of his or her particular peer group. A variety of studies have supported this categorization. Among the more prominent pieces of research upon which this distinction is made include these:

• In 1946, L. E. Hewitt and Richard Jenkins examined case files from the Michigan Child Guidance Clinic. They found "overinhibited" children (shy, anxious, and seclusive); socialized, generally gang delinquents; and "unsocialized" aggressive children (psychopaths) who were assaultive, defiant, and guiltless. Because of the inadequacy of case records, these three descriptions fitted only a minority of children (Glaser, 1978). The neurotic delinquents seem to have benefited most from psychiatric treatment (Glaser, 1978).

• In 1952, Albert J. Reiss applied similar but more refined techniques to the study of 1110 male probationers. He found high consistency on the ratings: 12% had "defective superegos" (psychopaths), 22% were neurotic, and 66% were "socialized."

• By 1959, J. D. Grant and M. Q. Grant had developed a "maturity scale" that systematically differentiated psychopaths from other types of criminals.

• In 1964, Herbert C. Quay demonstrated the utility of factor analysis as applied to delinquent inmates of institutions. Again, he found three basic types of offenders, including the psychopathic.

• In 1974, Ted Palmer reported on the results of an extended program of community treatment for delinquents. Palmer also found three types of criminals. The community treatment appeared to help "power-oriented," deceptive, manipulative youths (some of whom, presumably, were psychopaths).

• And, in 1979, T. Gannesbauer and J. Lazerevitz found three types of offenders in the American Air Force: conformist ("socialized"), neurotic, and antisocial (psychopaths). These groups differed not only in personality, but also in family backgrounds, Air Force performance, and type of offense.

Clearly, these and other studies indicated that criminal psychopaths can be differentiated from other criminals and require special forms of treatment. Such research rendered obsolete any attempt to develop a "general" theory of crime, its nature, or its "cure."

The studies also indicated some degree of overlap and ambiguity among the different categories. Most importantly, as I have already urged in considering the noncriminal psychopath, the research has not yet differentiated the criminal from the noncriminal psychopath (see Monahan & Splane, 1980).

LACK OF GUILT

With some consistency, psychological tests have revealed the criminal psychopath's basic lack of guilt. Originally, Linder (1943) administered Rorschach tests to both "normal" convicts and psychopathic convicts. He found that psychopaths exhibited a lack of guilt and an almost complete egocentricity. Other investigators using the Rorschach noted similar findings (Bowlus and Shotwell, 1947; Heuser, 1946; Kingsley, 1956).

Many analysts using the TAT (the Thematic Apperception Test) have reached similar conclusions. The tester presents a series of rather vague pictures to the subject and requests that he or she make up a story about them. The stories then can be graded on the basis of the amount of guilt (or anxiety about forbidden actions) that the subject showed. In comparisons of psychopaths, other delinquents, residents of an orphanage, and a random sample of high school students, Silver (1963) noted a marked lack of guilt feelings among psychopaths, and Berg (1963) found similar tendencies on the TAT in a different sample.

Using another technique, other psychologists have discerned the psychopath's guiltlessness. The Rosenzeig Picture-Frustration Test, for example, presents cartoons depicting a person undergoing frustration. The subject records his or her response as to how the person will act. Comparisons of male psychopathic delinquents and other types of delinquents have indicated that psychopaths attribute less guilt to the person's reactions than do nonpsychopaths (Holzberg & Hahn, 1952; McCord & McCord, 1956).

Using the MMPI, a questionnaire that measures psychopathic qualities such as a lack of guilt, Megargee, Bohn, and their associates (1979) illustrated the usefulness of this instrument in differentiating between types of offenders. Bohn (Megargee & Bohn, 1979) found, for example, that the MMPI can be applied to prison management. By using the classifications in making prison dormitory assignments, he found that the rate of assaults within the prison declined 46% from a period when the MMPI was not used.

As Hare (1970) suggested, "These studies do not mean, of course, that the psychopath is unaware of the discrepancy between his behavior and societal expectations, but rather that he is neither guided by the possibility of such a discrepancy nor disturbed by its occurrence [p. 25]."

To argue that the psychopath is guiltless does not mean that he or she is "valueless" or lacks preferences. Based on an elaborate, systematic theory, Milton Rokeach and his associates developed a Value Survey that has been used on a variety of samples, including criminals (see Rokeach, 1972; Rokeach, 1973). In general, Rokeach's research has indicated that people's cognitive structures differ in three basic dimensions:

1. People hold beliefs ranging from "the primitive" (*"I believe this is my mother"*) to "inconsequential" (*"I believe steak tastes better than chicken"*). Rokeach points out that "authority" beliefs based on conscience (*"The Pope is infallible in matters of faith and morals"*) are more easily changeable than "primitive" beliefs. As the psychopath is particularly deficient in "authority" beliefs, he or she should be most susceptible to change in this area.

2. In addition, people adhere to a limited set of attitudes: "a relatively enduring organization of beliefs around an object or situation predisposing one to respond in some preferential manner [Rokeach, 1972, p. 112]."

3. On the third level of cognitive organization, Rokeach (1973) holds that people hierarchically organize their most enduring beliefs (values) as "terminal values" that represent the endstate of existence that the person wishes to achieve (e.g., "a comfortable life," "social recognition," "wisdom") and modes of achieving these instrumental values including ambition, courage, imagination, honesty, etc. As Rokeach and other investigators have already demonstrated that men and women, different national groups, people of varying political stances, etc., differ significantly from one another, one would expect similar differences between psychopaths and other groups.

Differences between those defined as psychopathic and others are predicted on the basis of differences already found between criminals and other groups. Although the evidence is incomplete, preliminary surveys using the Value Survey indicate that there are differences between criminals and national samples. Cochrane (1971), for example, recorded differences between prison inmates matched for sex, age, and race on the Rokeach Value Survey and a national sample. The prison inmates had been convicted of crimes ranging from homicide to narcotics violations. Cochrane does not indicate how many of his subjects were psychopaths, but his results are suggestive. Male inmates named "happiness" and "pleasure" more often as their instrumental values. "This value pattern suggests a self-centered concern with hedonism accompanied by a lesser concern with religion, the plight of others, their nation, or the world beyond [Rokeach, 1973, p. 135]." Yet, both male and female convicts rated "wisdom" as one of their highest terminal values, much higher than non-inmates. "Is 'wisdom' ranked high by inmates," Rokeach asks, "because it is a virtue they do not possess, a virtue which, had they possessed more, would have kept them out of jail? Or, is it a virtue they perceive themselves as possessing and therefore more able to outsmart society and the police? We do not know [p. 134]."

Similarly, the pattern of values chosen by female inmates presents an interesting and as yet uninterpreted finding: They exhibited a greater desire for excitement than the national sample of females but also placed a greater value on such qualities as a sense of accomplishment and freedom.

Although both male and female convicts ranked honesty as an important value, they did so less frequently than those outside of the prison. This fits well with previous findings that children who steal or who cheat in the classroom rated honesty lower than those who did not (Rokeach, 1973).

Clearly, the nature of value systems among psychopaths requires further research as the state of present knowledge is only suggestive rather than conclusive. Theoretically, psychopaths should highly rate "a comfortable life," an "exciting life," "freedom," and "pleasure" as their most significant values—while downgrading such other values as "mature love," "true friendship," and "equality." Whether more intelligent psychopaths would tell the truth or would merely offer platitudes that they conceived to be useful to them would require careful attention and the use of sophisticated physiological measures. As the Rokeach research with other groups indicates that they can be changed by confronting them with discrepancies in their values (Rokeach, 1973), it would represent a significant advance to see if the same results could be achieved with psychopaths.

LACK OF ANXIETY

Psychological measurements of the psychopath have usually confirmed the picture of him as relatively lacking in anxiety. Thus, in some situations, such as a prison escape or a real trial, psychopaths can act more effectively than other people. In other situations, the very lack of anxiety leads criminal psychopaths to commit more errors and overestimate their capacity to master a task.

In Russia, A. E. Lichto and N. Ya. Ivanov (1976) described a marked lack of anxiety in their psychopathic patients. They compared psychopaths with other delinquents, schizophrenics, and tubercular patients. Whether criminal or "normal," psychopaths had the least anxiety of any group.

In America, A. Bedford and D. McIves (1978) compared various types of psychiatric patients on the "Foulds General Instability Scale." They, too, found that psychopaths reported less depression and less anxiety than either neurotics or "normal" people.

In Germany, Michael Kerzondorfer (1977) applied Cattell's 16 PF test (one measure of anxiety) and used it with psychopathic, neurotic, schizophrenic, alcoholic, and highly depressed people. The test accurately differentiated psychopaths and indicated that they less often suffered from anxiety attacks.

All of these studies were done on males. One scholar has, however, investigated the same phenomenon among females. Cathy S. Widom (1978) measured the responses of female offenders to the "Special Hospitals Assessment Inventory." She noted that the women fell into four basic types: primary (or more criminal) psychopaths, secondary psychopaths, the "over-controlled" (presumably neurotic) person, and the normal. The primary psychopaths suffered from relatively little anxiety. The females definitely resembled male psychopaths in their response to the test. Quite rightly, the author suggested that there should be more research on female psychopaths as there is a dearth of information about them.

To some degree, as the physiological evidence has suggested, this lack of anxiety may be "functional" for the psychopath: he or she is not disabled or, indeed, crippled by unrealistic waves of anxiety. Nonetheless, a lack of anxiety can lead to errors in judgment and planning. Several studies have demonstrated that the criminal psychopath pays such a price for his relatively carefree, insensitive existence.

In one study of gambling behavior, for example, Richard Siegel (1977) compared psychopathic criminals to other types of criminals. Each group was provided with an equal amount of money with which to gamble. Possibly in reaction to their lack of anxiety, psychopaths gambled the most recklessly—*particularly* when the results were most uncertain. This may have been fun for them, but they also ended up with the least winnings. Siegel hypothesized that the psychopaths may have given way to "magical thinking" (i.e., a belief that they would win whatever the odds against them).

In a somewhat similar vein, D. Schalling and A. Rosén (1968) have used the Porteus Maze test on psychopaths and others. During increasingly difficult trials, the subjects traced their way through various mazes. The test requires planning and foresight. Again, as perhaps one result of his lack of anxiety, the psychopath made the most errors due to carelessness and poor planning.

In another psychological test, M. J. Lonstein (1952) compared groups of psychopathic, neurotic, and normal veterans in a hospital. He asked them to participate in a test that required the subject to roll a marble toward a target. The more accurate the person, the greater were his rewards. In addition, the experimenter asked each person to estimate his degree of success. The psychopaths were the most unrealistic in their estimates of their success. Moreover, as the test progressed and the experimenter informed the subjects of their accuracy, most normal and neurotic subjects lowered their estimates. Psychopaths, on the other hand, did just the opposite. Such an unrealistic pattern of aspiration would support the opinion that the psychopath lacks anxiety (Hare, 1970).

LACK OF EMPATHY

Many psychologists and sociologists view the psychopath's lack of empathy—his inability to put himself in the shoes of others, to sympathize with their plight, or to see himself as others see him—as the defining trait of psychopathy (Dinitz, 1978). Gough (1948) argued that psychopaths cannot take the role of other people. He cannot foresee the social consequences of his action and is often surprised by society's reaction to his behavior. Indirect support for this hypothesis has come from various sources, particularly studies of "normal" women. Reed and Cuadra (1957) found that student nurses who scored high on a scale related to psychopathy did not predict as well as others how they would be described by their peers. In another test, psychopathic women and a sample of student nurses took the sentence completion test (Simon, Holzberg, & Unger, 1951). The psychopathic women much more frequently chose responses that ignored the wishes or concerns of other people.

INTELLIGENCE

Psychopathic criminals have about the same intelligence level as nonpsychopathic criminals (Gurvitz, 1947), and the total psychopathic population may actually be more intelligent than the normal population. In addition, it should be recognized that there may well

115

be certain qualitative differences in the psychopath's intelligence level when compared to other people. Sherman (1957), for example, has shown that psychopaths have a more retentive memory than do neurotics or normal subjects. Other investigators have found that psychopaths do not differ significantly from other criminals, except that psychopaths score lower on verbal comprehension than do nonpsychopathic delinquents (Hecht & Jokovic, 1978). Alfred Heilbrun (1979) also compared psychopathic criminals and nonpsychopathic convicts. Whereas the groups were similar, psychopaths who were lower in intelligence had more often committed impulsive, violent crimes (Heilbrun, 1979). If replicated, these studies would indicate that psychopaths with the greatest powers of retention, concentration, and general intelligence are, like other people, least likely to be caught and imprisoned.

SOME PSYCHOLOGICAL CORRELATES OF PSYCHOPATHY

Research by psychologists and sociologists has added to our knowledge about the psychopath in a variety of ways:

• Reliable measures now differentiate the psychopathic criminal from the neurotic or socialized criminal. On a theoretical level, such a discovery makes it virtually impossible to develop a theory of crime that applies to every criminal. On a practical level, the differentiation of psychopaths from other criminals allows for more sophisticated methods of treatment.

• Tests ranging from the TAT and the Rorschach to the MMPI have confirmed clinicians' suspicions that criminal psychopaths lack a stable conscience, although they may well have their own distinct set of values.

• Studies in many different nations have shown that the criminal psychopath lacks anxiety. For good or evil, the psychopath proceeds through life unfettered by the normal or neurotic anxieties suffered by other people.

• On various psychological measures, the criminal psychopath demonstrates a lack of empathy or sensitivity for other people. He or she is also likely to misunderstand the feelings of others.

• The criminal psychopath exhibits the same range of intellectual capacities as do other criminals or noncriminals. In fact, in some regards, the criminal psychopath may score higher than others but this relative superiority may be masked because of his impulsivity.

Psychological and physiological research can be of immense aid in understanding the psychopath and diagnosing his disorder. Yet, as

Edward Sagarin (1975) pointed out, there can be great difficulties in relating personality patterns to any form of deviance. First, Sagarin argues, personality is not an "original cause, except in those instances where the factor can be traced to hereditary or congenital conditions [p. 90]." Thus, the psychopath's lack of guilt or lack of anxiety or inability to relate to other people cannot, in itself, be considered the cause of his behavior but possibly a result of other, unmeasured conditions. Second, cause and effect may easily be confused. The psychopath, for example, may mistrust other people because they have treated him cruelly—or, possibly, his mistrust of others may lead them to suspect him. Third, as Sagarin noted, "if a sample of psychopaths comes from people who have been arrested, it may be the arrest that produced the very real psychological problems that one is seeking to identify [1975, p. 90]"—or, of course, it could be the obverse.

Thus, as most psychological and physiological research is based on people who have already been identified as criminal psychopaths, we must be very cautious in concluding that we are dealing with patterns of causation.

Psychological measures should be treated as useful diagnostic tools and not as infallible indicators of causation.

Clinical Judgment

In the end, the detection of psychopathy—once the disorder has begun—rests on the reasonable judgment of psychiatrists, psychologists, social workers, sociologists, judges, police, and others who have dealt directly with this and other mental problems. Tests of skin conductivity or the MMPI and the Rorschach are very useful shortcuts, but a final diagnosis of psychopathy must rest on a knowledge of the actual symptoms and behavior of psychopathic persons.

A variety of studies utilizing the behavior and signs of psychopathy—as opposed to a rigid adherence to a particular nosology —have demonstrated a high degree of reliability among diagnosticians in differentiating the criminal psychopath from other criminals and noncriminals (see Cleckly, 1976; Hare, 1970; McCord & McCord, 1964; Reid, 1978; and Smith, 1978). These and other investigators agree on a minimal definition of the psychopath as guiltless, loveless, insensitive, and asocial. The great discrepancies of diagnoses typical of the nineteenth century and the first half of the twentieth century have largely disappeared. Nonetheless, various sources of bias still becloud the diagnosis and we should be aware of them.

DIFFICULTIES IN DIAGNOSING PSYCHOPATHS

There are many difficulties facing any person who deals with psychopaths, but one should take special note of these:

1. Noncriminal psychopaths whose behavior is in tune with the mores of their particular society have seldom been investigated in depth, except by rare anthropologists and psychologists.

2. As cultures differ widely in their encouragement of different forms of behavior, diagnoses of psychopathology also differ. Spanish-speaking males in America, for example, react to frustration and stress with passive resignation and a withdrawal from others, whereas North American non-Spanish males tend to react with aggression (Diaz-Guerrero, 1967). Thus, in a sample of mental patients matched on various social variables, deFundia, Draguns, and Phillips (1971) found that Argentine patients were relatively free of aggression in comparison to their North American counterparts.

3. Even within the same culture, clinicians may be handicapped by their own stereotypes. Richard Warner (1978), for example, found that clinicians in America diagnose people differently depending on their sex. Although the patients had the same symptoms, clinicians tended to identify men more often as "antisocial" and women as more "hysterical." Despite the identical clinical features of the patients, the clinicians apparently dealt with men and women differently because of their own beliefs about the "proper" roles of men and women. In fact, Viola K. Brown (1977) noted that black female delinquents are as violent and aggressive as black male delinquents.

4. If the clinician does not possess other information about the person, the psychopath's elusive "charm" may often mask his symptoms (Cleckly, 1976; Smith, 1978). In nonthreatening interviews with Belgian psychopaths and nonpsychopaths, Livré (1978) found that psychopaths kept less distance from the interviewer, used more gestures, and had more eye contact—all supposed clues to the nature of "normal," extroverted people.

5. Many clinicians believe that psychopaths "burn out" after age 35. "His [or] her behavior becomes less spectacular and less overtly hostile, and the inadequate or unstable components find a modicum of adjustment in some respects [Reid, 1978, p. 50]." This may or may not be true (see Chapter 8) but, in any case, older psychopaths learn to present a less aggressive facade to the diagnostician.

6. Those who reject the diagnosis of psychopathy on a priori grounds, may fall prey to the psychopath's manipulations and endanger the rest of society. Clark and Pencycote (1976), for example,

have traced the case of Patrick McKay, a notorious English psychopath. McKay had been diagnosed early in life as a dangerous psychopath. At age 15, on suspicion of murder, he was committed to a mental hospital. Lawyers and correction officials did not, however, accept the concept. McKay was released and committed a variety of muggings and killings in 1974.

7. Historically, clinicians have often confused the psychopath with other types of deviants or with people suffering from mental disorders. The advent of more sophisticated physiological measures, psychological tests, and more experienced clinical judgment should correct this error.

THE PSYCHOPATH AND SOCIALIZED CRIMINALS

Encouraged by the use of less definite psychiatric terms such as "antisocial personality," some clinicians have dangerously confused psychopaths with *socialized criminals*. John Clausen (1957) has argued that many traits of the psychopath could be found among lower-class slum adolescents: "inability to form deep and lasting attachments . . . lack of concern with the rights of others and emotional poverty [p. 267]."

Clausen and others have, however, overlooked the fact that delinquents, gangsters, or Mafia members who emerge from such environments have strong attachments to their particular groups and a high level of guilt if they violate their group's norms.

Others such as Richard Jenkins (1966), for example, demonstrated that such "socialized" delinquents retain strong ties with their peers. Sheldon Glueck (Glueck & Glueck, 1950) showed that only a tiny minority of delinquents could be labeled as psychopathic and relatively few could be diagnosed as mentally disordered in any way. And Taylor (1975) noted that socialized delinquents are not free of anxiety as is the psychopath. Thus, to confuse "socialized" criminals with psychopaths reveals a strong, perhaps middle-class bias, rather than a verifiable clinical judgment.

PSYCHOPATHS AND PSYCHOTICS

Psychopaths have, at times, also been confused with *psychotics*. Hoch (1972) observed that some schizophrenics act in an antisocial way and have been diagnosed as psychopaths. Some "sexual psychopaths"—who demonstrated delusions, depression, and high anxiety—have also been mislabeled (Glueck, 1954). The distinction should be clear. Psychotics in general suffer from delusions and hallucinations; psychopaths do not. Psychotics may be autistic and withdrawn from reality; psychopaths are rational—within the confines of their own pleasure and pain. Psychotics suffer from a high degree of anxiety and guilt; psychopaths do not.

In childhood and adolescence, the pre-psychotic may be withdrawn, guilty, and introverted. He or she may feel inferior, shy, and "queer"—long before the onset of delusions or hallucinations (McCord, Porta, & McCord, 1962). This is in stark contrast to the psychopath's pattern of guiltlessness and asocial behavior.

PSYCHOPATHS AND PARANOIA

One type of psychosis, *paranoia*, can easily be mistaken for psychopathy. Without extensive psychological tests, it is sometimes extremely difficult to draw a distinction between paranoids who suffer from delusions of persecution and of grandeur and psychopaths.

The case of Charles Starkweather, killer of 11 people, illustrates the problem (Reinhardt, 1960). Starkweather set off on his killing orgy with an equally psychopathic lover, Caril Fugate, in 1957. While Caril watched, Starkweather killed 3 of her family. When finally apprehended, neither exhibited any guilt. In fact, they reported that they had "joyous" sexual encounters in the house that contained the bodies of Caril's family.

Psychologist James Reinhardt interviewed Starkweather in his prison cell and found no evidence of guilt in the man. "I never witnessed a sign of genuine remorse [p. 16]," Reinhardt commented. When asked about killing a little girl, Starkweather responded "What could we do with the kid? Do you think we could take her with us [p. 16]?"

Starkweather had long been plagued by the desire to kill, and by a feeling (or knowledge) that everyone hated him. His final actions before the death sentence illustrated his long-term desire: "If I'd killed as many people as I've shot at myself I'd killed a thousand [p. 99]." His liaison with Caril stirred his emotions: "Guess it wuz already there 'cause it came easy to me," he said, "and seemed like it wuz somethin I'd been waiting fer [p. 69]."

Caril Fugate, later released on parole after some years in prison, had encouraged his psychopathic tendencies. After a lifetime of loneliness, Starkweather believed that he had found a "true love." She certainly served as erotic stimulation for him, but when they were caught she quickly deserted him.

Reinhardt felt that Starkweather was merely paranoid. Clearly, he suffered from delusions and hallucinations. He felt that "Death" visited him in his cell and he could draw a picture of "Death" for the psychologist. He also believed that Jesus came to see him. On one level, then, Starkweather could be considered as a paranoid schizophrenic.

Yet, psychiatrists who participated in his trial exhibited a rare degree of unanimity in declaring him psychopathic. Psychiatrists for the prosecution said that he suffered from a "personality disorder" and that he was neither legally nor mentally sane. Defense psychiatrists agreed. One of them added that "Pumping bullets into a human is no different to Starkweather than pumping bullets into a rabbit [Reinhardt, 1960, p. 11]." Starkweather went to his death, although expert witnesses on both sides agreed that he was incapable of premeditation.

The "Son of Sam" and Charles Manson—notorious killers of the 1970s—offer other examples of the thin line between a paranoid psychosis and psychopathy.

THE "SON OF SAM"

The "Son of Sam" (David Berkowitz) killed six persons and left seven wounded during a killing spree in 1977. When finally apprehended, Berkowitz—a mild-mannered, amiable postal worker—freely admitted the crimes but added, with a slightly quizzical smile, that his neighbor's dog had ordered him to commit them. He had killed the dog. On the surface, Berkowitz seemed paranoid but intensive psychological and physiological examinations, including a brain scan, failed to confirm that diagnosis. During his brief stay in the Army, Berkowitz had experimented with drugs and various esoteric religions. On the basis of this background, one psychiatrist labeled him as unfit to stand trial and as "emotionally dead" (Conway & Siegelman, 1979). Yet, in 1980, Berkowitz renounced all of his previous testimony and declared that he was guilty of the crimes and that his neighbor's dog had not ordered him to commit the murders. He cited his membership in a satanic cult as the reason for his actions. Who would care to guess when he really told the truth?

MANSON AND HIS FAMILY

Charles Manson and his "family" present a third puzzling case. One could argue that Manson and his girls were psychotic rather than

121

psychopathic. The "Manson Family" committed a series of murders in 1969: all were unmotivated, except by Manson's belief that he was a new "Christ" and had been licensed to start a war of retaliation against the rich and blacks. Manson—an illegitimate child who spent 17 of his first 32 years in jail for burglary, car theft, forgery, and pimping—seduced or "hypnotized" various girls into acting as his surrogates in a variety of killings. Manson interpreted the Book of Revelations in the Bible as a scenario for a new apocalypse. Influenced by "Scientology," the Beatles, and by a cult called the "Church of Final Judgment," Manson believed that the Bible outlined for him a battle-plan of mass killings. He convinced three women—Susan Atkins, Patricia Krenwinkel, and Leslie Van Houton—that he was the prophet of a new order. They followed him in massacring a movie star and various other people (Conway & Siegelman, 1979).

Although Manson was eager to give interviews before the murders, Manson cut off all interviews by 1980. By then, the state had incarcerated him for life. Again, without a careful examination, it is difficult to say whether Manson suffered from a psychosis or psychopathy. His life history, however, suggests that he was a psychopath and that his stories of delusions of grandeur were merely a cover (Conway & Siegelman, 1979).

THE PSYCHOPATH AND NEUROTICS

In contrast to psychosis, the distinction between a psychopath and a *neurotic* seems quite reasonable. The neurotic individual suffers from intense anxiety; the psychopath does not. The neurotic often feels guilty, under tension, and inhibited; the psychopath does not. The neurotic usually represses or suppresses his hostility toward others; the psychopath does so only if it is to his immediate advantage.

Research indicates that psychopathy and neurosis seem to be at disparate ends of a continuum of mental disorder. Mason (1944), for example, demonstrated that neurotics and psychopaths in the American Army were entirely different types of people, although both may have been incarcerated for various crimes. Sheldon and Eleanor Glueck (1950), in their classic study of delinquents, found that neurotic traits actually appeared more often among nondelinquent slum dwellers than among delinquents of the same social group. Neurotic alcoholics suffer from a dependency conflict, often feel guilty, and seek love from anyone who will offer it—characteristics that are the antithesis of the psychopath (McCord, McCord, & Gudeman, 1960).

THE PSYCHOPATH AND THE ACTING-OUT NEUROTIC

The *"acting-out neurotic,"* which Franz Alexander classified with the psychopath, often engages in criminal behavior, but he or she differs radically from the criminal psychopath. Acting-out neurotics suffer from intense anxiety and a compulsion to commit a particular action—child molesting, child abuse, forgery, shoplifting, arson, etc. Moreover, they tend to remain fixated on a particular obsession and seek relief of their anxiety by repeatedly committing the same action. Such a person is, of course, quite different from the psychopath.

Acting-out neurotics are similar to psychopaths only in the sense that they may commit crimes. Their motives and character structure differ dramatically. During my years working in correctional institutions, I have met a famous, rich actress who felt compelled to shoplift goods from a well-known store; a child molester who, even after he married, still yearned for the "perfect relationship" with an 11-year-old boy; and a rapist who attacked women because of a desire for power rather than lust. These people were not psychopaths. They suffered from guilt, anxiety, and compulsion. They often come to the attention of psychiatrists because they genuinely wish to change their behavior.

In more specific terms, I should cite the case of a neurotic San Quentin convict whom I will call "Tom." Born in a rural Kentucky town, Tom had been literally strung up by the thumbs and beaten by his father. Unknown to the highly religious father, his mother was the madam of a local house of prostitution. Tom had been taught from early childhood to despise anything to do with sex.

In rebellion against his father, Tom ran away to California. There he committed a variety of crimes: burglary, car theft, and pickpocketing. These crimes would occur in a definite pattern: Tom would feel sexual urges, he would find somebody to satisfy him, and then feel tremendous guilt. To relieve his anxiety, Tom would commit a crime—usually in full view of police or other authorities—and receive a punishment. The punishment served to relieve his anxiety and guilt. Shortly the cycle would recur again. After sexual fulfillment, Tom would once again commit some other action in a way to assure him punishment.

At San Quentin Tom became one of the prison's "tough guys" but he still cried with shame, felt self-conscious and guilty. Basically, he abhorred all sexual relations with women or men:

"Ever since I can remember," he wrote me, "everything concerning sex has been embarrassing to me. . . . As I grew older, I began to desire relations with women, but because of my acute embarrassment, those relationships I did have with them were unsatisfactory. . . . I feel the desire to satisfy my sex impulses, while at the same time, I feel disgust for such things [personal communication]."

Obviously, this man suffered from a conflict, intense anxiety, and a high level of guilt. His crimes stemmed from the fact that he wanted to be punished because of his supposed evil deeds.

PSYCHOPATHY AND VICTIMS OF BRAIN DAMAGE

Victims of serious *brain damage* may also superficially resemble psychopaths in their impulsivity, aggressiveness, and irritability. Whereas the psychopath may suffer from some form of subtle brain damage (see Chapter 5), he or she differs from the person who, because of accident or disease, has undergone extensive, obvious damage to the brain. People who have had chronic neurological problems or who have suffered acute damage to the brain as an aftermath of an accident or a lobotomy sometimes act in a psychopathic manner. Neurological test batteries, however, easily distinguish such people from psychopaths (Smith, 1978, p. 32).

CONCLUSIONS

Thus, advances in clinical judgment, supplemented by physiological or psychological tests, have now made possible the following distinctions:

- Psychopaths differ from socialized criminals in their lack of guilt, absence of ties to other human beings, and low level of anxiety.
- Psychopaths stand in contrast to psychotics who are characterized by hallucinations, anxiety, and delusions, although at times, psychopaths resemble people who are in a paranoid state.
- Psychopaths contrast with neurotics whose behavior is characterized by guilt and anxiety.
- Although perhaps equally criminal, psychopaths differ from acting-out neurotics in their levels of guilt, anxiety, and empathy.
- Psychopaths can be differentiated from brain-damaged individuals by standard neurological examinations.

Although difficulties remain in the diagnosing of psychopaths, as ideological, class, or sex biases may cloud the judgment of the diagnostician, detection has become relatively exact. As the concept of psychopathy has been clarified, researchers have gathered an impressive amount of information about the mysteries of causation. What remains to be solved is how most of us grow up as "civilized" beings while a few become impulsive, destructive beings. "Unsocialized, untamed, and uninstructed," as Sheldon Glueck (1956) has argued, "the child resorts to lying, slyness, subterfuge, anger, hatred, theft, aggression, attack, and other forms of asocial behavior [p. 156]." Why, then, do some adults become psychopathic whereas the majority do not?

References

Alexander, Franz. The neurotic character. *International Journal of Psychoanalysis*, 1930, *11*:292– 313.

Aniskiewicz, A. A. Autonomic components of vicarious conditioning and psychopathy. *Journal of Clinical Psychology*, 1979, *40*:379– 390.

Arieti, S., *The intrapsychic self*. New York: Basic Books, 1967.

Bedford, A., & McIves, D. Foulds general instability scale and psychopath 16 PF scores and their relation to psychiatric mood and state. *Journal of Clinical Psychology*, 1978 (April).

Berg, P. S. Neurotic and psychopathic criminals. Ph.D. dissertation, Michigan State University, 1963.

Bittner, E., & Messinger, S. *Criminology review yearbook*. Beverly Hills, Calif.: Sage Publications, 1980.

Bowlus, D. E., & Shotwell, A. A Rorshach study of psychopathic delinquents. *American Journal of Mental Deficiency*, 1947, *52*:23– 30.

Brown, V. K. Black female gangs. *International Journal of Offender Therapy and Comparative Criminology*, 1977, *21*(3):210– 215.

Clark, T., & Penycote, J. *Psychopath: The case of Patrick McKay*. London: Routledge, Kegan Paul, 1976.

Clausen, J. A. Social patterns, personality and adolescent drug use. In A. H. Leighton, J. A. Clausen, and R. N. Wilson (Eds.), *Explorations in social psychiatry*. New York: Basic Books, 1957.

Cleckly, H. *The mask of sanity*. St. Louis: Mosby, 1976.

Cochrane, R. The structure of value systems in male and female prisoners. *British Journal of Criminology*, 1971, *11*:73– 79.

Conway, F., & Siegelman, J. *Snapping*. New York: Delta, 1979.

de Fundia, T. A., Draguns, J. C., & Phillips, L. Cultural and psychiatric symptomology. *Social Psychiatry*, 1971, 617– 620.

Diaz-Guerrero, R. Socio-cultural premises, attitudes, and cross-cultural research. *International Journal of Psychology*, 1967, *2*:79– 88.

Dinitz, S. Chronically antisocial offenders. In J. Conrad and S. Dinitz (Eds.), *In fear of each other*. Lexington, Massachusetts: Lexington, 1978.

Elliot, F. A. Neurological aspects of antisocial behavior. In W. H. Reid (Ed.), *The psychopath*. New York: Brunner/Mazel, 1978.

Emmons, T. D., & Webb, W. W. Subjective correlates of emotional responsivity and stimulation seeking in psychopaths, normals, and acting-out neurotics. *Journal of Consulting and Clinical Psychology*, 1974, *42*:620.

Eysenck, H. *Crime and personality*. Boston: Houghton-Mifflin, 1964.

Ganessbauer, T., & Lazerevitz, J. Classification of military offenders. *Crime and Delinquency*, 1979 (Jan.), *25*(1):42– 54.

Glaser, D. *Crime in our changing society*. New York: Holt, Rinehart, and Winston, 1978.

Glueck, B. Psychodynamic factors in the sex offender. *Psychiatric Quarterly*, 1954, *28:*1– 21.

Glueck, S., & Glueck, E. *Physique and delinquency*. New York: Harper, 1956.

Glueck, S. & Glueck, E. *Unraveling juvenile delinquency*. Commonwealth Fund, 1950.

Gouch, H. G. A sociological theory of psychopathy. *American Journal of Sociology*. 1948, *53:*359– 366.

Grant, J. D., & Grant, M. Q., A group dynamics approach to the treatment of nonconformists in the navy. *American Academy of Political and Social Science Review*, 1959, *322:*126– 135.

Gul'dan, V. V., & Ivannikov, V. A. Traits of the formationed use of past experience in psychopathic personalities. *Zhurnal Neuropatologi i Psikhiatrii*, 1974, *74:* 374–375.

Gurvitz, M. Intelligence factors in psychopathic personality. *Journal of Clinical Psychology*, 1947, *3:* 194– 196.

Hare, R. D. *Psychopathy*. New York: Wiley, 1970.

Hare, R. D. Paper on psychopathic behavior. NATO, Paris, 1975.

Hare, R. D. Preference for delay of shock as a function of its intensity and probability. *Psychonomic Science*, 1966, *5:*393– 394.

Hare, R. D., & Cox, D. Psychophysiological research on psychopathy. In W. H. Reid (Ed.), *The psychopath*. New York: Brunner/Mazel, 1978.

Hare, R. D., Frazelli, J., & Cox, D. Psychopathy and physiological responses to threat from an adversive stimulus. *Psychophysiology*, March, 1978.

Hinton, J., & O'Neil, M. Pilot research of psychophysiological response profiles of maximum security hospital patients. *British Journal of Social and Clinical Psychology*, 1978, *42:*213– 218.

Hecht, I. H., & Jokovic, G. J. The performance-verbal IQ discrepancy in differentiated sub-groups of delinquent antisocial boys. *Journal of Youth and Adolescence*, 1978, *31:*211– 214.

Heilbrun, A. Psychopathy and violent crime. *Journal of Consulting and Clinical Psychology*, 1979 (June), *6:*359– 380.

Heuser, K. D. The psychopathic personality: Rorshach patterns of 28 cases. *American Journal of Psychiatry*, 1946, *103:*105– 112.

Hewitt, L. E., & Jenkins, R. L. Patterns of maladjustment. Illinois Department of Public Welfare, 1946.

Hoch, P. H. *Differential diagnosis in psychiatry*. Chicago: Science House, 1972.

Holzberg, J. D., & Hahn, F. The picture frustration test as a measure of hostility and guilt reactions in adolescent psychopaths. *American Journal of Orthopsychiatry*, 1952, *22:*776– 797.

Jenkins, R. Review of psychopathy and delinquency. *American Journal of Orthopsychiatry*, 1957, *3:*45.

Kaplan, S. D. A visual analog of the Funkenstein test. *Archives of General Psychiatry*, 1960, *3:*383– 388.

Keller, O. J. The criminal personality or Lombroso revisited. *Federal Probation*, 1980, *21:*37– 43.

Kerzondorfer, M. Diagnostic usefulness of Cattel's 16 PF. *Zeitshrift für Klinische Psychologie*, 1977, *6*(4):317– 321.

Kingsley, L. A. A comparative study of certain personality characteristics of psychopathic and non-psychopathic offenders. Ph.D. dissertation, New York University, 1956.

Lichto, A. E., and Ivanov, N. Ya. The psychocharacterological diagnostic inventory for adolescents. Ministry for Public Health, Leningrad, 1976.

Lidberg, L. Excretion of adrenalin and noradrenalin as relation to real life stress and psychopathy. *Reports from the Laboratory for Clinical Stress* (Stockholm), 1976, 47:221.

Lidberg, L., *et al.* Urinary catecholamines, stress, and psychopathy. *Psychosomatic Medicine*, 1979 (March).

Lindner, R. The Rorschach test and the diagnosis of psychopathic personality. *Journal of Criminal Psychopathology*, 1943, 5:69–93.

Livré, B. Psychopaths and non-verbal behavior. *Journal of Abnormal Psychology*, 1978 (December).

Loeb, J., & Mednick, S. A prospective study of predictors of criminality: Electrodermal response patterns. In S. Mednick and K. O. Christiansen (Eds.), *Biosocial bases of criminal behavior*. New York: Gardner Press, 1977.

Lonstein, M. J. A comparative study of level of aspiration variables in neurotic, psychopathic, and normal subjects. Ph.D. dissertation, University of Kentucky, 1952.

Lykken, D. The psychopath and the lie detector. *Psychophysiology*, 1978, 24:319–320.

Lykken, D. T. A study of anxiety in the sociopathic personality. Ph.D. dissertation, University of Michigan, Ann Arbor, 1955.

McCord, W., & McCord, J. *Psychopathy and delinquency*. New York: Grune and Stratton, 1956.

McCord, W., McCord, J., & Gudeman, J. *Origins of alcoholism*. Stanford: Stanford University Press, 1960.

McCord, W., Porta, J., & McCord, J. The familial genesis of psychoses. *Psychiatry*, 1962, 25:60–71.

Martinson, R. What works? *The Public Interest*, 1974, 35:22–54.

Mason, I. An index of the severity of criminalism or psychopathy. *U.S. Army Medical Department Bulletin*, 1944, 75:110–114.

Mednick, S. A biosocial theory of the learning of law-abiding behavior. In S. L. Messinger and E. Bittner (Eds.), *Criminology review yearbook*, Beverly Hills: Sage, 1980.

Mednick, S., & Christiansen, Karl O. *Biosocial bases of criminal behavior*. New York: Gardner Press, 1977.

Megargee, E. I., & Bohn, M. J. *Classifying criminal offenders*. Beverly Hills: Sage, 1979.

Monohan, J., Splane, S. Psychological approaches to criminal behavior. In S. Messinger and E. Bittner (Eds.), *Criminology review yearbook* (Vol. 2). Beverly Hills, Sage, 1980.

Morrison, H. L. The asocial child: A destiny of the sociopath? In W. H. Reid (Ed.), *The psychopath*. New York: Brunner/Mazel, 1978.

New York Times, October 29, 1980.

Newsweek. Scanning the Human Mind. Sept. 29, 1980.

Palmer, T. The youth authority's community treatment project. *Federal Probation*, 1974 (March), 28:3–20.

Quay, H. C. Personality dimensions in delinquent males as inferred from the factor analysis of behavior ratings. *Journal of Research on Crime and Delinquency*, 1964, 1:33–37.

Quay, H. C. Psychopathic personality as pathological stimulation seeking. *American Journal of Psychiatry*, 1965, 122:180–183.

4. The Problem of Identification

Raskin, D. A reply to Lykken. *Psychophysiology*, 1978 (March).

Raskin, D., & Hare, R. Psychopathy and detection of deception in a prison population. *Psychophysiology*, 1978 (March), *14*:811–812.

Reed, C. F., & Caudra, C. A. The role taking hypothesis in delinquency. *Journal of Consulting Psychology*, 1957, *21*:386–390.

Reid, H. C. The psychopath in rural areas: Special considerations. In W. H. Reid (Ed.), *The psychopath*. New York: Brunner/Mazel, 1978.

Reiss, A. J. Social correlates of psychological types of delinquency. *American Sociological Review*, 1952 (December), *17*:710–718.

Reinhardt, J. *The murderous trial of Charles Starkweather*. Springfield, Illinois: Thomas, 1960.

Rokeach, M. *Beliefs, attitudes and values*. San Francisco: Jossey-Bass, 1972.

Rokeach, M. *The nature of human values*. New York: The Free Press, 1973.

Sagarin, E. *Deviants and deviance*. New York: Praeger, 1975.

Sanchez, J. (curator). The private papers of Robert Martinson. New York: CUNY Graduate Center, 1980.

Schalling, D., & Levander, D. Spontaneous fluctuations in EDA during anticipation of punishment in two delinquent groups differing in anxiety proneness. Report 238, Psychological Laboratory, University of Stockholm, 1967.

Schalling, D., & Rosén, A. Porteus maze differences between psychopathic and non-psychopathic criminals. *British Journal of Social and Clinical Psychology*, 1968, *7*:224–228.

Sherman, L. J. Retention in psychopathic, neurotic, and normal subjects. *Journal of Personality*, 1957, *25*:721–729.

Siegel, R. Probability of punishment and suppression of behavior in psychopathic offenders and non-psychopathic offenders. *Journal of Abnormal Psychology*, 1977 (Winter), *63*:119–120.

Silver, A. W. TAT and MMPI psychopathic deviant scale differences between delinquent and non-delinquent adolescents. *Journal of Consulting Psychology*, 1963, *27*:370.

Simon, B., Holtzberg, J. D., & Unger, J. A study of judgment in the psychopathic personality. *Psychiatric Quarterly*, 1951, *25*:132–150.

Skrzpek, G. J. The effects of perceptual isolation and arousal on anxiety, complexity, preference, and novelty in psychopathic and neurotic delinquents. *Journal of Abnormal Psychology*, 1969, *74*:321–329.

Smith, R. J., *The psychopath in society*. New York: Academic Press, 1978.

Stafford-Clark, D., Pond, D., & Doust, J. W. L. The psychopath in prison. *British Journal of Delinquency*, 1951, *2*:117–129.

Sutherland, E. Sexual psychopath laws. *Journal of Criminal Law, Criminology and Police Science*, 1950, *40*:543–554.

Taylor, A. J. Correspondence. *Bulletin of the British Psychological Society*, 1975, *28*:285–286.

Tunk, E., & Duma, S. Cartazine in the dyscontrol syndrome associated with limbic system dysfunction. *Journal of Nervous and Mental Disease*, 1977 (January).

Warner, R. The diagnosis of antisocial hysterical personality disorders. *Journal of Nervous and Mental Disease*, 1978 (December), *166*:839–845.

Widom, C. S. An empirical classification of female offenders. *Criminal Justice and Behavior*, 1978, *2*:183–187.

Yochelson, S., & Samenow, S. *The criminal personality*. New York: Aronson, 1976, 1977.

III

The Origins of
the Psychopath

5

Is There a Physical Base?

We are all born psychopaths. . . . We are born
without repressions.
Harry Lipton, psychiatrist
"The Psychopath," *Journal of Criminal Law,*
Criminology and Police Science, 1952.

We enter this life without guilt, without a conscience, and without an instinctive love for particular individuals. At birth, we are helpless creatures, dependent on others, and ruled by our random impulses. Slowly, in a groping fashion, we learn the mores of our society and, usually, we come to love the parents who feed us and to control our whimsical desires. We internalize what society teaches us about "proper" behavior and develop a conscience. Unless we are raised as Iks or Alorese, we come to understand that certain rules supersede our own immediate calculations of pleasures and pain. Yet, some persons—psychopaths—remain at an immature level of development, cannot form loving attachments to other people, and apparently never develop a set of inner controls.

Intrigued by the evidence that psychopaths are psychologically insensitive, exhibit "childlike" neural rhythms, have different hormonal excretions, and fail to respond to physical punishments, some scholars have suggested that psychopathy may be caused by a deep physical malfunction.

The critical evidence on these issues comes from five fields of inquiry:

1. Physiological measures of the psychopath's insensitivity (Rotenberg, 1978)
2. Studies of a "genetic" predisposition to psychopathy (Newkirk, 1957)
3. Evidence concerning chromosomal abnormalities in psychopaths and other criminals (Reid, 1978)
4. Investigations of differences in physique and character (Glueck, 1956)
5. Studies of neurological dysfunction in psychopaths (Elliott, 1978)

Each of these areas of inquiry demands serious consideration. If, in fact, psychopathy has a physical basis, our society might require extraordinary measures to "cure" physiological defects, or "genetic engineering," or, at the extreme, elimination of the genetically or physiologically "unfit." I do not advocate any of these solutions. I merely want to point out the somber realities of the physiological approach and the policy results that might flow from it.

Few, if any, scientists would argue that a crude, direct relationship exists between psychopathy and physiology; even fewer would maintain that some people are "born" as psychopaths. Even advocates of a physical explanation for the disorder generally add that social and physical factors interact to produce the syndrome.

The evidence allows several interpretations:

1. Psychopaths may have innate neural dysfunctions, defects in their chromosomal structure, or slowness in cortical responsiveness that might make them prone to their particular disorder (Rotenberg, 1978).
2. Psychopaths may have suffered physical ailments—encephalitis, epilepsy, or birth damage—that affected their neural structures and make them relatively incapable of internalizing the inhibitions that their particular society dictates (Henderson, 1939).
3. It could also be that psychopaths suffer sufficient environmental deprivation to affect their neural structure (Rotenberg, 1978).
4. One can also speculate that the typically impulsive behavior of child psychopaths—hitting their heads against a wall, throwing themselves out of a crib, running in the path of a car—could

often result in severe neural damage and produce a psycho-pathic pattern (Elliott, 1978).

Physiological Insensitivity

Overwhelming evidence indicates that the psychopath is physio-logically insensitive, relatively incapable of learning from physical cues, and that he or she fails to exhibit the usual skin conductivity responses. Yet, psychopaths have a normal, if not superior range of intelligence. And careful experiments have demonstrated that psychopaths are consciously aware of the goal of conditioning exper-iments even if they do not show it physiologically.

Ziskind and his colleagues found that equal numbers of psychopaths and "normal" subjects will verbally respond in a correct fashion when subjected to aversive conditioning. Yet, corresponding skin conductivity responses appeared only in "normal" subjects. Moreover, among psychopaths who did react to the conditioning ex-periment, the effects did not persist over time. Ziskind attributes this anomalous finding to some type of neurological dysfunction (Ziskind, Syndulko, & Maltzman, 1978).

Rather than explaining this lack of physical insensitivity by post-ulating an innate physical factor, Mordechai Rotenberg (1978) rea-sonably suggested that society may encourage differential forms of physical insensitivity, lack of anxiety, and "cool" detachment. Rotenberg argues cogently that "low arousal or lack of anxiety even in the face of stress . . . may indicate . . . a high degree of adjustabil-ity to uncertainty and to the danger of arousing stimuli [p. 187]."

Rotenberg argued that such insensitivity may be either socially functional or dysfunctional and that these insensitivities arise as a result of formal or informal training during the person's life history. Rotenberg postulated that the psychopath's crucial traits can be traced to "an early history of desensitization to anything emotional [p. 188]." That control over emotional response can and does occur in many varied situations.

For example, parachutists have been trained to have little anxiety just before jumping (Epstein, 1967); police officers develop a "veneer of hardness," increasingly legitimizing the use of violence as their years of service progress (McNamara, 1967; Toch, 1970). Even Israeli high school students who have been trained as electricians have less reaction to shock than do institutionalized delinquents (Rotenberg, 1978). From this point of view, then, environmental experiences can produce diminished physiological responses rather than the responses resulting from a specific set of physical characteristics.

On the basis of this reasoning, Rotenberg speculated that psychopaths (insensitive) and neurotics (oversensitive) lie at opposite ends of a physiological continuum. As the psychopath is insensitive, Rotenberg suggested that the psychopath might be treated by "sensitivity training." Generally, Rotenberg (1978) posited that psychopathic subjects might be affected by exciting stimuli or by stimulants such as adrenalin that would decrease the psychopath's insensitivity and thereby increase learning ability.

Other scientists have attributed the psychopath's insensitivity to a single autonomic defect: a diminished function of catecholamine-secreting neurons. Such a defect would decrease physiological sensitivity, interfere with emotion-laden decisions, and lead a person to perceive events in an extremely biased, socially incorrect manner (Lindner, Goldman, Dinitz, & Allen, 1970). The scientists who have proposed this idea do not argue that the autonomic defect is necessarily innate. "It is as conceivable," they note, "that the defect is 'congenital' and 'innate' as that it is 'environmental' or 'acquired.' The location and character of the postulated neuronal defect is obscure [Lindner et al., 1970, p. 266]." Nonetheless, evidence from disparate parts of the body—the heart, skin, and eye pupil—has led some investigators to hypothesize that the psychopath suffers from a genetic inferiority.

As Sarnoff Mednick has put it, "The electrodermal recovery rate . . . is a highly hereditary attribute, since it is much more similar in identical than in fraternal twins. Therefore, persons born with a slow rate, which is conducive to psychopathy, will less readily learn to inhibit delinquent or criminal urges if they are punished for misconduct [Mednick, quoted in Glaser, 1978, p. 145]." If this is true, studies of the psychopath's heredity versus those who are not psychopathic becomes highly relevant.

The Genetic Approach

Here we enter into a mystifying realm. Although many scientists have conducted studies of the psychopath's heredity, we still do not possess any definitive knowledge. Beginning with Pinel, Pritchard, and Lombroso's contention that some criminals are born and not made, scholars have accumulated knowledge that—on the surface—might support the contention that criminal psychopaths suffer from genetic defects.

A variety of studies in the first half of the twentieth century indicated that criminal psychopaths disproportionately came from a disordered lineage. More often than usual, the ancestral histories of psychopathic patients revealed a high incidence of crime, epilepsy, alcoholism, or some other form of social or physical maladjustment (see Cruz, 1939; Gottleib, 1946; Mohr, 1947; Partridge, 1928). Such evidence led Newkirk (1957) to declare flatly that "psychopathic traits are inheritable [p. 175]."

These studies all suffered from the same faults. The authors defined their psychopathic subjects in an extremely broad fashion, often confusing "maladjusted" people with psychopaths. Their studies provided no way to differentiate the relative effects of nature versus nurture. And generally, they failed to provide a control group so that the ancestry of psychopaths could be compared with that of other people.

In the 1930s, several geneticists attempted to correct these deficiencies by studying large samples of twins and siblings and comparing their subsequent life histories. As identical twins have an identical genetic background, they should—if psychopathy were inherited—lead more closely parallel lives than fraternal twins. Franz Kallman's (1939) pioneering study in 1939 produced puzzling evidence. Indeed, he found that schizophrenia seemed to have a genetic base (identical twins more often resembled each other psychologically than did fraternal twins) but the same pattern did not hold for psychopaths. Children of psychopaths more often resembled their parents than they did siblings. Kallman concluded that the incidence of psychopathy did not follow the lines of closest blood kinship and that other factors—such as parental influence—must be responsible for the disorder.

Other scientists during the 1930s also examined samples of twins. Although they did not focus specifically on psychopathy, Johannes Lange (1930) and A. J. Rosanoff (1943) provided much suggestive evidence concerning criminal histories in general. Lang found that 77%

of identical twins and only 12% of fraternal twins had similar prison records. After studying the criminal patterns of 400 pairs of twins, Rosanoff found the same, if lower, correspondence in the prison histories of the identical twins in his sample.

Although these studies were hailed as indicating that genetic destiny determined criminal behavior, critics attacked the research on several grounds. They argued that neither Lange nor Rosanoff had sufficiently established the identical nature of their twin pairs and that they relied on dubious sources for estimating the extent of crime. Even if it proved true that identical twins behaved criminally in a fashion more similar than fraternal twins, Edwin Sutherland (1960) contended that this might be due to the fact that parents during the 1930s treated (and even dressed) identical twins in a similar fashion.

Attempting to unravel this puzzle proved an extremely difficult task. In 1947, E. T. Slater presented the case histories of nine pairs of identical twins who had been raised in separate environments from birth. Seven people had turned out to be psychopathic, others neurotic. Slater found that only two pairs of twins possessed similar life histories (Slater, 1948). He tentatively concluded that a genetic basis for the disorder might exist but that environmental forces played the dominant role.

EEG PATTERNS

During the second half of the twentieth century, scientists employed more diversified, sophisticated techniques for measuring a possible genetic basis for psychopathy. Alas, the results remain ambiguous and unconvincing.

One positive correlation between psychopathic behavior and possible ancestral roots has emerged from studies of EEG patterns. As it has been well-established that slow-wave EEG activity is associated with cortical underarousal (two neurological symptoms of the psychopath), Knott and his colleagues (1953) set out to discover if this neural pattern had a genetic basis. They examined the EEG rhythms of 86 psychopaths, their biological parents, their foster parents, and a normal population. Knott found that the psychopathic patients and their biological parents closely resembled each other in abnormal slow-wave neural activity. In contrast, they found no relationship between the EEG records of 9 psychopathic subjects and their 18 foster parents. Such findings suggest that some of the cortical differences between psychopaths and other people might be genetic in nature.

Yet, as Robert Hare (1970) ably argued, the evidence does not preclude other explanations. The similarity in EEG waves between children and their parents might arise from the effects of their environments or, one could argue, that the parents suffered from certain EEG abnormalities and the children reflected these through learning. It is even conceivable, as N. E. Miller (1966) suggested, that parents reward behavior that reflects slow-wave activity and underarousal. Knott and his colleagues (1953) rejected these hypotheses on grounds that adopted psychopaths did not resemble their foster parents.

The debate on the heritability of EEG patterns remains in limbo, as experimenters have found so few cases of psychopaths raised away from their biological parents. Further, the age at which the twins were separated was usually not specified. Assuming that learning factors affect EEG patterns, the influence of the original parents might take effect at a very early age. Thus, some of the cortical activity of psychopaths might be attributed to heredity while environmental factors may also play an important role.

Further evidence that an hereditary factor may exert some influence on the criminal behavior of people has been gathered by Sarnoff Mednick and his associates (Mednick, Schulsinger, Higgins, & Bell, 1974). In Copenhagen, they studied the sons of criminal fathers who had experienced little contact with their fathers. They compared this group of people who had a criminal adoptive father, or a non-criminal biological father, and a group of control cases matched by age, occupational status, and residential area. Because, in Denmark, officials of foster home agencies try to place adopted sons in foster homes that closely resemble their original environments, one might expect few differences between the various groups. Mednick found that biological sons of criminal fathers tended to adopt a criminal pattern in later lives—regardless of the environment in which they had been placed. Nonetheless, the majority of adopted children of criminal fathers did not develop a criminal record and the adoptive father seemed to have an equally strong effect on the child.

Fini Schulinger (1977) also compiled data on 57 adopted cases of "psychopaths" and compared them to 854 adoptive and biological relatives. She found a higher relationship of mental disorders among biological than adoptive relatives. Schulinger defined psychopathy, however, as including alcoholism, drug addiction, and "impulse-ridden" personalities who may or may not have been psychopaths. Consequently, it becomes extremely difficult to locate a specific link in her study between psychopathic behavior and a genetic background.

Danish investigators have also found that the galvanic skin response recovery rate was slowest among adopted criminal sons of noncriminal fathers. As Daniel Glaser (1978) observed, "This highly hereditary characteristic of the autonomic nervous system seemed very closely related to crime. . . . It may foster criminality by impeding ability to learn from a noncriminal environment the inhibitions necessary for a crime-free life [p. 148]."

HORMONAL EXCRETIONS

Hormonal excretions from the endocrine glands are partly hereditary in origin although there is evidence that environmental influences affect them. As we have previously noted, the production of epinephrine (adrenaline) is severely limited in psychopaths. Sexual hormones released into the bloodstream by endocrine glands may possibly bear some relation to aggressive behavior. The injection of androgens (male hormones) into animals increases aggression. Progesterone (a female hormone related to some androgens) reaches its low point during menstruation in women. It is also during this period that about 50% of all violent crimes committed by women occur (Shah & Roth, 1974).

Clearly, however, violence cannot be equated with psychopathy. Further, it is by no means evident that androgen levels correlate with aggressive behavior in human males. Moreover, the vast majority of women do not commit violent crimes during their menstruation period. Thus, the relationship between psychopathic behavior and hormone excretion as well as its hereditary basis remains obscure. Some of the most thorough investigators of the possible genetic base of psychopathy have failed to find a definitive link.

In Denmark, Karl O. Christiansen reviewed all studies of criminality among twins up to 1977 (Mednick & Christiansen, 1978a). He could find only eight identical pairs of twins—using strict standards of monozygocity and definitions of crime—who had been raised completely apart from each other and their parents from birth. Within this tiny, but scientifically important group, he found no conclusive evidence of a genetic basis for psychopathy.

Using a more comprehensive sample of 3586 pairs of Danish twins, Christiansen (Mednick & Christiansen, 1977) noted only a slightly higher rate of "concordance" in criminal patterns between monozygotic versus dyzygotic pairs. The same pattern held for males and females. Christiansen concluded, however, that his evidence did not provide strong support for a hereditary thesis.

In Sweden, Michael Bohman (1978) examined 2000 people, as well as their biological and adoptive parents. Although he noted a significant correlation between alcoholism in the biological parents and alcoholism in the children, he could not discover a significant genetic connection with psychopathic behavior.

In 1978, Reni Cadout investigated 246 adoptees who had been separated at birth from their "antisocial" parents. The researcher found some evidence among females that hysteria, psychosomatic ailments, and severe mood swings might have a genetic component. In contrast, the study uncovered no evidence for a genetic basis of psychopathy.

CONCLUSIONS

In summarizing the research linking ancestry and psychopathy, one may reasonably conclude:

1. Identical twins, even when raised in separate environments, tend to exhibit similar behavior.
2. Slow-wave EEG activity and cortical underarousal seem to reflect partly hereditary, partly psychological differences between psychopaths and other people.
3. Biological children of psychopathic parents more often exhibit a psychopathic syndrome than do offspring of nonpsychopathic parents.
4. Hormonal excretions that relate to psychopathy may have a genetic link.

Most studies of psychopathic inheritance indicate, at best, only a tenuous connection between heredity and psychopathic behavior.

Whatever weight we ascribe to genetic factors, three considerations can be borne in mind:

1. The most significant studies indicate that most people who have a "psychopathic" inheritance do not become psychopaths when raised in a normal social environment (Mednick & Christiansen, 1977).
2. Most people who exhibit signs of possibly hereditary origin— slow EEG waves, cortical underarousal, a lack of adrenalin—do not become psychopaths (Rotenberg, 1975).
3. Conversely, most psychopaths do not have a "psychopathic" ancestry or symptoms of cortical or hormonal malfunction that might conceivably be traced to a genetic base (Mednick & Christiansen, 1977).

Lacking either necessary or sufficient reasons for ascribing psychopathy to inheritance, we cannot assume that they are "born" as psychopaths (see Reid, 1978).

Chromosomal Abnormalities

Studies in the 1960s indicating that the presence of an extra Y chromosome in males might bear some relation to severely aggressive behavior have caused a flurry of attention (Montague, 1968). The initial results seemed to indicate that certain unusual combinations (such as XYY instead of the normal male pattern of XY) could be related to psychopathy. The idea of the "born criminal" again raised its head—although the occurrence of the XYY complement is *not* inherited but reflects an unknown abnormality in the separation of the sex chromosomes during formation of the sperm.

A few sketchy reports from Scottish maximum security prisons indicated that inmates convicted of violently antisocial behavior had an extra Y chromosome (see Reid, 1978). Subsequent reports suggested that a chromosomal imbalance might predispose a person to abnormally violent behavior, but that there was no evidence to regard the XYY syndrome as directly causal (Baker, 1972). By 1975, Robins had concluded that the evidence for the role of XYY or XXY chromosomes as a determinant of aggression was, at best, flimsy.

Yet, after the first publication of reports that a few males might have an extra Y chromosome (the 47, XYY pattern), defense lawyers leapt to the conclusion that such a chromosomal distribution might be used as a reason for acquitting their clients of violent crimes. In 1968, Parisian lawyers entered a plea for a murderer on grounds that he was insane because of XYY chromosomes (Glaser, 1978). They succeeded in reducing the man's sentence. Simultaneously, an Australian murderer received acquittal on the same grounds—that his XYY syndrome led to an excess of masculinity and thus, to insanity. The notorious case of Richard Speck in America—the murderer of eight nurses—lent further appeal to the claim when Speck's lawyers argued that his crime was due to an XYY syndrome. (Later microscopic examination actually revealed that Speck had a completely normal 46, XY pattern.)

Exaggerated journalistic accounts have led to a series of studies by the National Institutes of Mental Health in the United States to determine the exact impact, if any, of an XYY anomaly (NIMH, 1970). These studies indicated that the XYY syndrome was extremely rare in the general population, but somewhat higher—sometimes as much as 20 times higher—in hospitals for the criminally insane (Glaser, 1978).

The early results proved confusing. No one discovered a specific link between psychopathy and the XYY syndrome. In fact, criminals who were supposedly "oversexed" with an extra masculine chromosome committed *less* violent crimes, including rape, than did others (Borgaonkar & Shah, 1974). The one known case of XYY identical twins exhibited distinct differences in social behavior (Rainer, Abdullah, & Jarvick, 1972). The only genuine correlations that showed up in these studies were that XYY men tended to be taller and of less intelligence than the average for their family. Although only about one man in 1500 to 3000 of the average population has an XYY syndrome, some 2 or 3% of aggressively antisocial people fitted this pattern (Hare, 1970).

International studies have increasingly questioned the hypothesis that XYY chromosome patterns are related to antisocial behavior, let alone to psychopathy. Saleem Shah (1974), for example, found no relation between antisocial, violent behavior and the XYY pattern. In France, Benezech and Bourgeois (1976) failed to discover a "criminal chromosome." Money and his associates (1979) noted that antiandrogen therapy reduces the crimes of sex offenders (all of whom had a normal XY syndrome) but had no effect on violent XYY prisoners.

Clearly, the research provides little to substantiate the conclusion that chromosomal abnormalities bear a major relationship to crime. At most, they suggest that physiological bases might account for a tiny percentage—in combination with social factors—of criminal offenses. No one has demonstrated a direct connection with psychopathy.

Physique and the Psychopath

One's bodily constitution—a presumed result of heredity as influenced by environment—has long been a popular explanation of crime. Lombroso originally attempted to demonstrate a relationship between physique, character, and crime. In the twentieth century, Ernst Hooton (1939) pioneered in trying to associate crime with physique. He attempted to prove that convicts were physically inferior to "normal" people. Indeed, they were—when compared to his biased samples of lifeguards, firemen, and military men.

William Sheldon (1949) noted contradictory results to those of

Hooton. Sheldon measured three dimensions of the anatomy that he assumed correlated with personality traits: "endomorphs" tended to be fat and relaxed; "ectomorphs" were thin, introverted, and anxious; "mesomorphs" were muscular, aggressive, and extroverted. Delinquents exhibited distinctly more of the "mesomorphic" traits than did nondelinquents. Although charged by many sociologists with using subjective measures and of ignoring the influence of the environment on his subjects, Sheldon was actually a convinced supporter of social explanations for crime and psychopathy.

Rigorous studies of physique and crime have supported Sheldon's original contentions. In 1950, Sheldon and Eleanor Glueck (1950, 1956) examined the body proportions of 500 delinquents and 500 nondelinquents selected from Boston slums. Without assuming a necessary connection between constitution and heredity, the Gluecks reported that delinquents had a larger, more homogeneous and generally mesomorphic body build than did nondelinquents. (In passing, it should be mentioned that measures of physique were done independently of any knowledge as to which subject had a delinquent record.) They concluded that 60.1% of delinquents had a mesomorphic physique, far more than nondelinquents. Subsequent studies supported the Gluecks' contention that bodily constitution should be considered as one among many other factors that affect criminal behavior (Shah & Roth, 1974).

Some interpreters, such as the British psychologist Eysenck (1964), have argued that a mesomorphic physique is related to delinquency and to psychopathy because such a constitution is correlated with extroversion. Extroversion, he further claimed, impedes learning from punishment and renders the individual less readily conditioned by pain. Although Eysenck's theory would fit with other evidence about the psychopath, the position has received relatively little support (Hare, 1970).

Sociologists proffer a simple explanation for the finding regarding deviance and body type. Many criminal activities, particularly crimes committed by adolescents, require a mesomorphic physique. Mesomorphic youths should be more successful in fighting, mugging, breaking and entering, as well as maintaining their status within a gang. Thus, so the argument goes, mesomorphs are socially selected for their activities because of their physique. Physically identical people from middle-class environments will, however, choose socially acceptable activity such as football playing or other sports.

It would appear, then, that research relating crime to physique, like other findings regarding crime and physical attributes, is inconclusive—and remains in the realm of speculation.

Neural-Physical Dysfunction and the Psychopath

Neural physiologists have produced a large, impressive, and mounting body of evidence that psychopaths suffer from neural dysfunction or a defect in their autonomic nervous system (located mainly outside the brain). Such malfunctions might be traced to the person's genetic background, to accidental damage or disease, or even to the effects of the environment.

One source of evidence comes from the study of brain-damaged people. As far back as 1848, physicians have noticed a similarity between psychopaths and people who have suffered severe brain damage. In the famous "crow-bar case" of 1848, a diligent, responsible worker suffered from an explosion that rammed a 4-ft long crowbar through his head. Somehow, although he survived the accident, his behavior dramatically changed. He deserted his wife and children, fell prone to explosive outbursts of rage, and became "a childish kind of crook: profane, obstinate, and given to outbursts of temper [Henderson, 1939, p. 111]."

Less dramatic brain injuries have also been correlated with similar changes in behavior. Brain surgery has led some patients to lose their original foresight, control over their behavior, and their conscience (Freeman & Watts, 1945). Other forms of brain damage have often been linked with the appearance of a "psychopathic" behavioral syndrome (Kennedy, 1954). A few scientists, such as Thompson (1953), concluded that *all* psychopathic behavior results from cerebral injury. Elliott (1978), in summarizing studies of brain injury, reported in 1978 that there was ample evidence that prefrontal lobectomy, head injuries, or frontal lobotomy could result in a "ruthless disregard for the feelings and interests of spouse, children, and associates [p. 200]."

Clearly, however, brain injuries or operations do not always have the same results. After trauma, people may become more inhibited, more sociable, more aggressive, or may exhibit any number of other unpredictable reactions. Therefore, psychopathy cannot be attributed to obvious head injuries.

The evidence is, however, suggestive when complemented by studies of people who have suffered from various forms of neurological disease. In 1939, David Henderson reported that victims of encephalitis, cholera, and epilepsy were sometimes transformed from "models of virtue" into psychopaths. In 1942, American psychiatrists recorded evidence of pseudopsychopathic behavior in children who suffered from such diseases (Bender, 1942).

An American epidemic of encephalitis (sleeping sickness) in the 1920s and 1930s lent general credence to the belief that neural diseases could lead to psychopathic behavior. Some 30% of the victims radically changed after the acute phase of the disorder had disappeared. Specifically, as Kinnier Wilson (1940) described the aftermath of the disease: "The moral and social sense of the patient suffers eclipse [p. 146]." Observing the same phenomenon, Lauretta Bender (1962) reported that "these children are destructive and impulsive. . . . They are indifferent to punishment. When they express remorse, this does not modify their behavior [p. 178]." Kanner (1968) found that such children "lost any feelings of empathy. . . . Threats, punishment, rewards, and admonitions have, at best, only temporary results. Any regret . . . is transitory and impulsive behavior continues [p. 100]."

Temporal lobe epilepsy can sometimes result in behavior that resembles the psychopathic pattern and it is possible that subclinical epilepsy—detected by examination of the blood and spinal fluids—may result in a psychopathic syndrome (Elliott, 1978). Nonetheless, such reactions are relatively rare, amounting to from 4.8% to 17% of patients with temporal lobe epilepsy (Bingly, 1958; Currie, 1971; Rodin, 1973).

Moreover, some observers have found little if any evidence that psychopathy results from postvaccinal encephalitis (Puntigam, 1950), or from childhood meningitis and encephalitis (Essen-Moller, 1956). Similarities undoubtedly exist between some psychopaths and victims of brain diseases but theorists have yet to explain why so few psychopaths have a history of epilepsy and why so few epileptics develop a psychopathic syndrome.

Thus, as Frank Elliott (1978), an expert on neurological aspects of antisocial behavior, reasonably argued, "Organic disorders tend to produce a 'partial' psychopath rather than the fully fledged classical picture. . . . This does not exclude the possibility that physical insults in early life may delay maturation and the acquisition of adult social values and responses, thereby producing classical psychopathy [p. 147]."

The development of the EEG—an electrical measure of brain impulses—allowed further examination of the psychopath's neurology. Without attributing a genetic or even neurological cause to the psychopath's aberrant behavior, students of the psychopath discovered in the 1940s that their patients exhibited an unusual pattern: a high proportion of spike waves (associated with impulsive, aggressive behavior) and a preponderance of slow, theta undulations (perhaps indicating a low level of cortical arousal) (Hill & Watterson, 1942).

A variety of studies suggested that a large segment of psychopaths—some 32% to over 65%—displayed this pattern (Bradley, 1942; Gottleib, 1946; Hill & Watterson, 1942; Sessions-Hodges, 1945; Silverman, 1944). Random surveys of normal individuals indicated that less than 15% had a similar configuration (Gibbs & Lennox, 1943).

Only one major study of the psychopath's brain waves seemed to contradict the prevailing evidence. In 1946, Ostrow and Ostrow selected 440 inmates of a federal prison. Sixty-nine of these appeared to be guiltless, lacking in empathy, and highly impulsive. The Ostrows labeled this group as psychopathic. They compared the EEG patterns of the psychopaths with other types of prisoners. Fifty percent of the psychopaths did, indeed, exhibit abnormal waves, but so did 65% of conscientious objectors and 80% of schizophrenics. Clearly, the personalities of conscientious objectors differed radically from those of psychopaths. The Ostrow study pointed up the need for a clear definition of psychopathy. The varied findings suggested that some researchers had intermingled various personality types in selecting their cases.

Initial enthusiasm in the 1940s over the EEG studies led some scientists to conclude that a neural dysfunction created psychopathy and that all psychopaths suffered from the same disorder (Sessions-Hodges, 1945).

Research in the 1950s and 1960s did not confirm such a universalistic description of psychopaths' neural structures but continued to lend support to the thesis that many psychopaths had been victimized by some form of neural disorder (Ehrlich & Keogh, 1956; Ellinton, 1954).

The evidence accumulated that psychopaths exhibited EEG abnormalities. The results of studies of both adolescent and adult psychopaths showed remarkable consistency—approximately 50% of psychopaths exhibited EEG abnormalities, particularly in slow-wave activity (Ehrlich & Keogh, 1956; Knott, Platt, Ashby, & Gottlieb, 1953; Stafford-Clark, Pond, & Doust, 1951). In addition, Hill (1952) reported that 14% of highly aggressive psychopaths had abnormal slow-wave activity specifically located in the temporal lobes of the cerebral hemisphere. Only 2% of "normal" subjects, 4.8% of schizophrenics, and 2.8% of average prison inmates had the same pattern. Positive spike activity—correlated with explosive outbursts, a lack of guilt or anxiety—characterized 40 to 45% of criminal, aggressive psychopaths (Kurland, Yeager, & Arthur, 1963).

By 1978, neurologist Frank Elliott felt confident in attributing a high proportion of psychopathic behavior to some physical cause since such high proportions of both psychopaths and their parents exhibited abnormal EEGs and "almost all of the clinical features of the psychopath can be produced by physical disorders of the brain [Elliott, 1978, p. 146]."

CONCLUSIONS

Because of the mounting evidence from the 1940s onward, it would be tempting to conclude that psychopathic behavior reflects some type of brain abnormality caused by heredity, injury, or disease. Before jumping to such a conclusion, however, one should remember one relevant fact. Although an extraordinarily high proportion of psychopaths have an unusual EEG pattern, some 50% do not. Thus, even if a neural dysfunction were established, any explanation would have to account for this anomaly. Thus, the EEG evidence is hardly conclusive but it is suggestive of several possible interpretations:

• Because adult psychopaths and normal children resemble each other in EEG patterns, some investigators have concluded that psychopaths suffer from *cortical immaturity.* Kiloh and Osselton (1966) demonstrated that slow-wave activity, noted in both children and psychopaths, indicated delayed cerebral maturation. And histologic research on the nervous system shows a gross correlation between cortical maturation and EEG data (Scheibel & Scheibel, 1964). Even if one accepted the cortical immaturity hypothesis, however, a crucial question would remain: Why are psychopaths slow in cortical maturation?

• The presence of localized EEG abnormalities led some scholars to the belief that psychopathy emerges from a *structural disorder* within the brain (Kiloh & Osselton, 1966). Other investigators have suggested that the disorder, disease, or damage occurs primarily in the hypothalamic area—that region of the brain that regulates behavior and controls inhibition (McCord & McCord, 1956).

• A third, somewhat similar explanation is that psychopaths suffer from a dysfunction in the underlying *temporal and limbic mechanisms* (Hare, 1970). The limbic system has inhibitory effects on behavior, particularly behavior related to fear. Lesions in the limbic mechanisms could well interfere with learning to inhibit a punished response. Thus—either because of an inherent characteristic or because of past learning experience—a person suffering from a dysfunction in the limbic system would tend to respond with the same behavior, even if it had previously been inhibited because of punishment.

SIGNS OF NEURAL DISORDER

Further evidence that psychopaths more often suffer from some form of neural disorder has come from the study of abnormal signs of neural functioning—unusual reflexes, tics, and tremors—as well as the medical histories of psychopaths.

In 1943, Silverman and Lindner independently established some basic physiological differences between psychopaths and others. Silverman found that 21% of his psychopathic subjects exhibited eccentric reflexes and severe tremors. Lindner compared psychopathic criminals with other criminals by measuring their reactions to an electric shock. He warned the subjects 1 min before the shock by ringing a bell. Instruments recording galvanic skin responses indicated that psychopaths showed less physical tenseness, although this increased during the shock. After the experiment had ended, psychopaths tended to revert to normal physiological levels more quickly than the control group.

Other scientists found a far higher proportion of dysfunctional physical signs among psychopaths than in control groups. One group of investigators noted that 76% of psychopaths, as opposed to only 9% of a "normal" control group, exhibited signs of neurological disorder such as a flickering movement of their fingers or an equivocal plantar response (Sessions-Hodges, 1945). In 1951, another group of British scientists headed by Stafford-Clark compared psychopaths who had suffered from epilepsy or a definite head injury with nonpsychopathic criminals and with psychopaths who had no recorded history of neural disorder. Surprisingly, psychopaths who had no history of epilepsy or head injury had the greatest number of outward signs of neurological disorder. Fifty-two percent of psychopaths in this category, as compared with 24% of nonpsychopathic prisoners, had neurological symptoms.

A majority of investigators, however, have discovered histories indicative of cerebral lesions among psychopaths. From 36% to 45% of psychopaths reportedly had once suffered from dystocia, tumors, birth trauma, childhood head injury, anoxia, convulsions, or epilepsy

(Gottlieb, Ashley, & Knott, 1946; Silverman, 1943; Stafford-Clark, 1951). In contrast, only about 9% of the general population have such histories (Sessions-Hodges, 1945).

Once again, the evidence is not strong. The majority of psychopaths did not have a history of neural disorder, and some "normal" people who did have not turned into psychopaths.

Nonetheless, the high proportion of criminal psychopaths who exhibited neural disorders has remained an intriguingly consistent finding. One promising attempt to explain it has been made by neurologists who have explored the hypothalamic region of the brain.

The Hypothalamus and the Psychopath

The hypothalamus regulates various inhibitory mechanisms within the human body. Along with cortical areas, it helps in the establishment of associational patterns. Together with the limbic system, the temporal lobes, and the medial frontal cortex, the hypothalamus has an important relationship to the expression of aggressive, emotionally charged behavior. Some scientists have speculated that the hypothalamus may be the physical base of conscience: the neural area where learned reactions to moral customs are stored. As antisocial aggressive behavior almost invariably results when the hypothalamus is damaged. Some scholars have argued that a defective hypothalamus—whether caused by damage, disease, or a genetic defect—might be one of the major causes of psychopathy (Henderson, 1939; Sessions-Hodges, 1945).

Animal research has offered some support for this suggestion. Fulton and Ingraham operated on cats in 1929. They surgically damaged the hypothalamic region. Playful, normal cats turned into vicious, aggressive, and rageful animals. Even touching them after the operation produced rage. East (1945) showed that total removal of the thalamic area of dogs produced a similar condition of chronic rage. In human beings, verified lesions in the hypothalamic area have almost invariably induced anger, aggression, and antisocial behavior (Alpers, 1944).

This disorder differs from that of "explosive rage": a condition characterized by sudden, unprovoked assault on friends or strangers. Most often this "dyscontrol syndrome" occurs in cases of temporal lobe epilepsy, postoperative brain tumors, or head injuries not specifically located in the hypothalamus (Elliott, 1978). "Explosive rage" can usually be cured by medication and, unlike psychopathy, is accompanied by feelings of guilt and, at times, convulsions after the incident has occurred.

As the history of those who have suffered specific damage to the hypothalamus indicates that they develop a genuinely psychopathic syndrome of guiltlessness, egocentricity, and total disregard for others, there is a strong suggestion that certain types of head injury, even in the intrauterine stage, may produce such behavior. Most children who have suffered this injury have not been subjected to emotional deprivation (Elliott, 1978).

Early autopsies performed on psychopaths did not originally reveal a hypothalamic defect (Sessions-Hodges, 1945). More sophisticated techniques in Australia have, however, uncovered definite malfunctions in the hypothalamic area. Girgus (1977), for example, has dissected the brains of 42 highly aggressive, antisocial individuals. Blocks taken from their brain tissue indicated dysfunctions throughout the limbic system, particularly the hypothalamus.

It should be recognized that even autopsies may not reveal a particular defect and that it is extremely difficult to locate the source of such injury in the childhood histories of criminal psychopaths. In any case, damage to the hypothalamus does not seem to be a necessary and sufficient cause for the disorder but must be supplemented by some other causal factor.

Neural-Physiological Arousal in Psychopaths

Some new clues concerning the psychopath's cortical functions appeared in the 1960s and 1970s as investigators further examined the problem of cortical arousal. As we have noted (Chapter 4), abundant evidence indicates that psychopathy bears a definite relation to a lowered state of cortical arousal, a chronic need for stimulation, and a lack of response to experimental punishments (Hare, 1970; Lykken, 1953; Petrie, 1967; Quay, 1965). In addition, a lack of arousal could be related to hypothalamus damage (Elliott, 1978).

Clearly, psychopaths exhibit less of a galvanic skin response to threatening stimuli and they are slower in returning to a normal level (Glaser, 1978). Sarnoff Mednick (1977) interpreted these results as due to an interaction between environmental and physiological factors: Persons born with a slow rate of return after arousal will less readily learn to inhibit delinquent or criminal urges even if they are punished. Mednick believes that the electrodermal recovery rate is a highly hereditary attribute as it is more similar among identical than fraternal twins and, as we have noted, it is more similar among biological parents of adopted children than among adoptive parents and the adoptees.

Some experiments have indicated that the slow cortical arousal rate of psychopaths might be increased by dosages of epinephrine (Allen, Lindner, Goldman, & Dinitz, 1969). The assumption that recidivism might be reduced by injecting prisoners with arousal-inducing drugs was suggested but never experimentally tested (Goldman, Dinitz, Lindner, Foster, & Allen, 1974). Obvious and quite well-taken objections to the manipulations of human subjects have hindered, if not stopped such experiments.

Nonetheless, sociologists such as Daniel Glaser (1978) who are social theorists of the causes of crime and object to the concept of psychopathy itself, have commented, "Much more conclusive evidence for a genetic influence has been produced by the recent research . . . than was ever before available [p. 147]." Glaser recognizes the objections to the use of arousal-inducing drugs, but suggests that "procedures might be designed to be compatible with both legal concerns and scientific rigor [p. 147]."

Although the evidence is overwhelming that psychopaths have a lower rate of cortical arousal, the specific reasons for this have remained obscure: hereditary factors might play a dominant role but so, too, could experiential and learning factors as well as specific damage to the hypothalamus (Hare, 1970).

Hyperactive Children and Psychopaths

Hyperactive children—highly impulsive, sometimes aggressive, chaotic people—make life a shambles for their parents, often establishing a criminal record, and sometimes leading disastrously unhappy lives as adults. Understandably, this syndrome has at times been equated with psychopathy. The hallmarks of the disorder are extremely agitated, impulsive behavior and a severe inability to focus attention and concentration.

The causation of the disorder remains a mystery. Some scholars attribute it to disorders that, as in the psychopath, may create brain damage. Encephalitis victims commonly exhibit the syndrome. Yet, extensive research on brain damage among such children has failed to reveal a definitive pattern. Although the disorder runs in families, studies of adoptive parents and hyperactive children have not revealed a clustering of the syndrome. Contrary to the results with psychopaths, the injection of certain stimulants—amphetamines, methylphenidate, and remoline—have the effect of reducing restlessness and increasing the levels of norepinephrene in the brain.

There is little scientific evidence to link hyperactivity in children with psychopathy. They probably constitute two separate disorders. Nonetheless, it is possible that hyperactive children grow into adults who disproportionately produce psychopathic descendants. James R. Morton (1979) compared matched groups of men and women who had once been hyperactive with a control group. He found that the formerly hyperactive parents had an unusually high proportion of psychopathic children but that their children did not show high rates of schizophrenia. This finding could be attributed to the parental patterns of the once hyperactive children.

Conclusions

Myriad difficulties have confronted those who have undertaken research on the physical basis of psychopathy. Vague, encompassing definitions of the psychopath have often included people who did not exhibit the psychopathic syndrome of guiltlessness, lovelessness, asociality, and insensitivity. "Normal" psychopaths, who may well differ significantly in their physical characteristics, have not been included in the vast majority of studies. Various hypotheses concerning the physical nature of criminal psychopaths have been suggestive but theoretical explanations of the findings have not allowed discrimination between (a) criminal psychopaths who exhibit the particular physical trait; (b) nonpsychopaths who also possess it; and (c) criminal psychopaths who do not have the particular attribute.

Nonetheless, the evidence drawn from criminal psychopaths strongly suggests the following conclusions:

- Psychopaths are physiologically insensitive and relatively incapable of learning from physically punishing cues. This may be due to some form of neurological dysfunction or to forms of "training" (in early or later life) that desensitize the person to certain emotional events, or to some innate deficiency.
- Although certain measures of physical insensitivity—such as the electrodermal recovery rate—are highly inheritable, proof does not exist that this factor plays a paramount role in creating psychopathic personalities.

- Psychopaths exhibit slow-wave and spike EEG activity. Certain pieces of research indicate that this characteristic is inheritable.
- Some evidence indicates that children more often resemble their biological parents than their adoptive parents in criminal (although not necessarily psychopathic) behavior.
- Hormonal excretions, such as a lack of epinephrine, may have a partly hereditary base and might be linked to psychopathy.
- Chromosomal abnormalities have little relation to crime in general and no proven link to psychopathy.
- Criminals, including criminal psychopaths, differ from the average population in possessing a "mesomorphic" physique. The evidence indicates that such a physiological difference might possibly contribute to criminal behavior but usually through a process of social selection.
- More than others, psychopaths have suffered from diseases such as encephalitis, brain injuries, or symptoms such as tics, and tremors, and abnormal EEG patterns indicative of neural disorder. This high incidence of neurophysiological dysfunction might be attributed to a number of factors: cortical immaturity, a structural disorder within the brain, or malfunctions of the temporal and limbic systems. Each of these differences could, in turn, be explained in terms of genetics, pre-birth injuries, early diseases, or environmental influences and "accidents."
- However caused, it appears that defects in the hypothalamic area may play a major role in psychopathy.
- Psychopaths generally exhibit a lowered state of cortical arousal that might be genetic or environmental in origin.
- Hyperactive children appear to suffer from an unknown disorder that differentiates them from psychopaths. As adults, however, they produce an unusually high incidence of psychopathic children.

Although highly speculative and completely dependent on further studies of "normal" psychopaths and a random sample of the general population, one may hypothesize that criminal psychopaths significantly differ from other people in their low level of cortical arousal, their inability to learn from punishment, neurophysiological dysfunctions, and more specifically, damage to their hypothalamic area.

It could well be that these organic differences mark the dividing line between criminal psychopaths (who have been well studied) and "normal" psychopaths (who remain unstudied). It is not beyond the realm of possibility to suggest that psychopaths who end up in prisons and mental hospitals suffer from a number of neuro–physiological difficulties and are, therefore, more impulsive, violent, aggressive, and more liable to be labeled as deviant than are "normal" psychopaths. Only future research can discern whether the "normal" psychopath—a relatively controlled, suave, smooth, and nonaggressive person—exhibits fewer signs of neurophysiological disorder than do criminal psychopaths.

At this point in history, one fact seems apparent: No one has discovered a "bad seed" that flowers into psychopathy. At times, "The public's need for a simple explanation of complex phenomenon has outstripped the progress of careful thought and research [Reid, 1978, p. 178]." In the 1930s, a genetic explanation of psychopathy gained prominence; in the 1940s and 1950s, explanations of the phenomenon in terms of neural defects seemed in their ascendance; the 1960s and 1970s marked a period when the cortical arousal level of the psychopath became measurable—and a chromosomal theory of causation went into decline.

Nonetheless, the evidence cited in this chapter strongly indicates that a high proportion of psychopaths do suffer from a neuro–physiological dysfunction that may, perhaps, have genetic origins, or occur during the first few days after birth, or in the intrauterine stage. Unless blinded by biases, few could deny the accumulated evidence.

Evidence from throughout the world has supported the thesis that psychopaths do differ physically from other people. In Finland, Virkunnen (1979) noted the same basic physical traits of psychopaths as in America. In addition, when he compared psychopaths to both other criminals and to normal subjects, Virkunnen found that psychopaths are low in serum cholesterol. In Belgium, Bourdouxhe (1975) reported that psychopaths show a lower level of cortical activation, EEG abnormalities, a deficit in the secretion of amines, and a slow galvanic skin response recovery rate. She has concluded that psychopaths are incapable of learning proper social behavior because they cannot learn conditioned responses of fear or anxiety.

Nonetheless, however much weight one assigns to possible physical factors, one must carefully assess the evidence that indicates that a psychopathic syndrome emerges because of environmental influences and the total life experience of the person.

References

Allen, H.E., Lindner, L., Goldman, H., & Dinitz, S. The social and bio-medical correlates of sociopathy. *Criminologica*, 1969 (Feb.), 4:68–75.

5. Is There a Physical Base?

Alpers, B. Hypothalamic destruction. *Psychosomatic Medicine*, 1944, *2:*286.

Baker, D. Chromosome errors and antisocial behavior. *Critical Reviews in Clinical Laboratory Sciences*, 1972 (Jan.), *3:*41–101.

Bender, L. Post-encephalitic behavior disorders in childhood. In J. B. Neal (Ed.), *Encephalitis*. New York: Grune and Stratton, 1942 (reprinted 1962).

Benezech, M., & Bourgeois, M. Medico-psycho-social syndrome of polygonosomies. *Encéphale*, 1976, *2:*305–315.

Bingly, T. Mental symptoms in temporal lobe epilepsy and temporal lobe glioma. *Acta Psychiatry Scandinavia* (Suppl. 120), 1958, 1–151.

Bohman, M. Some genetic aspects of alcoholism and criminality. *Archives of General Psychiatry*, 1978, *18:*313–317.

Borgaonkar, D. S., & Shah, S. The XYY chromosome: Male—or syndrome? In A. G. Steinberg and A. G. Bearn (Eds.), *Progress in medical genetics* (Vol. X). New York: Grune and Stratton, 1974.

Bourdouxhe, S. Concerning psychopathy. *Feuillets Psychiatriques de Liège*, 1975, *8:*17–26.

Bradley, G. E.E.G. patterns of children with behavior disorders. *Connecticut State Medical Journal*, 1942, *6:*773–777.

Cadout, R. Psychopathology in adopted-away offspring of biological parents with anti-social behavior. *Archives of General Psychiatry*, 1978, *18:*219–230.

Christiansen, K. L. A preliminary study of criminality among twins. In S. Mednick and K. O. Christiansen (Eds.), *Biosocial bases of criminal behavior*. New York: Gardner Press, 1977. (a)

Christiansen, K. L. A review of studies of criminality among twins. In S. Mednick and K. O. Christiansen (Eds.), *Biosocial bases of criminal behavior*. New York: Gardner Press, 1977. (b)

Cruz, J. Estudio de las Personalidades Psicopaticas en Neutra Criminalidad. *Archives Criminalidad Neuropsiquiatria*, 1939, *3:*38–50.

Currie, S., Heathfield, K. W., Henson, R. A., & Scott, D. F. Clinical course and prognosis of temporal lobe epilepsy. *Brain*, 1971, *94:*173–190.

East, W. N. Psychopathic personality and crime. *Journal of Mental Science*, 1945, *91:*426–466.

Ehrlich, S. K., & Keogh, R. P. The psychopath in a mental institution. *A.M.A. Archives of Neurology and Psychiatry*, 1956, *76:*286–295.

Ellington, R. J. Incidence of E.E.G. abnormality among patients with mental disorders of apparently non-organic origin. *American Journal of Psychiatry*, 1954, *III:*263–275.

Elliott, F. A. Neurological aspects of antisocial behavior. In W. H. Reid (Ed.), *The psychopath*. New York: Brunner/Mazel, 1978.

Epstein, S. M. Toward a unified theory of anxiety. In B. A. Maher (Ed.), *Progress in experimental personality research*. New York: Academic Press, 1967.

Essen-Moller, E. Individual traits and morbidity in a Swedish rural population. *Acta Psychiatria et Neurology* (Supp. 100), 1956, 15.

Eysenck, H. J. *Crime and personality*. Boston: Houghton-Mifflin, 1964.

Freeman, W., & Watts, J. W. Prefrontal lobotomy: The problem of schizophrenia. *The American Journal of Psychiatry*, 1945, *101:*739–748.

Fulton, J. J., & Ingraham, F. D. Emotional disturbances following experimental lesions to the base of the brain. *Journal of Physiology*, 1929, *90:*353.

Gibbs, E. L., & Lennox, W. G. Classification of epileptic patients and control subjects. *Archives of Neurology and Psychiatry*, 1943, *50:*111.

Girgus, M. Social implications of the dyscontrol syndrome; Neuropsychiatric correlates. *Australian and New Zealand Journal of Psychiatry*, 1977 (Dec.), 30.

Glaser, D. *Crime in our changing society*. New York: Holt, Rinehart and Winston, 1978.

Glueck, S., & Glueck, E. *Unraveling juvenile delinquency*. New York: Commonwealth Fund, 1950.

Glueck, S., & Glueck, E. *Physique and delinquency*. New York: Harpers, 1956.

Goldman, S., Dinitz, S., Lindner, L., Foster, T., & Allen, H. A designed treatment program of sociopathy by means of drugs. Ohio State University Program for the Study of Crime and Delinquency, 1974.

Gottleib, J. S. Primary behavior disorders and the psychopathic personality. *Archives of Neurology and Psychiatry*, 1946, *56:*381–400.

Hare, R. D. *Psychopathy*. New York: Wiley, 1970.

Henderson, Sir David. *Psychopathic states*. New York: Norton, 1939.

Hill, D. E.E.G. in episodic and psychopathic behavior. *E.E.G. and Clinical Neurophysiology*, 1952, *4:*419–442.

Hooten, E. *Crime and the man*. Cambridge: Harvard University Press, 1939.

Kallman, F. J. *The genetics of schizophrenia*. New York: Augustine, 1939.

Kanner, L. *Child psychiatry*. Springfield, Illinois: Thomas, 1968.

Kennedy, A. Psychopathic personality and social responsibility. *Journal of Mental Science*, 1954, *100:*873.

Kiloh, L., & Osselton, J. W. *Clinical electroencephalography*. Washington: Butterworth, 1966.

Knott, J. R., Platt, E. B., Ashby, M. C., & Gottleib, J. S. A familial evaluation of the electroencephalogram of patients with primary behavior disorder and psychopathic personality. *E.E.G. and Clinical Neurophysiology*, 1953, *5:*363–370.

Kurland, H. D., Yeager, C. T., & Arthur, R. J. Psychophysiologic aspects of severe behavior disorders. *Archives of General Psychiatry*, 1963, *8:*599–604.

Lange, J. *Crime and destiny*. New York: Boni, 1930.

Lindner, R. Experimental studies in constitutional psychopathic inferiority. *Journal of American Psychopathology*, 1943, *3:*252–273.

Lindner, L., Goldman, H., Dinitz, S., & Allen, H. Antisocial personality type with cardiac lability. *Archives of General Psychiatry*, 1970 (Sept.) *23.*

Lipton, H. The psychopath. *Journal of Criminal Law, Criminology, and Police Science*, 1952, *40:*584–596.

Lykken, D. T. A study of anxiety in the sociopathic personality. Ph.D. dissertation, University of Michigan, Ann Arbor, 1953.

McCord, W., & McCord, J. *Psychopathy and delinquency*. New York: Grune and Stratton, 1956.

McNamara, J. H. Uncertainties in police work. In D. J. Bordua (Ed.), *The police*. New York: Wiley, 1967.

Mednick, S. A. A bio-social theory of the learning of law-abiding behavior. In S. A. Mednick and K. O. Christiansen (Eds.), *Biosocial bases of criminal behavior*. New York: Gardner Press, 1977.

Mednick, S. A., Schulsinger, F., Higgins, J., & Bell, B. *Genetics, environment and psychopathology*. New York: Elsevier, 1974.

Millner, N. E. Experiments relevant to learning theory and psychopathology. *Proceedings of the 18th International Congress of Psychology*, 1966.

Mohr, P. Die Forensische Bedeutung der Psychopathen, *Schweiz Archives Neurology Psychiatry*, 1947, *60:*244–268.

Montague, A. Chromosomes and crime. *Psychology Today*, 1968, *2:*42–49.

5. Is There a Physical Base?

Money, J. 47, XYY and 46, XY males: Antiandrogen therapy plus counseling. *Dissertation Abstracts*, 47, 1979.

Morton, J. R. Diagnosis of adult psychiatric patients with childhood hyperactivity. *American Journal of Psychiatry*, 1979, *21*:313.

National Institutes of Mental Health. Report on the XYY chromosomal abnormality. Public Health Service Publication No. 2103, Rockville, Md., 1970.

Newkirk, P. R. Psychopathic traits are inheritable. *Diseases of the Nervous System*, 1957, *18*:52–54.

Ostrow, M., & Ostrow, M. Bilaterally synchronous paroxysmal slow activity in the encephalograms of non-epileptics. *Journal of Nervous and Mental Disease*, 1046, *103*:346–358.

Partridge, G. E. A study of 50 cases of psychopathic personality. *American Journal of Psychiatry*, 1928, 7:953–973.

Petrie, A. *Individuality in pain and suffering*. Chicago: University of Chicago Press, 1967.

Puntigam, F. Verursacht die Encephalitis post Vasscinationen bei Jugendlichen kriminogene Personlichkeits-veranderungen?", *Ost. Ztchr. Kinderheik Kinderfursorge*, 1950, *4*:142–159.

Quay, H. C. Psychopathic personality as pathological stimulation seeking. *American Journal of Psychiatry*, 1965, *122*:180–183.

Rainer, J. D., Abdullah, S., & Jarvick, L. F. Kyy Karyotype in a pair of monozygotic twins: A 17 year life history study. *British Journal of Psychiatry*, 1972 (May), *120*:543–548.

Reid, W. H. Genetic correlates of antisocial syndromes. In W. H. Reid (Ed.), *The psychopath*, New York: Brunner/Mazel, 1978.

Rosanoff, A. J. The etiology of child behavior difficulties. *Psychiatric Monographs*, 1943, *1*:413.

Rodin, E. A. Psychomotor epilepsy and aggressive behavior. *Archives of General Psychiatry*, 1973, *28*:210–213.

Robbins, L. N. Discussion of genetic studies of criminality and psychopathy. *Proceedings of the American Psychopathological Association*, 1975, *63*:117–122.

Rotenberg, M. Psychopathy, insensitivity, and sensitivization. *Professional Psychology*, 1975, *49*:167–171.

Rotenberg, M. Psychopathy and differential insensitivity. In R. Hare and D. Schalling (Eds.), *Psychopathic behavior: Approaches to research*. New York: Wiley, 1978.

Scheibel, M. E., & Scheibel, A. B. Some neural substates of postnatal development. In M. Hoffman and L. Hoffman (Eds.), *Review of child development research* (Vol. 1). New York: Russell Sage Foundation, 1964.

Schulinger, F. Psychopathy and environment. In S. Mednick and K. O. Christiansen (Eds.), *Biosocial bases of criminal behavior*. New York: Gardner Press, 1977.

Sessions-Hodges, R. The impulsive psychopath. *Journal of Mental Science*, 1945, *91*:476–482.

Shah, A. S. The 47 XXY chromosomal abnormality. In W. R. Smith and A. Kling (Eds.), *Issues in brain/behavior control*. New York: Spectrum, 1974.

Shah, A. S. & Roth, L. H. Biological and psychophysiological factors in criminality. In D. Glaser (Ed.), *Handbook of criminology*. Chicago: Rand McNally, 1974.

Sheldon, W. H. *Varieties of delinquent youth*. New York: Harper & Row, 1949.

Silverman, D. Clinical studies of criminal psychopaths. *Archives of Neurology and Psychiatry*, 1943, *50*:18.

Silverman, D. The E.E.G. of criminals. *Archives of Neurology and Psychiatry*, 1944, *52*:38–42.

Simmons, D. J., & Rockwell, F. The electroencephalogram studies of psychopathic personalities. *Archives of Neurology and Psychiatry*, 1946, *55:*410–413.

Slater, E. T. Psychopathic personality as a genetical concept. *Journal of Mental Science*, 1948, *94:*277.

Stafford-Clark, D., Pond, D., & Lovett Doust, J. W. The psychopath in prison. *British Journal of Delinquency*, 1951, *2:*117–129.

Toch, H. H. Psychological consequences of the police role. In A. E. Niederhoffer and A. S. Blumberg (Eds.), *The ambivalent force*. Waltham: Gina, 1970.

Thompson, G. N. *The psychopathic delinquent*. Springfield, Illinois: Thomas, 1953.

Virkunnen, M. Serum cholesterol in anti-social personality. *Neuropsychobiology*, 1979, *5*(1):27–30.

Wilson, S. A. K. *Neurology* (Vol. 1). London: Edward Arnold, 1940.

Ziskind, E., Syndulko K., & Maltzman, I. Aversive conditioning in the sociopath. *Pavlovian Journal of Biological Science*, 1978 (Oct.– Dec.) *13:*199– 205.

The Social Causes
of Psychopathy

Please mam put my tiny mind at ease
tell Judge and Jury on your knees
they will LISTEN to your cries of PLEAS
THE GUILTY ONE is you not me
these last words I speak
Tell them you are guilty
Please, so then mam, I'll be free,
Daughter Mary
Mary Bell, murderer, age 11, quoted in
G. Sereny, *The Case of Mary Bell*
(New York: McGraw-Hill, 1973).

Mary Bell did not go free. In 1968, an English court convicted her of strangling Martin Brown, 4 years old, and Brian Howe, 3. She and a retarded accomplice slashed the boys with razors and cut their hair after killing them (Sereny, 1973). Psychiatrists unanimously declared that Mary Bell was a child psychopath. The court found her guilty of manslaughter and sentenced her to detention for life because of the "diminished responsibility" associated with psychopathy in English law.

The girl confessed her crimes to a matron in jail. "She felt nothing," the matron said, "I've never seen anything like it. She said all those awful things they had done but she didn't *feel* a thing [Sereny, 1973, p. 54]."

A psychiatrist, T. M. Orton, asked Mary how someone who was strangled would suffer before he died. "Why, if you are dead," she said, "you're dead. It doesn't matter then [Sereny, 1973, p. 60]." Orton later commented, "I've seen a lot of psychopathic children but I've never met one like

Mary: as intelligent, as manipulative, or as dangerous [Sereny, 1973, p. 65]."

Another matron in jail allowed Mary Bell to play with a cat on a window ledge. When the matron turned her back, Mary tried to strangle it. As the matron grabbed the cat from her, Mary calmly said, "Oh, she doesn't feel that, and, anyway, I like hurting little things that can't fight back [Sereny, 1973, p. 180]."

Gitta Sereny, who closely investigated Mary Bell's history, could not accept a "bad seed" explanation of her actions. The girl had, however, suffered a series of near-fatal "accidents": an overdose of sleeping pills that her mother used, a fall out of a window, a collision with a lorry, and another overdose of iron pills (perhaps administered by her mother). Any one of these accidents could have damaged her brain.

Yet, when the court sentenced the girl to life detention, the judge instructed the detention attendants that Mary's background was "unimportant for the staff to know [Sereny, 1973, p. 236]." Mary Bell was incarcerated at the Special Unit at Red Bank along with 22 boys. The staff knew nothing about her except for her crimes.

> "Is this really possible?" Gitta Sereny asked. "Can anyone severely disturbed ever be effectively helped without understanding of the background—the root causes of the disturbance? If—in this mysterious domain of human behavior—we deny the relevance of past experiences, what are we left with? What is there to build on but a shell? . . . In the light of overwhelming proof that what she represents is a severe manifestation of widely and indeed universally existing problems, this attitude begins to look like an almost deliberate act of self-persuasion. Is this, one begins to wonder, something we are all tempted to do: to hide from that which is too difficult to face? To obliterate that which is too stark? [1973, p. 252]."

When Gitta Sereny began to unearth Mary Bell's past through interviews with her relatives, she asked, "When are we going to learn that no relationship can hold darker dangers than the one between mother and child gone wrong [1973, p. 259]?"

Investigation revealed that Mary's mother was a person who frequently disappeared from home for weeks at a time, repeatedly tried to force the child out of the home, and rejected Mary from birth. The mother bore the child on May 26, 1957. Her first reaction on seeing the baby was, "Take the 'thing' away from me! [Sereny, 1973, p. 193]." The mother tried to leave the child in department stores where someone might pick her up; Mary later recalled these episodes and also the fact that her mother had cut off her hair before making forays to dispose of her. The mother later explained the shavings as attempts to rid the child of lice; one might speculate that Mary's own engagements in cutting the hair of children she had killed might have occurred because of vestigial memories of her own humiliation. The mother hated her child, but after Mary had committed the murders, she vainly tried to sell Mary's stories to newspapers.

Mary Bell's grandmother later speculated, "I suppose the only way all this could have been prevented—the only right thing would have been if *Betty* [the mother] had been under a psychiatrist since she was small [Sereny, 1973, p. 181]."

Mary's father was of little comfort to her. When the mother periodically disappeared to enjoy city life, the father came to their home. He pretended to be "an uncle" so that welfare payments would not be cut off. He was an alcoholic and a criminal; Mary later visited him in prison. He was quite open about his shiftless existence. "Nobody wants to work," he said. "As long as I have my pint, I don't need money [Sereny, 1973, p. 211]."

From early childhood, authorities knew of Mary's situation but no one took any action. During her first days in school, Mary kicked other children, bit them, and attempted to choke the smaller ones. One teacher recalled that she found Mary crying in the playground. "I asked her what was the matter.'Nobody wants to play with me.'" The teacher responded, "You musn't do such nasty things to them [Sereny, 1973, p. 205]."

Mary Bell's case raises the distinct possibility that highly rejected children behave in a manner that triggers more rejection from other people, thus creating a vicious circle.

After her conviction, English authorities could find no suitable way of detaining her for life. Lacking substitutes, they committed her to a secure institution for boys. There, her condition did not markedly improve. She refused to see her mother, the only person who occasionally volunteered to visit her. She falsely accused a teacher of sexual abuse. She played games with her guards and constantly cheated. When told that she could not cheat, she responded, "*I can.*"

An unloved, asocial, insensitive, and guiltless child, Mary Bell exhibited all of the traits of the adult psychopath. Few little girls, as far as we know, commit murder. Yet, as Sereny concluded, "Mary's *crime* seems rare—her *condition* is not [1973, p. 231]."

Experience of Psychopaths in Childhood

A German legend—perhaps true, perhaps not—recounts one of the more cruel experiments of Frederick II. In the 1400s, it is reported, he ordered that a group of infants should be brought to his castle and given everything they wanted—except love. Bereft of all affection, according to legend, all of the children died.

EARLY DEPRIVATION

Few would suggest that a background devoid of love invariably produces early death. Yet, in a series of classic studies, Spitz (1958, 1962) found impressive evidence that deprivation results in early mortality and stunted emotional and intellectual development. Spitz compared children raised in a nursing home and a foundling home. Both homes had admirable hygienic conditions and excellent food. The two groups of children were intellectually equal at the time of their incarceration. The difference lay in the fact that the nursing home children received daily care from their mothers while the foundling home children were raised by a handful of nurses who necessarily had to divide their time among a large group of children. After 4 months in the two homes, the foundling group showed a much higher rate of infection and a higher mortality rate. In their second and third years of life, few of the foundling home children could walk or talk. In later studies, Spitz found that children raised in foundling homes exhibited a retarded level of sexual and emotional growth.

Experiments with "fake," unsocial mother substitutes who have "raised" baby monkeys have shown similar results (Harlow & Harlow, 1962). Apparently, social stimulation, if not actual love, is necessary for both human and higher animal development.

A great amount of evidence indicates that the vast majority of psychopaths, like Mary Bell, have experienced a childhood that resembles the deprivation suffered by Spitz's foundling home children or Harlow's experimental monkeys. Their backgrounds have taught hate, not love; mistrust, rather than trust; cruelty, rather than kindness. Early emotional deprivation—parental rejection, neglect, animosity, or absence; parental inconsistency, cruelty, or aggression—brutalizes the potential psychopath, deprives him or her of a stable conscience, and makes it impossible for the psychopath to comprehend the feelings of others.

Researchers in the 1920s and 1930s first reported the almost universal pattern of rejection in the backgrounds of psychopaths. In 1928,

Partridge found that all of the psychopaths in an American reform school hated their parents and reported that they had been rejected as children. In 1933, Knight found a similar pattern when she compared highly aggressive children to very submissive ones. All of the mothers of the aggressive children (some of whom may not have been psychopathic) said that they disliked their children and that they had to use severe physical punishment in dealing with them. The submissive children, in contrast, had been overprotected by their mothers. Field (1940) later investigated 25 children who had a psychopathic syndrome. All but 2 came from families where the mothers rejected their children, exhibited signs of mental disorder, and reported that their mothers had treated them cruelly.

In 1942, Haller also reported a pattern of maternal rejection in psychopaths who had been paroled from a mental institution. He argued that the severely rejected child wants love more than other adults—in the same fashion that a starved person craves food. All of these studies, conducted with males labeled as psychopathic, placed the blame for their subjects' condition on maternal rejection.

Subsequent studies in the 1940s indicated paternal rejection and maternal neglect (or indulgence) as a primary constellation in the backgrounds of psychopaths. Although they may well have dealt with "acting-out neurotics" rather than psychopaths, various psychoanalysts noted that their patients exhibited a syndrome of paternal rejection and maternal indulgence (if not actual approval for deviant behavior) among their parents. Szurek (1942) recorded cases where children attacked others with a hammer or a knife and showed little guilt. Mothers of such children supposedly gained pleasure from a martyrdom complex and allowed the children to roam at will. Heaver (1943) found that typical child psychopaths hated their stern, authoritarian fathers but that the mothers either neglected the children or allowed them to indulge in every whim. And Greenacre (1945) concluded that her patients at a New York hospital had similarly neglectful mothers while the fathers remained distant, mean, rejecting figures. Greenacre wrote that the fathers of her psychopathic subjects were "stern, respected, and often obsessional . . . remote, preoccupied, and fear inspiring [p. 197]." The frivolous mothers neglected or indulged their children.

Such studies of children could well be criticized because they dealt with primarily middle-class families and the children may not have definitively shown the psychopathic syndrome. Other studies of the psychopath, however, continued to uncover a background of parental rejection—sometimes from the father, more often from the mother.

One interesting experiment by Robert Lindner (1944) involved the hypnoanalysis of eight criminal psychopaths. Under hypnosis, all of his patients reported brutal childhood experiences, hated their fathers, and viewed their mothers as virtually irrelevant.

Jenkins and Hewitt (1944) found that psychopathic children compared with hundreds of other cases from child guidance clinics had been reared by rejecting parents who hated each other as well as their child. The parents aggressively abused such children. In 1960, Jenkins concluded that "the product of this background is a child of bottomless hostilities and endless bitterness, who feels cheated in life, views himself as the victim . . . and is grossly lacking in guilt over his misconduct [p. 326]."

The evidence has continued to amass that psychopaths have suffered from severe emotional deprivation in childhood. (See, for example, Bowlby, 1952; Craft, 1961; Friedlander, 1947; Jenkins, 1960; Rabinovitch, 1951.)

CRITICISM OF STUDIES OF PARENTAL REJECTION

Yet, influential critics in the middle of the twentieth century have not let this mass of evidence pass uncriticized. The "dean" of studies of psychopaths, Hervey Cleckly, commented in 1959:

> I have not regularly encountered any specific type of error in parent–child relation in the early history of my cases. . . . I am increasingly impressed with the difficulty in obtaining any reliable evidence of what was felt twenty or thirty years ago. . . . Assumptions about infantile, and even intrauterine, experiences are sometimes made solely on the basis of analogy and symbolism. The methods can be used with such elasticity that it is not difficult to "discover" in the unconscious virtually anything the investigator chooses to seek [1975, p. 584].

Psychoanalysts can, of course, reconstruct any background they wish from the selective memories of their patients; parents may consciously or unconsciously filter their real sentiments toward the child; and the actual reconstruction of the past of any person requires the combined skills of an historian, a psychiatrist, and possibly, a geneticist.

Such considerations have led some researchers to question whether a link exists between childhood experience and any form of adult behavior, including psychopathy (Clarke & Clarke, 1976; Clinard, 1974; Jessor and Jessor, 1977; Yarrow, Campbell, & Burton, 1968). They have criticized the fact that many studies of the interaction between childhood experience and adult activity have depended on simultaneous interviews with the subjects and the parents, or on the memories of the subjects themselves. These are, of course, legitimate objections, but a variety of longitudinal studies have outdated them.

In 1959, W. McCord, J. McCord, I. Zola, and J. Gudeman traced subjects of the Cambridge–Somerville Study whose family backgrounds had been investigated in the 1930s and whose criminal and alcoholic records had been independently ascertained when the subjects reached adulthood (McCord, McCord, and Gudeman, 1960; McCord, Zola, & McCord, 1959). These researchers found significant relationships between the early family background of the subjects and their later adult behavior.

Following this first empirical evidence that childhood decisively affects adult behavior, other investigators found striking evidence— again gathered "blindly" between childhood and adulthood—that family backgrounds and early socialization markedly affect adult character (Block, 1971; J. McCord, 1979; Robins, 1966).

The last half of the twentieth century has produced ever more convincing evidence that psychopaths suffer from an extraordinarily deprived emotional environment—whether one attributes it to the mother or the father or to their social structure. Reports have been gathered from longitudinal studies, the person's recollections, his or her reactions under hypnosis, accounts by the parents about the child, and measurements of the person's childhood as well as adulthood. Any one source could be suspect. The combination of diverse approaches to the same problem—all of which produce similar information—makes it extremely plausible, if not inescapable to reach a logical conclusion: *Psychopaths have suffered from emotional deprivation, punishment, neglect, ostracism, or some other form of early socialization that severely cripples their ability to identify with other people, empathize with them, or learn societal values.*

The Cambridge–Somerville Study indicated not only a statistical correlation between early environmental deprivation and violent crimes in adulthood, but it produced evidence that specific backgrounds lead to violence. Potential murderers (not all psychopathic) came from homes devoid of love. Their mothers either neglected them completely or tried to dominate every aspect of their lives. Their fathers were generally highly aggressive men. Typically, the parents disciplined the eventually violent criminals in an erratic manner. Counselors in the 1930s predicted that 16 boys would commit acts of violent aggression. In fact, some 20 years later, of the 14 persons who had been judged as violent criminals, only 1 was not included in the original group of 16 (W. McCord, 1968).

Using different approaches, Albert Bandura and Richard Walters demonstrated in a carefully controlled study that early rejection in childhood highly correlates with unsocialized aggressive behavior in adolescence (Bandura & Walters, 1959).

These studies dealt only with people who had been caught and labeled as violent; further, there is no evidence that everyone in the samples was psychopathic. Other studies have concentrated completely on psychopathic children and produced similar results. Laurette Bender (1947), for example, examined some 800 children at New York's Bellevue Hospital. She found a classical syndrome among her child patients: no guilt, an inability to identify with others, aggressiveness, and impulsivity. The children could manipulate others but felt no affection for them. After investigating their backgrounds, Bender noted that all of the children had been raised in an environment of maternal or paternal neglect, particularly during the first years of their lives. "We know that the critical time," she wrote, "is the first year; any significant break in parent relationships or any period of deprivation under five years may be sufficient to produce this personality defect [p. 501]."

LOSS OF PARENTS

Some authors have particularly highlighted the loss of parents early in life as a causative factor in psychopathy (Craft, Stephenson and Granger, 1964; Greer, 1964; Gregory, 1958; Oltman & Friedman, 1967). A significant study by Lee N. Robins (1966) based on a comparison of child guidance clinic referrals and normal subjects showed that most psychopathic subjects came from broken or impoverished homes and had psychopathic or alcoholic fathers. Robins particularly stressed the importance of a psychopathic father in the home, rather than the actual separation of parents entailed by a broken marriage.

Investigating the later lives of deviant children, Robins found that psychopathic fathers played a paramount role in producing psychopathic children. Typically, the fathers had a long history of antisocial behavior, arrests, alcoholism, and desertion of the family. Cold but authoritarian fathers, however, did not produce psychopathic children. From Robin's point of view, the fathers played a determinant role as children who did not have a severely antisocial father or who were raised by psychopathic mothers (but not psychopathic fathers) seldom developed the syndrome (1966).

A series of studies have focused on parental inconsistency in the disciplining of psychopaths. Ullmann and Krasner (1969) observed that the parents of pre-psychopathic children "reward both 'superficial conformity' and 'underhanded nonconformity.' Because the parent behaves arbitrarily and inconsistently, punishment is the result, but it is unpredictable. . . . A frequently observed behavior is that of a child either lying to avoid punishment or making superficial responses such as 'I'm sorry and I won't do it again.' The child has then been rewarded for escaping punishment without feeling guilt [1969, p. 454]." Maher (1966) also suggested that the parents of pre-psychopathic children do not punish them, if the child acts in a "cute" fashion and promises not to repeat his behavior. Such inconsistencies in childrearing may help to explain why psychopaths who generally have little empathy for others can manipulate them "like puppets on a string [Smith, 1978, p. 62]."

Regardless of the particular culture, the pattern of parental rejection leading to psychopathy remains basically the same. In France, Hochman (1976) reported that psychopaths have usually been raised by rejecting, erratic mothers. The fathers are typically distant or absent. In Uruguay, Perez-Sanchez (1977) reported a similar pattern. Finnish investigators have noted that a higher proportion of psychopaths have undergone childhood deprivation and that they seek to deprive others (Tor-Björn, 1974; Virkunnen, 1976). Within the Chicano culture of America, Castellano (1978) discovered that paternal absence created a higher incidence of psychopathic behavior among Mexican-American girls. And John Lingdon and Fernando Topia (1977) reported that children who tortured animals all came from chaotic homes characterized by parental aggressiveness. One key factor seems to be that rejected children all over the world fail to learn to trust other human beings (Erik Erickson's first "stage" of human development) (Evans, 1976; Schuster, 1976). This lack of trust seems only natural as rejected children have been treated with cruelty, inconsistency, or neglect.

UNANSWERED QUESTIONS ABOUT PSYCHOPATHS

Two further questions about the background of psychopaths remain unanswered:

First, does the potentially psychopathic child behave in a manner that causes his parents to react in a rejecting, inconsistent fashion? It could well be that the child's asocial, sullen, guiltless, aggressive behavior causes the parents to treat him in a similar manner. The parents' way of treating the child could be both a cause and an effect of the child's behavior. Hare (1970) observed that "psychopathy may very well represent the outcome of interaction between the characteristics (possibly congenital) of the child and the socialization techniques employed [p. 101]."

As interesting as this hypothesis is, certain difficulties make it relatively implausible: (*a*) we do not as yet possess sufficient evidence to regard a child's potentially psychopathic behavior as congenital; and (*b*) I find it difficult to believe that certain adult characteristics of the parents of psychopaths—such as their high incidence of criminality, alcoholism, and desertion—could actually be caused by the child's behavior. It is possible, of course, to suggest that a father's negligence and his child's psychopathy originate from the same biological factor but, as the previous chapter has indicated, such an explanation must remain at the level of speculation.

Second, does emotional deprivation necessarily result in a psychopathic pattern? Many studies have shown that parental rejection eventuates in aggressiveness, a lack of ability to learn from experience, little emotional depth, and antagonism toward society and its institutions—all potentially psychopathic traits (Burgum, 1940; Levy, 1937; Newell, 1936; Symonds, 1939; Wolberg, 1944). Yet, other researchers have found that rejected children respond in many different ways: submissiveness, self-reliance, or "clinging," attention-seeking behavior (Bowlby, 1952; Lewis, 1954). Some studies have demonstrated that rejection in childhood correlates with deviant but nonpsychopathic adult behavior such as psychoses, alcoholism, and sexual problems (McCord, McCord, and Gudeman, 1960; McCord, McCord, and Verden, 1962; McCord, Porta, and McCord, 1962).

REJECTION AND PSYCHOPATHS

Thus, research on unloved children suggests that rejection, in and of itself, may not produce psychopathy. Virtually all psychopaths have been rejected. But the obverse does not hold true: Rejected children may become psychopaths but sometimes follow other paths in life. What is the *differentia specifica?*

Rejected Children and Psychopathy

The severity of rejection that children experience and their isolation from other human beings may be a major element in turning some rejected children—but not all—into psychopaths.

The Fels Research Institute (1945), for example, has found that children who are "actively rejected"—subjected to hostility, conflict, quarrels, and resentment—usually reacted with aggression and guiltless behavior. Other children who had been rejected but indifferently neglected by their self-interested parents tended to respond by withdrawing, becoming self-sufficient, or by highly dependent behavior. Schactel and Levi (1945) found similar results among nursery school children who responded to a Rorshach test.

Children who have been separated from their parents and institutionalized at a very early age seemed particularly subject to psychopathic tendencies. Goldfarb (1945) compared institutionalized children with those raised in foster homes during their first 3 years of life. Goldfarb argued that institutionalization had "primitivized" the children. He reported a typical psychopathic syndrome: "A meagerness of feeling for other humans" and "the absence of anxiety following acts of hostility, cruelty, or unprovoked aggression [p. 411]." Lowrey (1940) also studied institutionalized children who had been deprived of parental care during the first 2 years of their life. He found asocial, hostile tendencies in the children and labeled them as "isolated personalities."

World War II unfortunately provided a "natural experiment" in isolating children. Nazi attacks provoked the evacuation of children from London to isolated camps. Later studies of these children indicated that many of the children experienced a "stunted" growth in conscience and that they could not control their antisocial tendencies (A. Freud & D. Burlingham, 1944).

John Bowlby's (1956) classic work on isolated children who have been deprived of affection in their early years indicated "that the more complete the deprivation in the early years, the more isolated and asocial the child [p. 118]."

Yet, it is also clear that *complete* isolation of a child results not in psychopathy but in an almost total retardation of the child. As one would predict, because of a high death rate, there are very few cases to illustrate this hypothesis.

Kingsley Davis (1940) documented one extreme case of childhood deprivation. In 1940, child welfare officials discovered a child of 5 who had spent her life in closets or locked with her arms above her head. Because she had been born illegitimately, her grandparents had consistently and severely punished the child. By age 5, she could not walk, talk, feed herself, or show any emotion but rage. After eventual placement in a foster home, she began to develop the rudiments of a human character, but she remained extremely retarded and almost "inhuman."

Thus, it would appear that total deprivation of a child results in a total retardation of personality. Severe rejection or institutionalization of a person leads to the development of a psychopathic syndrome.

Other aspects in the child's environment also contribute to the unloved child taking some path other than psychopathy. The severity of rejection, in itself, seems critical but certain idiosyncratic factors in the child's background also lead to particular results. To refer to the Cambridge–Somerville deviants again: a common strain of rejection ran through the backgrounds of various sorts of deviants but, as I have remarked, only a handful became psychopaths.

Alcoholics in the study contrasted sharply with the psychopaths. The typical alcoholic was reared in a middle-class family, full of stress and quarreling. Typically, his mother varied between overt rejection of the child and loving indulgence. The father was a cool, distant man who taught his son to use escapist mechanisms to avoid the pitfalls of life. As an adult, the alcoholic continued to long for love but found sustenance in hard drinking (McCord, McCord, & Gudeman, 1960).

Male psychotics, in contrast, were raised by "smothering" mothers who actively tried to dominate them. Their fathers were passive, ineffectual men. Neither actively demonstrated love for the children. Often, both parents exhibited signs of mental disorder. Uneducated to meet adult crises and, perhaps, unable to do so, the psychotics crumbled in the face of their problems and sought to return to a symbolic state of maternal domination (McCord, Porta, & McCord, 1962).

Sexual deviants were typically raised by sexually promiscuous fathers who cared little for their children. They usually married sexually stimulating, if anxious mothers (McCord, McCord, & Verden, 1962). As a group, homosexuals were exposed to authoritarian, rejecting, and sexually anxious mothers (McCord, McCord, & Verden, 1962).

As I have previously argued, such evidence indicates that parental rejection can produce varied results (McCord, 1968). No single, overarching explanation for deviant behavior can be defended. Theories that help to explain one form of behavior, such as membership in a delinquent gang, have little, if any, relevance to explicating the biochemical basis of psychoses or the manipulative behavior of "normal" psychopaths. Contrary to the prevailing sociological view— whether put forward by structuralists, labeling theorists, or critical sociologists—longitudinal studies suggest that certain early experiences and resulting personality characteristics predispose a person to "choose" a course of deviant behavior.

A particular experience, such as parental rejection, however, does not, in itself, determine the person's life. The form of the rejection, the attributes of the parents, the model that the parent represents, his or her subculture, and many other factors—perhaps including the biological characteristics of the child and certainly his or her general social milieu—help to decide their fate.

Some Effects of General Cultural and Social Forces

Emotional deprivation, which seems so closely related to the psychopath's lack of conscience and warped ability to love, does not occur in a vacuum. Sometimes, as I have noted, entire societies may develop psychopathic tendencies. Other social influences, far beyond the control of the individual or his or her parents, may also play a role: the occurrence of a major social disaster, such as war, which can separate children from their parents, one's social-class position, or even the technological complexity of a particular society.

THE EFFECTS OF A MAJOR SOCIAL CRISIS

Some great social disaster, such as the Iks' loss of their hunting land or the massive disruptions caused by the outbreak of a major war, can seriously affect relationships between parents and children. Studies of children forcibly separated from their parents during World War II suggest that they often developed a psychopathic pattern (Freud & Burlingham, 1944; Pritchard and Rosensweig, 1942). Children from Nazi concentration camps also exhibited a similar pattern (Szondi cited in Bowlby, 1952). Fortunately, perhaps because of certain physiological differences, the majority of such children did not turn out to be psychopaths.

171

Although "normal" psychopaths seem to come from all social strata, a variety of studies indicate that criminal psychopaths more often emerge from lower-class environments. Economic deprivation, greater familial disorganization, being raised in a (generally) urban environment, the anonymity of lower-class social life, and many other factors may account for this relationship. The Fels Research Institute and the Harvard Laboratory for Human Development have shown that lower-class parents were less demonstrative to their children, more distant from them, and more overtly rejecting (Baldwin, Kalhorn, & Breese, 1945; Sears, Maccoby, & Levin, 1956). In addition, a comprehensive survey of New Haven showed that the incidence of severe "antisocial reactive disorders" (which undoubtedly included some psychopaths) had the highest incidence in the lower social classes (Hollingshead & Redlich, 1958). From a different point of view, John Whiting and Irwin Child surveyed many cultures and found that discipline based on the withdrawal of love, rather than physical punishment, resulted in a higher level of guilt (Whiting and Child, 1953).

Many sociologists have implicitly challenged these findings—at least as they apply to criminals in general. They have used anonymous self-reports where people check off the crimes they have committed (Gibbons, 1970; Short & Nye, 1958). These studies indicate that virtually everyone will admit to committing some crime during their lives and criminal behavior extends over a broad spectrum of social classes. Yet, people who are actually incarcerated generally admit to more offenses and to more serious violent crimes (Silberman, 1978).

Moreover, in a cohort study of 10,000 boys in Philadelphia, Wolfgang (1972) found a high proportion (35%) had developed an official criminal arrest record by age 18. The truly chronic offenders—those who had been arrested for an average of 8.5 crimes each—comprised only 18% of those boys who had been officially labeled as delinquent, but they committed 83% of all serious crimes. We would expect that these hard-core delinquents had a number of criminal psychopaths in their ranks. Typically (77%), they came from the lower social classes.

TECHNOLOGICAL COMPLEXITY AND CRIMINAL PSYCHOPATHY

In 1933, Mandel Sherman and Thomas R. Henry compared four communities in the Blue Ridge mountains: Two were developing rapidly and had experienced economic growth. The other two used technologically simple instruments of farming. The more simple communities produced more psychopaths: the people of these less advantaged villages "had slight guilt feelings and shallow emotional development. In general, they suffered from stunted emotional development [Sherman & Henry, 1933, p. 200]."

Studies of the Ik and Alorese tended to lend support to Sherman and Henry's original findings. Yet, it soon became clear that sheer "simplicity," technological underdevelopment, economic scarcity, and life in a stagnant society do not correlate with psychopathy. In a highly simple society such as the Hutterites, the existence of rigid social norms, strict rules, and a cohesive religion prohibit the development of psychopathic syndromes.

Later studies of technologically advanced, urbanized, and less homogeneous societies indicated that as technological complexity spreads, the general incidence of criminal behavior goes up (McCord & McCord, 1977).

This does not seem unusual as increasing technological complexity is usually accompanied by greater urbanization, more specialization in work roles, a higher divorce rate, and the disappearance of close communal bonds. All of these influences "free" the individual from intimate social ties, create an atmosphere of anonymity, and, relatively, allow each individual to follow his or her own life-style. At the same time, they correlate with an increase in crime. We do not know how many criminal psychopaths are included, but a clear pattern of criminal behavior has emerged in America between the 1930s and the 1980s as technology has advanced.

INCREASES IN THE GENERAL AMERICAN CRIME RATE

Despite somewhat romantic myths about gangsters, the actual incidence of crime in America was quite low in the 1930s (Silberman, 1978). Yet, America has a long history of violence—ranging from its revolutionary days, to conflicts on the frontier, to labor and racial tensions. Between 1933 and the late 1940s, however, the rate of homicide dropped by 50% and the rate of other violent crimes declined by 33% (Silberman, 1978). Many factors accounted for this change: a sense of community created by the depression and by war, a decline in foreign and black migration to Northern cities, and a decline in that age group (14–24) that traditionally has accounted for an unusually high proportion of violent crimes.

Between 1960 and 1975, the pattern dramatically changed: the incidence of serious crimes soared by 200% (Silberman, 1978). A part of this increase can be accounted for by a relative growth in the 14–24 age group, but the growth in serious crimes occurred in every age group. The pervasive (often) violent atmosphere of the mass media, the ready availability of handguns, the influx of new generations of migrants into decaying cities may account for some of this increase. Moreover, although the birth rate has decreased, we cannot expect an immediate reduction in the rate of serious crime for two reasons: (a) the absolute number of children is increasing; and (b) the growth in numbers of the 14- to 24-year-old group is particularly marked in urban slums and ghettos—the traditional breeding places of serious crime (Silberman, 1978).

Aside from the general demographic pattern, there is little reason to expect a general decline in violent crimes by the end of the century. The fundamental causes of America's high crime rate remain forceful. The heritage of violence, perhaps enhanced by the mass media, will continue to affect young, susceptible minds. Racist conditions, particularly as they influence Blacks, show no sign of disappearing. The fact that all Americans are offered the elusive goal of "success"—but some groups are denied the means to achieve success—encourages many to seek deviant routes to the achievement of their goals (Merton, 1957).

Some Prevailing Views about Criminal and Psychopathic Behavior

Unfortunately, most existing theories about the nature of crime—let alone criminal or "normal" psychopathy—do not present the type of synthesis that is required by the evidence. As various scholars have written comprehensive books about criminological theory, it is hardly necessary to reiterate their views (see Gibbons, 1978; Sykes, 1978). Some researchers merely dismiss the concept of psychopathy altogether and ignore physiological and clinical evidence (Gibbons, 1979). Others view psychopathy as one form of reaction to the strains produced by inconsistencies in a particular society (Merton, 1957). Such a position may go far in understanding differential crime rates or the incidence of various forms of mental disorder. It does not, however, explain the ubiquitous appearance of psychopathy throughout the world. Scholars such as Edwin Sutherland and Albert

Cohen regard deviance—and presumably psychopathy—as a reaction to labeling, a criminal subculture (Cohen, 1955; Sutherland & Cressy, 1960), and the learning process. Such theories do not explicate why psychopaths appear in noncriminal cultures or why certain familial constellations predispose people in a psychopathic direction.

In contrast, psychiatrists favor the use of case histories and explanations based on psychological predispositions (Jackson, 1960), but their position ignores the fact that entire groups, such as the Ik and the Alorese, exhibit a psychopathic syndrome and yet cannot be physiologically identical.

Labeling theorists (Becker, 1963; Erikson, 1966) helped to explain how a person becomes a member of a deviant subculture but leave us unenlightened about why the person originally committed himself to a particular way of life.

Geneticists and physiological psychologists have attempted to reduce psychopathy to a constitutional predisposition (see Chapter 5) but they have failed to explain why so many psychopaths do not exhibit signs of a physical disorder.

Some sociologists (Hirschi, 1969) have plausibly explained why certain delinquents have less attachment to others, less commitment to conventional behavior, and less belief in the validity of social rules. And various social psychologists, such as Albert Bandura, have brilliantly explained the origins of aggression in terms of social-learning theory, modeling, reinforced performance, and other factors (Bandura, 1979; Megargee & Bohn, 1979). Usually, however, they have failed to extricate the specific problem of psychopathic aggression from the more generalized concept of aggression itself.

No single theory, it seems to me, *has yet succeeded in explaining psychopathic behavior*. The cortical underarousal hypotheses seem useful in investigating individual psychopaths, but irrelevant in explaining the Iks. The subcultural approach may help us to understand much of the behavior of the Alorese, but adds little to comprehending the position of the lonely stranger in contemporary America. The tradition that stresses the concept of anomie can help to explicate America's high rate of crime, but does not inform us about what motivates a particular upper-class person such as Lizzie Borden or J. Pierpont Morgan.

Thus, in understanding a phenomenon as complex as psychopathy, it is clearly essential to achieve a closer collaboration between the various sciences: social scientists, physiological psychologists, geneticists, and psychiatrists must ally themselves in a joint attack.

A Neuro–Social Theory of Psychopathy

Physiological research on psychopaths—primarily of the criminal variety—has produced evidence that can be ignored only at the peril of a "reductionism" that attributes all behavior to social causes.

Through analysis of twin studies, the inheritability of slow cortical reflexes, examination of brain waves, and medical histories, physiologically oriented scientists have definitively established that a very high proportion of psychopaths suffer from neural disorders and various neural mechanisms that hinder their ability to learn from experience.

Yet, as I have argued, we cannot accept this impressive evidence as proof that physical causes create a psychopathic syndrome as some psychopaths do not have signs of a neural dysfunction, some "normal" people have a dysfunction but do not become psychopathic, and the exact relation between physical, genetic, intrauterine, and environmental factors as causes of the physical symptoms remains relatively unknown.

The environmentalist approach, on the other hand, offers some rather straightforward but, by no means conclusive, evidence.

- The vast majority of criminal psychopaths have undergone parental rejection, deprivation, or neglect during their childhood years. Some estimates suggest that all adult psychopaths have experienced severe emotional deprivation.
- Rejected children, however, do not necessarily turn into criminal psychopaths. Some become psychotics, alcoholics, sexual deviants, or other types of human beings who are labeled by society as deviant. Clearly, then, parental rejection does not in and of itself lead to psychopathy.
- Institutionalized children often exhibit the psychopathic syndrome. Again, however, the majority do not.
- General social factors—such as position in the lower social class, disruptions in life caused by major crises such as war, and increased technological complexity—certainly bear a relationship to criminal behavior in general. Although there has been a general increase in criminal behavior since the 1960s, we do not know how much of this phenomenon should be attached to psychopathic behavior *per se*.

Therefore, neither the environmental nor the "physical" theories of psychopathy offer a full explanation of this baffling pattern of behavior.

As virtually all studies of psychopaths have been conducted with institutionalized, usually criminal types, we lack information on the "normal" psychopath who operates well within the confines of his society's mores or laws.

A lack of information or an apparent contrast between different approaches should not lead us to despair in seeking the origins of psychopathy. The evidence warrants the belief that different hypotheses should be suggested about criminal psychopaths and "normal" psychopaths.

CRIMINAL PSYCHOPATHS

The evidence concerning criminal psychopaths suggests the following hypotheses:

1. *Severe rejection, but not total isolation, results in psychopathy.*
2. *Rejection, in combination with damage to such areas of the brain as the hypothalamus, results in psychopathy.*
3. *Rejection, in the absence of neural disorder, can result in psychopathy if other influences in the environment help to direct the person in a criminal direction.*

In the first case, severely rejected children—lacking love, rewards for socially approved behavior, and models with whom they could identify—do not develop a conscience, trust in others, or a willingness to consider the interests of other human beings. Such people end their lives as a "Billy the Kid" who neither understood nor cared about other human beings.

In the second case, a person might have a predisposition to criminal behavior because of a physiological inability to learn from punishment. When this is complemented by a failure of the parents to reward the child's conformity with love or to provide him with an environment where he learns the needs of others, the child would feel consistently rebuffed, he would never acquire the ability to empathize with others, and would doubt the sincerity of those who seek close relationships. He or she would not develop a conscience, but might instead develop into a Mary Bell.

In the third case, a rejected child might turn into a criminal psychopath if certain other conditions were present: (*a*) The child had a psychopathic model in his family; (*b*) The child experienced completely inconsistent punishments that leave him confused about what adult society expected; (*c*) The child was neglected and left unsupervised; (*d*) The child's environment provided other models—

"street" gang leaders, pimps, gangsters—who encouraged criminal behavior. If a person underwent all of these experiences, one would expect that a psychopathic individual might emerge.

Rejection, sometimes complemented by neural dysfunctions or general environmental experiences, seems to play a dominant role in the production of criminal psychopathy. These admittedly speculative hypotheses, I believe, reasonably synthesize the diverse and apparently conflicting discoveries about the criminal psychopath.

As few people have had the opportunity to study the "normal" psychopath, our hypotheses must remain even more speculative. Information from physiologists and from historians does, however, allow the consideration of several hypotheses.

"NORMAL" PSYCHOPATHS

The evidence suggests the following hypotheses, although only future research can substantiate them

1. *Normal psychopaths, like their criminal counterparts, have undergone a high degree of parental rejection.* Thus, they have little concern about others, a rudimentary conscience, and an inability to form close emotional relationships.

2. *Within industrialized societies, "normal" psychopaths are more intelligent than criminal psychopaths or the general population.* The greater intelligence of a J. Pierpont Morgan or a Hermann Goering allows them to adjust to if not lead their particular societies.

3. In certain subcultures, such as the Ik or the Alorese, psychopathic behavior is considered as normal. *This "normal" psychopathy is caused by a severe dislocation in the culture or by a cultural pattern that dictates that children should be raised without loving care.* It is clear, however, that a sheer lack of food will not transform people into psychopaths. Because of their original socialization, for example, the Uruguayan "cannibals" and concentration camp victims developed their own system of social stratification. The great majority did not become psychopaths, although they suffered from extraordinary deprivation.

4. According to twin studies and other sources, *"normal" psychopaths may have a greater genetic proclivity for their behavior than do criminal psychopaths.* Specifically, Mednick and Christiansen's studies have indicated that criminals raised in the upper classes in Scandinavia have less physically fearful responses to punishment than do those raised in a lower-class environment (Mednick & Christiansen, 1977). It is clear that membership in the lower class of any

nation—because of economic deprivation, or a higher tolerance for violent behavior, or discrimination, or a lack of opportunity—correlates with criminal behavior (Empey, 1978; Silberman, 1978; Sykes, 1978). Thus, a privileged member of the upper class avoids these social influences and may become a psychopath more often because of a specific genetic background.

5. As a corollary of this assumption, we can follow the evidence that indicates that *"normal" psychopaths have a higher level of cortical underarousal than do criminal psychopaths or the general population.* This may be caused by either physical or environmental forces.

6. It seems possible to suggest that *"normal" psychopaths have suffered less damage to their hypothalamic area than criminal psychopaths, but more than the general population.* "Normal" psychopaths seem relatively able to control outbursts of aggression, violence, and impulsive behavior. They can "turn on" charm, politeness, or manipulative behavior at will. Thus, they seem less likely than criminal psychopaths to have experienced diseases or injuries that have seriously impaired the regulatory area of the brain. As, on the other hand, "normal" psychopaths sometimes give way to extremely aggressive behavior—such as Lizzie Borden's axe killings of her parents—they possibly have suffered brain damage.

These hypotheses synthesize existing knowledge and are testable by current methods. Reasonable men can debate their validity, refute or support them by intelligently gathered data. To discuss them does not require unique assumptions about human nature or a dogmatic defense of physiological *versus* social causes of the problem.

Is Psychopathy on the Increase?

As I have already noted, some writers such as Norman Mailer, Alan Harrington, and Robert Smith believe that certain forces—well-advertised "hustler" styles of life, the decline of religion, the dominance of a "marketplace mentality"—have greatly increased the ranks of lonely strangers (Chapter 2).

Superficially, such assertions are absurd. In the 1930s, prison officials sometimes reported that 94% of their inmates were psychopaths (Sutherland & Cressy, 1960); today, by more careful diagnosis, no more than 10% would be so labeled. This apparent decline in criminal psychopaths is merely an artifact of the categorization process but it certainly lends little support to a belief that criminal psychopathy has increased. Although extremely difficult to measure, the rate of normal psychopathy—as judged by surveys, mental hospital commitments, contracts with mental health clinics—shows no marked increase between 1958 and 1980 (see Chapter 2).

One impressive but only suggestive source of evidence comes from the work of Charles Silberman (1978) who interviewed psychiatrists concerning the nature of their patients. Although not specifically focusing on the psychopath, Silberman noted some distinctive trends.

Silberman's review of representative court psychiatrists' records, in his opinion, indicates that young urban criminals more than in the past do not view their victims as fellow human beings. "Increasingly, psychiatric reports on juveniles arrested for murder are filled with phrases such as 'shows no feeling,' 'shows no remorse,' 'no discernible emotional reaction,' and 'demonstrates no relationship' [p. 63]." He recorded one psychologist's interview of a 14-year-old who had murdered a woman by setting her on fire:

Q: *Did you have a good night's sleep?*
A: *Yeah.*
Q: *. . . In the morning, what happened then? How did you feel? What was your mood? Did you feel upset at all, after you had poured gasoline on the woman and she burned to a crisp?*
A: *No. She didn't burn to a crisp.*
Q: *She didn't burn to a crisp?*
A: *No. She lived for a week before she died. It was just like on every other day. . . .*
Q: *Did you ever cry afterwards?*
A: *No. To tell you the truth, I had no feeling after I did it.*
Q: *No feelings at all?*
A: *No, I forgot all about it until they caught me [p. 63].*

Even without concluding that psychopathy is actually increasing, we must, however, acknowledge the fact that it represents a formidable threat at the present time. Society must face the complicated, perhaps insoluble problem of how the lonely stranger can be controlled or corrected. The answer may well be that "nothing works." I do not share such pessimism.

References

Baldwin, A., Kalhorn, A. L., & Breese, F. H. *Patterns of parental behavior. Psychological Monographs*, 1945, *3*:161–180.

Bandura, A. The social learning perspective. In H. Toch, (Ed.), *The psychology of crime and criminal justice.* New York: Holt, Rinehart and Winston, 1979.

Bandura, A., & Walters, A. *Adolescent aggression.* Chicago: Row Peterson, 1959.

Becker, H. S. *Outsiders*. New York: The Free Press, 1963.

Bender, L. Psychopathic behavior disorders in children. In R. Lindner and R. Seliger, (Eds.), *Handbook of correctional psychology*, New York: Philosophical Library, 1947.

Block, J. *Lives through times*. Berkeley: Bancroft, 1971.

Bowlby, J. *Maternal care and mental health*. Geneva, WHO, 1952.

Burgum, M. Constructive values associated with rejection. *American Journal of Orthopsychiatry*, 1940, *10:*319.

Clarke, A. D., & Clarke, A. D. B. *Early experience: Myth and evidence*. New York: Free Press, 1976.

Cleckly, H. *The mask of sanity*. New York: Grune and Stratton, 1975.

Clinard, M. B. *Sociology of deviant behavior*. New York: Holt, Rinehart and Winston, 1974.

Cohen, A. *Delinquent boys*. New York: The Free Press, 1955.

Craft, M. J. Psychopathic personalities. *The British Journal of Criminology*, 1961, *3:*217–230.

Craft, M. J. *Ten studies into psychopathic personalities*. Bristol: John Wright, 1965.

Craft, M. J., Stephenson, G., & Granger, C. A. A controlled trial of authoritarian and self-governing regimes with adolescent psychopaths. *American Journal of Orthopsychiatry*, 1964, *34:*543–554.

Davis, K. Extreme social isolation of a child. *American Journal of Sociology*, 1940, *45:*554–565.

Empey, L., *American delinquency*. Homewood, Ill.: Dorsey Press, 1978.

Erikson, K. T. *Wayward puritans*. New York: Wiley, 1966.

Evans, E. G. Behavior problems in children. *Child Care, Health, and Development*, 1976, *4:*417–418.

Field, M. Maternal attitudes found in 25 cases of children with primary behavior disorder. *American Journal of Orthopsychiatry*, 1940, *10:*293–311.

Friedlander, K. *The psychoanalytic approach to juvenile delinquency*. London: Kegan, Paul, Trench, and Tribner, 1947.

Freud, A., & Burlingham, D. *Infants without families*. New York: International Universities Press, 1944.

Gibbons, D. *Delinquent behavior*. Englewood Cliffs, New Jersey: Prentice-Hall, 1970.

Gibbons, D. *The criminological enterprise*. Englewood Cliffs: Prentice-Hall, 1978.

Goldfarb, W. Psychological privation in infancy and subsequent adjustment. *American Journal of Orthopsychiatry*, 1945, *15:*247–255.

Greenacre, P. Conscience in the psychopath. *American Journal of Orthopsychiatry*, 1945, *15:*495–509.

Greer, S. Study of parental loss in neurotics and sociopaths. *Archives of General Psychiatry*, 1964, 177–180.

Gregory, I. Studies of parental deprivation in psychiatric patients. *American Journal of Psychiatry*, 1958, *115:*432–442.

Haller, B. L. Some factors related to the adjustment of psychopaths on parole from a state hospital. Smith College Studies of Social Work, Vol. 13, 1942.

Harlow, H. F., & Harlow, M. Social deprivation in monkeys. *Scientific American*, 1962, *207* (No. 5):136–146.

Heaver, W. L. A study of 40 male psychopathic personalities. *American Journal of Psychiatry*, 1943, *100:*342–346.

Hirschi, T. *Causes of delinquency*. Berkeley: University of California Press, 1969.

Hochman, J. The mother's teeth. *Évolution Psychiatrique*, 1976, *41:*619–661.

Hollingshead, A., & Redlich, F. *Social class and mental illness,* New York: Wiley, 1958.

Jackson, D. *The etiology of schizophrenia.* New York: Basic Books, 1960.

Jenkins, R. L. The psychopathic or antisocial personality. *The Journal of Nervous and Mental Disease,* 1960, *131:*318–321.

Jenkins, R. L., & Hewitt, L. Types of personality structure in child guidance clinics. *American Journal of Orthopsychiatry,* 1944, *14:*84–94.

Jessor, R., & Jessor, S. L. *Problem behavior and psychological development.* New York: Academic Press, 1977.

Knight, E. A descriptive comparison of markedly aggressive and submissive children. Smith College Studies in Social Work, Vol. 4, 1933.

Levy, D. Primary affect hunger. *American Journal of Psychiatry,* 1937, *94:*643–652.

Lewis, H. *Deprived children.* London: Oxford, 1954.

Lindner, R. *Rebel without a cause.* New York: Grune and Stratton, 1944.

Lingdon, J., & Topia, F. Children who are cruel to animals. *Journal of Operational Psychology,* 1977, *8,* pp. 216–217.

Lipton, H., The psychopath. *Journal of Criminal Law, Criminology, and Police Science,* 1952, *40:*584–596.

Lowrey, L. G. Personality distortion and early institutional care. *American Journal of Orthopsychiatry,* 1940, *10:*576–586.

McCord, A., & McCord, W. *Urban social conflict.* St. Louis: Mosby, 1977.

McCord, J. Some child-rearing antecedents of criminal behavior in adult men. *Journal of Personality and Social Psychology,* 1979, *37*(9):477–486.

McCord, W. The personality of social deviants. In E. Norbeck, D. Price-Williams, and W. McCord (Eds.), The study of personality. New York: Holt, Rinehart and Winston, 1968.

McCord, W., & McCord, A. *American social problems.* St. Louis: Mosby, 1977.

McCord, W., McCord, J., & Gudeman, J. *Origins of alcoholism.* Stanford: Stanford University Press, 1960.

McCord, W., McCord, J., & Verden, P. Sexual deviance among lower-class adolescents. *International Journal of Social Psychiatry,* 1962, *8:*165–179.

McCord, W., Porta, J., & McCord, J. The familial genesis of psychosis. *Psychiatry,* 1962, *25:*60–71.

McCord, W., Zola, I., & McCord, J. *Origins of crime.* New York: Columbia University Press, 1959.

Maher, B. A. *Principles of Psychopathology.* New York: McGraw-Hill, 1966.

Merton, R. *Social theory and social structure.* New York: Free Press, 1957.

Mednick, S., & Christiansen, K. *Biosocial bases of criminal behavior.* New York: Gardner Press, 1977.

Megargee, E. G., & Bohn, M. J. *Classifying criminal offenders.* Beverly Hills: Sage, 1979.

Newell, W. H. The psychodynamics of maternal rejection. *American Journal of Orthopsychiatry,* 1937, *4:*387–401.

Oltman, J., & Friedman, S. Parental deprivation in psychiatric conditions. *Diseases of the Nervous System,* 1967, *20:*298–303.

Partridge, G. E. A study of 50 cases of psychopathic personality. *American Journal of Psychiatry,* 1928, *7:*953–973.

Perez-Sanchez, M. Considerations of psychopathy. *Revista Uruguaya de Psicoánlisis,* 1977 (October), 89–102.

Rabinovitch, R. D. A differential study of psychopathic behavior in infants or children. *American Journal of Orthopsychiatry,* 1951, *21:*231–237.

Robins, L. N. *Deviant children grown up.* Baltimore: Williams and Wilkins, 1966.

Rotenberg, M. Psychopathy and differential insensitivity. In R. Hare and D. Schalling (Eds.), *Psychopathic behavior.* New York: John Wiley, 1978.

Schactel, A. H., & Levi, M. B. Character structure of day nursery children as seen through the Rorschach. *American Journal of Orthopsychiatry,* 1945, *15:*213–222.

Schuster, R. Trust. *International Journal of Offender Therapy and Comparative Criminology,* 1976, *20*(2):17–20.

Sears, R., Maccoby, E., & Levin, H. *Patterns of child rearing.* Evanston: Row Peterson, 1956.

Sereny, G. *The case of Mary Bell.* New York: McGraw-Hill, 1973.

Sherman, M., & Henry, T. *The hollow folk.* New York: Crowell, 1933.

Short, J. F., & Nye, I. Extent of unrecorded delinquency. *Journal of Criminal Law and Criminology,* 1958, *49,* (No. 4):318–327.

Silberman, D. *Criminal violence, criminal justice.* New York: Random House, 1978.

Smith, R. J. *The psychopath in society.* New York: Academic Press, 1978.

Spitz, R. A. Hospitalism. In *The Psychoanalytic Study of the Child* (Vol. I). New York: International Universities Press, 1958.

Spitz, R. A. Autoeroticism re-examined. *The psychoanalytic study of the child* (Vol. XVII). New York: International Universities Press, 1962.

Sutherland, E. H., & Cressy, D. R. *Principles of criminology.* Philadelphia: J. P. Lippincott, 1960.

Sykes, G. *Criminology.* New York: Harcourt Brace Jovanovich, 1978.

Szurek, S. A. Notes on the genesis of psychopathic personality. *Psychiatry,* 1942, *5:*1–6.

Tor-Björn, H. *Psychiatrica Fennica,* 1974, 3, 241–248.

Ullman, L. P., & Krasner, L. *A physiological approach to abnormal behavior.* Englewood Cliffs: Prentice-Hall, 1969.

Virkunnen, M. The pedophiliac offender with anti-social behavior. *Acta Psychiatrica Scandinavica,* 1976, *3:*17–20.

Whiting, J., & Child, I. L. *Child training and personality.* New Haven: Yale University Press, 1953.

Wolberg, L. The character structure of the rejected child. *The Nervous Child,* 1944, *3:*74–88.

Wolfgang, M. *Delinquency in a birth cohort.* Chicago: University of Chicago Press, 1972.

Yarrow, M., Campbell, J. D., & Burton, R. V. *Child rearing.* San Francisco: Jossey-Bass, 1968.

IV

Changing
Psychopaths

Treatment of Adult Psychopaths

This disease is beyond my practice . . .
[Doctor, in *Macbeth*]

Conventional wisdom in the late twentieth century dictated that criminals, particularly adult psychopaths, could not be rehabilitated by any method. After reviewing several hundred studies of attempts to change criminals (including some psychopaths), Robert Martinson (1974) somberly commented, "With few and isolated exceptions, the rehabilitative efforts that have been reported so far have had no appreciable effect on recidivism [p. 216]." Accepting this reasoning, James Q. Wilson (1975), one of the most important writers on crime in the late twentieth century, concluded, "Wicked people exist. Nothing avails except to set them apart from innocent people [p. 10]."

Social policy reflected this scholarly pessimism. Many states reintroduced the death penalty. Some formerly progressive states, such as California and Maryland, abandoned "indeterminate" sentences, insisting instead that criminals should remain in jail according to arbitrary terms set by the state. This policy of mandatory sentences ensured that corrections officials had to release convicts on a specified date, regardless of whether they were ill or dangerous (Rubin, 1979). Rehabilitation, as an ideal, went into a precipitous decline.

In its place, some conservative politicians rejuvenated the concept of punishment ("just deserts"); others advocated a policy of sheer "incapacitation" (locking people up for a minimum of 3 years on the obvious assumption that during that period they could hurt nobody but themselves and their guards) (Wilson, 1975). Some scholars, convinced that many criminals, particularly psychopaths, "burn out" and cease their destructive behavior at older ages, toyed with the idea of incarcerating criminals until they were 50 (Morris, 1974). Even tentative advocates of this position, such as Norval Morris (1974), abandoned it when they considered the possible abuses of power: "If criminals are subjected to coercive control beyond that justified by the past injuries they have inflicted, then why not you, and certainly me? We find ourselves in the business of remaking man, and that is beyond our competence; it is an empyrean rather than an earthly task [p 70]."

Pessimism about rehabilitation particularly affected attitudes toward psychopaths, the most severe and presumably least tractable of offenders. Psychopathy has long been viewed as "untreatable," even when rehabilitative philosophies held sway in the 1950s. "As a probation or parole risk the psychopath's chances of failure are 100 percent," a psychologist summarized the general opinion about adult psychopathy. "There is no evidence to my knowledge that any psychopath has been cured by imprisonment—or by anything else [McCann, 1948, p. 131]." Another prison psychiatrist wrote: "The disease is of lifelong duration in almost every case [Darling, 1945, p. 14]." And Hervey Cleckly (1959), dealing primarily with private, noncriminal psychopathic patients, noted the general failure of psychotherapy and added, "All other methods available today have been similarly disappointing in well-defined adult cases of this disorder with which I am directly acquainted [p. 411]."

At times, pessimism about ever curing psychopaths has almost turned into a diagnostic standard: if an asocial person does not change his behavior, he is ipso facto a psychopath. Clearly, "incurability" must be eliminated from any diagnosis. First, it carries the danger of a "self-fulfilling" prophecy. Second, the very assertion—as it did when all schizophrenics were labeled as suffering from "incurable dementia praecox"—discourages innovative research.

Nonetheless, one must admit that most attempts to change the adult psychopath (a person over age 15) have been profoundly discouraging. Our society's primary response to criminal psychopaths has, of course, been imprisonment.

Incarceration

Institutionalizing the psychopath, even in environments specially designed to affect him or her, has almost universally failed. Incarceration does, of course, remove the psychopath from society but it accomplishes little more than that. And new generations continually appear on the scene, creating a great economic burden.

A British research team found that the average adult criminal diagnosed as psychopathic has already served seven terms in prison, twice the average of typical British convicts (Stafford-Clarke, Pond & Doust, 1951). Special prison environments created for the treatment of adult psychopaths in the United States have abysmally failed: about 70% of psychopaths commit another crime 36 months after their release (Kassenbaum, Ward, & Wilnet, 1971). In Switzerland, the special asylum of *Königsfelden* —which may have contained many types of criminals other than psychopaths—reported an overall failure rate of 60% within 2 years of the convicts' release (Mohr, 1947).

Some studies have indicated that incarceration has a serious disorganizing effect on psychopaths. Bauer and Clark (1976) traced psychopathic convicts and others during their prison careers. The longer the person remained in prison, the higher his or her score went on the "psychopathic deviance" section of the MMPI. Anne Newton (1980) produced an even more damning indictment of imprisonment and its effects on psychopaths. The rate of homicides committed by psychopaths who served prison terms and were eventually released increased eight times. At the very minimum, Newton found, "incapacitating Americans had done nothing to protect the public [p. 176]." At the same time, she noted that the abolition of training schools in Massachusetts during the 1970s had "little effect" on delinquency.

The impact of incarceration over a long period of time has seemed equally pernicious. Dynes (1979) traced the careers of psychopaths and a control group who had once been incarcerated. Although a minority of both groups, psychopaths accounted for 40% of all subsequent crimes. Over the 45-year period, the average psychopath had nine arrests, five convictions, and three subsequent incarcerations.

Mental hospitals have not proven a more acceptable alternative. Heaver (1943) reported that 60% of psychopaths treated in a mental hospital established a new criminal record within 2 years; Haller

189

found a recidivism rate among psychopaths to be 87% after only 6 months release from a mental hospital (Gibbons, Pond, & Stafford-Clarke, 1955). Watts and Bennett in Britain found no reason for excluding psychopathic patients from day hospitals but provided no evidence on the outcome of their cases (Watts & Bennett, 1978).

INCARCERATION AND TREATMENT

Many experiments have been conducted within prison or hospital environments in attempts to affect psychopaths. Group therapy of various types has been employed commonly. The army has used a "discussion group" variant with psychopaths discussing problems of personality development and relations to authority (Abrahams, 1947). Officials of the Chilicothe Reformatory established a "Little Alcatraz" for hard-core prisoners, many of them psychopaths, who underwent strict discipline but received group therapy (Glaser, 1978). San Quentin Prison used group therapy and psychodrama on psychopaths and, like all the other experiments, reported a high degree of success (Corsini, 1958). Despite claims that group therapy within prison had achieved success, few scholars have provided groups for comparison or follow-up studies. One exception is provided in the work of Craft and his colleagues (1964) comparing psychopaths who participated in self-governing group therapy and those who submitted to a more authoritarian type of individual counseling. After parole, the psychopaths committed twice as many offenses as did the control group.

Under the American tradition of justice, the great majority of all offenders are paroled after a certain period of incarceration. The evidence indicates that most criminal psychopaths will continue their depredations after serving a term of incarceration with or without group therapy.

Perhaps the most positive report on psychopath rehabilitation comes from Scandinavia, but even here the results are not propitious. Various Scandinavian countries have established small treatment facilities specifically designed to control psychopathic prisoners. These little prisons are humane, psychiatrically oriented, and designed both to teach the psychopath the consequences of his behavior but also to mitigate some of the rejecting, alienating experiences that he has undergone. In carefully controlled studies, however, it has been shown that the psychopathic prisons have the highest recidivism rate of other penal institutions within each nation. But this, in itself, would not be a condemnation as the "psychopathic" institu-

tions accept only the most severely asocial prisoners. Fifty-seven percent of prisoners at these institutions commit another crime after
their release (Bishop, 1975). This is, of course, a relatively high rate of
recidivism but one might find some small comfort in the fact that it is
the lowest rate of recidivism reported for released psychopaths in
Scandinavia.

The general failure of incarceration has led to a search for more
dynamic cures in group and individual psychotherapy outside of a
prison environment.

Group and Individual Psychotherapy

Attempts to treat the psychopath with psychoanalysis, psychotherapy, hypnotherapy, or other sophisticated techniques have produced highly contradictory results. Early studies reported in the literature dealt with only a handful of cases, did not utilize control or
comparison groups, often mixed together psychopaths with other
types of criminals, and failed to provide follow-up studies. Even when
interpreted most optimistically, these early studies produced highly
ambiguous results.

Lipton (1952) noted remarkable changes in psychopaths who received only intermittent counseling in prison: Robert Lindner (1945)
reported a high degree of success in hypnotizing and then treating
psychopaths; and another psychoanalyst, Schmideberg (1949), reported equally hopeful effects of psychotherapy. In contrast, Bromberg (1948) treated psychopaths in the Navy and reported less successful results, possibly because the psychopaths left the service and
terminated treatment before its completion; O'Malley reported that
"psychoanalysis as a therapeutic measure for the psychopathic personality . . . has proven a failure [O'Donnell, 1940, p. 15]"; and in
Germany only 1 of 23 psychopaths treated with psychoanalysis
showed any degree of improvement (Curran & Mallinson, 1944).

Other experimenters have claimed that their particular brands of
counseling radically affected presumed psychopaths. Yet, most have
failed to produce any convincing evidence. Samuel Yochelson and
Stanton Samenow (1977) treated some 240 inmates incarcerated for
reasons of insanity at St. Elizabeth's Hospital. They thought that all
of the patients were psychopaths because of the patients' propensity
to mistrust others and lie to them. The therapists attempted to break
down the lying pattern of the inmates and reveal to them their "true
selves." In essence, while calling the process "phenomenological," the

therapists used traditional methods of religious conversion. The inmates had to write down everything they did or thought. The therapists then spent from 10 hours to 5000 hours on each patient attempting to unveil their falsehoods. Although attracting wide publicity, the experimenters themselves claimed that they had made "functional, responsible" citizens out of only 13 of the original subjects—of course, at a huge cost.

Other attempts to provide intensive counseling for "violent, incorrigible adolescents" in a closed treatment center have made extravagant claims of success but have failed to provide replicable data (Agee, 1979).

Better controlled experiments have shown that almost any form of individual counseling is virtually useless for psychopaths. In France, Scharback (1977) noted that French psychopaths had proved impossible to treat with psychotherapy. In an extensive experiment where young American psychopaths were put into 18 different treatment groups in New York City, Robert Fishman (1977) found that none of them had a positive effect on recidivism.

A few psychotherapists believe that psychopaths proceed along a life path eventually leading to depression. They retain a hope that psychotherapeutic intervention at a later stage of life may produce sufficient depression in the psychopath so that he or she is willing to explore their inner life (Reid, 1978). So far no empirical evidence has been produced to substantiate this claim.

The preponderance of evidence, then, strongly suggests that psychopaths are immune to the possibly beneficial effects of psychotherapy or group therapy. This should not be surprising. The adult psychopath lacks the ability to identify with his or her therapist, does not possess the inner controls to adhere to such minor restrictions as keeping appointments, and is not plagued by the anxiety that pushes many neurotics into therapy. The lonely stranger generally believes that his or her problems are caused by society and not by their own inner dynamics.

At this point in history, traditional forms of psychotherapy have little relevance to the psychopath. Newer forms such as "transactional therapy" seem to have success with neurotic criminals but not the severely asocial or "manipulative" types (Jesness, 1975). Similarly, therapy based on "modeling" seems most successful with neurotic, passive individuals (Sarason & Glazer, 1973). The lack of success of traditional modes of therapy has led some experimenters to try "behavior modification," utilizing direct rewards or punishment.

Behavior Modification

Behavior modification with criminals has involved the use of either positive or aversive conditioning. Programs that emphasize positive conditioning may, as one example, operate a "token economy" within an institution. If inmates achieve certain "target goals" such as a lessening of aggressive behavior, they receive tokens that may be exchanged for privileges within the institution. Aversive conditioning involves the use of drugs, deprivation of privileges, electroshock, or other methods in an attempt to punish the offender in a systematic way for antisocial behavior.

Positive conditioning in a variety of forms has generally proved fairly successful with ordinary criminals (Gendrau & Ross, 1979). Elery Phillips (1973) reported on one such program where individuals were reinforced by a token economy for "appropriate" behavior. A follow-up study 1 year later compared the subjects to those who had undergone imprisonment or probation; the recidivism rate of the experimental group was 35% lower than the control groups. Jesness (1975) assigned 983 delinquents to two institutions, one of which emphasized behavior modification (a token economy). The program seemed particularly successful with offenders classified as "manipulators" than with others: recidivism rates were 25% lower for this group than for a similar group who had been assigned to the reformatory before the experiment took place. Other programs have reported equally impressive results (Doctor & Polakow, 1973; Douds, Englesjord, & Collingwood, 1977; Jenkins, 1974). And, as previously mentioned, psychopaths respond more favorably to direct monetary rewards (while in prison) than to punishment. While hopeful, these studies did not focus on psychopaths and often concentrated on offenders who were allowed to remain free in the community (Gendrau & Ross, 1979).

One study conducted by William Davidson and Michael Robinson (1975) centered on "hard core" chronic offenders who agreed to a "contract" of behavior modification. Eighteen months later, the arrest rate of the subjects had dropped from 3 to .46 a year. As this older teenaged group had been allowed to remain on the outside of prison, we do not know how many can be considered psychopathic.

The one specific study directed to psychopaths was based on the assumption that a blatant appeal to self-interest (through various rewards) and an attempt to demonstrate to the clients the discrepancy between the goals they sought and the means they used would prove particularly effective (Templeman & Wollersham, 1979). The researchers failed, however, to present any follow-up evidence to support their propositions.

Aversive therapy has also been applied to criminals in general and psychopaths in particular. For psychopaths, the rationale has often been that they fail to learn from normal punishments, as measured physiologically, and that more potent forms of punishment might change them. Sex offenders first received such treatment. On a voluntary basis, child molesters were shown pictures of young children. If they responded sexually to the pictures, they received electric shocks (Glaser, 1978). Supposedly, this reduced the recidivism rate, but the result might well be attributed to the voluntary nature of the program that attracted only those who most desired to change their behavior (Glaser, 1978).

Aversive conditioning has been widely used on prisoners defined as "untreatable," but the actual results have often been suppressed by correctional bureaucrats. In Iowa, prisoners who were regarded as having "severe behavior problems" were given apomorphine, a drug that induces continuous vomiting for up to an hour (Sykes, 1978). Prolixin has been used in various jurisdictions. This tranquilizer virtually paralyzes "unruly" prisoners. Anectine, a derivative of curare, temporarily cuts off breathing. It has been used in several prisons. While the inmate, usually a psychopath, stopped breathing, guards admonished him for his misbehavior (Mitford, 1973). The START program in Missouri strips intractable, assaultive, manipulative prisoners of all their rights and places them in strict segregation. If they obey their captors, the inmate gradually receives certain privileges on the assumption that he will learn new habits (Schenkenbach, 1973).

Obviously, such programs can force prisoners to conform while they are within the institution. There have been no long-run studies of the eventual effects of such "treatment." (The reader may, however, remember the case of one psychopath, Gary Gilmore, who was given massive doses of prolixin before his killings. His lawyers unsuccessfully tried to use this fact as a defense in his trial for murder.)

Outside the prison, some researchers have experimented with the use of electronic transmitters implanted in ex-convicts. They hope that the device will allow continued monitoring of the person and immediate deterrence if he deviates from society's norms (Schwitzgebel, 1971).

Aside from the fact that these techniques have no established effect on standard measures such as recidivism rates, they clearly raise visions of *1984* and *Clockwork Orange*. Quite naturally, various moral objections have been posed against aversive conditioning. Critics have attacked aversive therapy on various grounds: that it is an inhumane, cruel punishment disguised as rehabilitation; that it produces merely the "docility of a slave"; and that it has the potential for producing the "death of identity" (Sykes, 1978).

Although aversive conditioning may be criticized legitimately on both empirical and ethical grounds, positive conditioning offers some hope of changing psychopaths without destroying them. Rotenberg (1975) reasonably suggested that positive reinforcement—particularly aimed at making the psychopath aware of the suffering of others—might be reinforced by collective experiences and by stimuli that cater to the psychopath's need for exciting stimulation. Although unsupported as yet, positive experiments in behavior modification with psychopaths would appear to be constructive.

Drug Therapy

Various forms of drugs have been used not only for aversive conditioning, but with the definite hope that they could alter psychopaths permanently and not just by producing temporary conformity. As with any other human being, certain drugs have a calming, soothing effect on psychopaths that may make him or her more amenable to psychotherapy or, simply, custodial care.

The earliest experiments resulted in enthusiastic reports but, invariably, the long-term effects on the patient were not followed. Some prison psychiatrists found Pentothal Sodium and Sodium Amytal useful in establishing initial rapport with patients (Adatto, 1949; Freyhan, 1951; Train, 1947). Silverman (1944) reported that Dilantin Sodium affected the EEG waves of psychopaths and calmed them. Hill (1947) found that amphetamine sulfate improved the behavior of imprisoned psychopaths. Shovron (1947) noted that Benzedrine had little effect on English psychopaths, but Craft found that benactyzine positively affected "emotionally unstable" psychopaths (Craft, 1958; Tong, 1959). Lacking appropriate control groups and further studies, these early experiments did little more than boost the hopes of those who had faith in narcotherapy.

Uncontrolled studies of psychotropic drugs, often lacking the "double-blind" element, have also been conducted on psychopaths with ambiguous results. The findings of the best designed studies suggest that diphenylhydantoin (DPH) apparently has no effect on asocial behavior (Lefkowitz, 1969); stimulants, such as amphetamine, may reduce aggression but their long-term effect has not been studied (Kellner, 1978); in studies that were not double-blind, lithium apparently had a calming effect on psychopaths, and in controlled studies lithium reduced the level of overt aggression (Kellner, 1978).

Thus, lithium may tranquilize violent impulsiveness, but there is no indication that it affects psychopaths who are not subject to extreme aggressive tendencies or severe swings in mood (Kellner, 1978).

It is, of course, possible that new discoveries, such as the fact that the injection of adrenalin may increase the psychopath's excitement and his or her learning ability, may lead to dramatic changes in their current drug treatment. Greater rigor in drug therapy experiments and greater precision in the diagnosis of psychopaths should lead to a more rational "choice of drugs" in the treatment of the disorder. At this point in history, however, drugs appear to have little utility except in tranquilizing the extremely aggressive person.

Other Forms of Organic Treatment

Electric shock therapy, lobotomies, and mega-vitamin therapies have been used in a similarly cavalier and inconclusive way as have various drugs.

ELECTRIC SHOCK

Enthusiastic supporters of electric shock therapy have, at times, reported "beneficial" effects on psychopaths (Almansi & Impastate, 1947; Darling, 1945b). These studies, however, as did many others, suffered from the fact that many obviously nonpsychopathic people were included as subjects. In contrast, Green, Silverman, and Geil (1944) conducted a study of 24 psychopathic prisoners and noted that the majority of prisoners were unchanged by the experiment. These lack of results are not surprising, as electroshock therapy seems, at best, only to decrease the anxiety of patients: This is hardly a problem with psychopaths.

LOBOTOMIES

Lobotomies (the partial separation of other parts of the brain from prefrontal lobes) enjoyed a brief vogue in the 1940s but have been largely abandoned by contemporary psychiatrists. At most, psychiatrists employed this type of psychosurgery for severe "incurable" cases. Original reports, each limited to an operation on a single patient, indicated that surgical trauma to the prefrontal lobes decreased aggressive behavior (Banay and Davidoff, 1942; Freeman and Watts, 1945; Nilson, 1949). Darling and Sandall (1945) used this technique on 18 "antisocial" inmates of a mental hospital and reported that 17 improved. They did not specify their standards of improvement (1945). In contrast, Robin (1958) found no evidence in a controlled follow-up study that leucotomy beneficially affected psychopaths and Falconer and Shurr (1959), after a comprehensive review of the literature, concluded that any generalizations concerning psychosurgery await long-term follow-up studies. The possible side effects of such surgery—a high mortality rate and the possibility of turning the person into a "vegetable"—have curtailed the use of this technique.

NUTRITIONAL TREATMENT

In the 1970s, some researchers argued that a type of unspecified biochemical defect produces all forms of criminality and that it can be corrected by a nutritional regimen (Hippchen, 1976). Without defining their theoretical base or calling on research on psychopaths, some physicians administered massive doses of vitamins to psychopaths and other criminals. As during the period of initial enthusiasm over electroshock therapy and psychosurgery, advocates of this approach claimed huge successes. George von Hilsheimer (1977), for example, reported that they had achieved 86% "success" with incorrigible, uncooperative adolescents. They focused on the restoration of ACTH balance and a nutritional program. They left the definition of "success" undefined and did not measure recidivism rates. Until the time when researchers become more specific both theoretically and empirically, "mega-vitamin" programs remain a questionable approach to the problem of psychopathy.

Community Treatment

Standing at the opposite extreme from those who demand organic therapy for individuals are those who believe that changes in social groups—families, schools, or an entire community—may beneficially affect psychopaths. Experts in the area of "community treatment" advocate the use of family communication, the development of behavioral contracts, "diversion" from the usual court processes, and immediate responses to individual and family crises in the community as the best response to crime. A variety of programs have demonstrated the potential of this approach. Terry Wade (1977) showed that intervention in family crises can reduce recidivism rates for second offenders by a rate of 45%. Herbert Quay and Craig Love (1977) used counseling, job placement, and academic training with adolescents and, after a 1-year follow-up study, found that re-arrest rates were 8–40% lower than in a control group (1977). Marvin Bohnstedt's (1978) review of 11 California projects reported that recidivism had been reduced by 16–35% during a 6-month period. These experiments were conducted on young offenders and there is some doubt that psychopaths who commit more serious crimes were included in the samples. Bohnstedt's survey indicates, however, that community programs worked best with "high-risk" offenders, some of whom may have been psychopaths (1978). James Beck's review in 1979 confirms this conclusion (1979).

The most enthusiastic reports concerning community treatment have come from La Playa, Puerto Rico, an impoverished slum (Silberman, 1978). The Centro de Orientación y Servicios has provided medical services, community "advocates," counseling, and a variety of other services. The number of older delinquents has dropped by 85% since the center was organized in 1970. There has been no focus, however, on adult psychopaths, and the slum, while abysmally poor, is almost "benign" according to one close observer: "Although burglary and theft are widespread, robbery and murder are rare events; there is remarkably little criminal violence [Silberman, 1978, p. 446]." Whether the lessons of Puerto Rico can be translated to the harsher, more violent ghettos of New York, Chicago, or Phoenix remains an open question.

Thus, it appears that various forms of community treatment may be well adapted to ordinary crime and delinquency, but their relevance for adult psychopathy has yet to be established.

Incapacitation

Led by James Q. Wilson, a political scientist, some observers who have had little experience in criminal justice have thrown up their hands at any prospect of rehabilitating or even deterring criminals. They advocate locking up all felons for a long period of time in order to remove them from society. Recognizing the dismal results of past attempts, adult psychopaths would head the list of those who would be "incapacitated."

Using figures that could not be replicated, Wilson (1975) estimated (from a study by City College of New York Engineers, Shlomo and Reuel Shinnar) that the crime rate in New York State could be reduced by two-thirds if all felons received a sentence of 3 years. Wilson later said that such a sentence would decrease crime rates by 20%. Wilson did not advocate abandoning all efforts at rehabilitation or at making prisons more humane. Yet, he argued that the mere removal of criminals from the street would drastically reduce the crime rate.

Superficially, the argument sounds reasonable. Yet, it ignores the fact that new generations of criminals (and psychopaths) are continuously produced. Adherents of the position also refuse to recognize the impact of prison on inmates, usually, as we have seen, a negative effect. Wilson and his followers tend to minimize the economics of his program that would probably double the cost of imprisonment (Sykes, 1978). They also forget that criminal organizations, such as the Mafia, can easily recruit new members while some of their cohorts are in jail (Sykes, 1978).

In dealing with psychopaths, advocates of incapacitation may have some evidence to support their position. Contrary to some studies, Charles McCreary and Ivan Mensh (1977) showed that MMPI profiles of offenders aged 16 up to 85 indicated that male offenders decreased in impulsivity, asocial behavior, and "psychopathic deviance" as age advanced. It could be that psychopaths learn as age increases, or that aging itself has an effect in terms of responses to the MMPI. In any case, even advocates of incapacitation do not recommend holding prisoners until they are in the 60–85 year range.

International studies have shown that incapacitation would have little effect on adult psychopaths or even other criminals. Bilos (1974) in Australia tested Wilson's proposition that those states that incapacitate a large proportion of the criminal population in jails would have, all things being equal, a lower rate of crime. Investigating the crime rates in Australia, Canada, and America, Bilos found the obverse of Wilson's contention: The more people are incarcerated, the higher the rate of crime. One could, of course, argue that the higher rates of crime result in a higher imprisonment rate. In any case, the facts lend no support to the theory of incapacitation.

Empirical estimates in America have shown that mandatory sentences advocated by Wilson would have very little effect on crime rates. In Columbus, Ohio, for example, studies have shown that a policy of 5-year sentences for all felons would have failed to prevent the great majority of violent crimes (Conrad, 1980). A 3-year sentence for any felony would have prevented 11% of adult crimes and only

16% of 2892 violent crimes in 1973. The monetary cost of a 5-year sentence in Ohio would have been about $1.5 billion. The human cost is incalculable.

On the whole, therefore, the empirical evidence does not support claims that strict mandatory sentences would truly incapacitate the criminal or psychopathic population (Van Dine, Conrad, & Dinitz, 1978).

Milieu Therapy

Many have argued that the only possible cure for the adult psychopath is to lodge him or her in a nonpunitive, consistent environment that totally changes the circumstances of their life (Aichhorn, 1935; Granick, 1977; W. McCord & J. McCord, 1964; Redl & Wineman, 1954; Toch, 1980). Such an environment, so the argument goes, would allow the person to identify with noncriminal people, replacing mistrust with trust, reorienting the psychopath from his or her punitive view of others, and rewarding them consistently for socially acceptable behavior. Some experiments have been carried out on young people but relatively few on the adult psychopath. The reasons are obvious: The adult psychopath usually requires a maximum security institution, a huge staff of counselors as well as guards, and years of re-training. Society has seldom been willing to pay the exorbitant cost. And critics have complained that psychopaths were merely being pampered.

The previously mentioned Scandinavian experiments approached this ideal. In England, Maxwell Jones (1952, 1956) established "therapeutic communities" in mental hospitals that provided intensive group therapy and involved psychopathic patients. Tentative follow-up studies have suggested that these autonomous units reduced violence and recidivism (Rosow, 1955; Shostack, 1956).

Attempts at establishing a therapeutic community within a prison have often failed due to the opposition of guards, the public, or powerful convicts. An aborted experiment in California showed that a therapeutic environment within a prison reduced recidivism rates for released convicts for 1 year, but did not have an effect after 2 years (Robinson & Kevotkian, 1967). In America, only one institution has even approximated the goals of milieu therapy for adult psychopaths: Patuxent, Maryland. This unique environment has consistently received praise (Carney, 1978; Rapport, 1975), but has been hampered by changes in the law, a lack of money, and a dearth of public political support. Nonetheless, the institution has achieved a remarkably low recidivism rate (Carney, 1978).

From the outside, Patuxent Institution appears to be a typical, gray-walled, grim American prison. Inside, it contains those people who are defined by Maryland law as evidencing severe criminal tendencies, "emotional imbalance," and an inability to adjust to parole—in a phrase, the most "high-risk" prisoners. It, however, differs dramatically from other maximum security prisons in that each prisoner has a private cell; all are under the care of mental health professionals, and everyone receives psychotherapy.

Until the late 1970s, all prisoners served indeterminate sentences. They gradually worked their way up from the bottom tier, where they had no privileges, to the top tier where self-awareness and self-control were valued and prisoners were allowed extraordinary privileges. The institution involved a total treatment process including: (*a*) acceptance (including the roles they play in prison); (*b*) control; (*c*) support (psychotherapy for severe psychopaths); and (*d*) learning (rewards related to later school and job performance).

Patuxent reports a 7% recidivism rate for those who received full treatment—usually people who spent 4 years in the institution. Obviously, this is a far lower rate of crime than is usually reported for the average prison (some 80%). Other investigators have reported equal success in milieu treatment in mental hospitals (Liebman & Hudlund, 1974).

In 1977, the state of Maryland drastically changed the Patuxent experiment. The legislature removed indeterminate sentences, made participation at Patuxent voluntary, and cut funds for the institution. One psychologist who was deeply committed to the experiment sadly commented, "Our culture is becoming ever more punitive . . . and more reluctant to spend tax money on criminals. Those of us who still believe that criminals can and should be treated are clearly out of step [Carney, 1978, p. 283]." Yet, on the basis of experience at Patuxent, he triumphantly stated: "We know that even though the history of the treatment of sociopathy has been filled with frustration, it has in recent years also had many successes. The sociopath is not untreatable [Carney, 1978, p. 284]."

Conclusions

Any review of experiments in changing adult psychopaths must conclude with the somber observation that psychopaths have strongly resisted the great majority of attempts to alter their behavior:

- Incarceration, as such, does not reduce the rate of recidivism of adult psychopaths. The longer the imprisonment—unless it lasts well into old age—the more likely a released psychopath is to repeat or increase his crimes.
- Individual and group therapy appears to have little effect on adult psychopaths, despite the claims made on the basis of case histories or experiments.
- The effect, if any, of positive behavior modification on adult psychopaths has not been established, but it may offer some hope.
- Aversive conditioning experiments with adult psychopaths have generally failed.
- Drug therapy has had little demonstrable effect. Lithium perhaps serves to tranquilize extremely aggressive, moody psychopaths.
- The effects of other forms of organic treatment on adult psychopaths are discouraging, but largely unmeasured.
- The utility of community treatment for adult psychopaths has yet to be confirmed.
- The incapacitation of adult psychopaths through the imposition of mandatory sentences seems to have little effect on general crime rates.
- Milieu therapy with adult psychopaths appears to reduce their recidivism rate. The very few experiments with this approach have, however, been hampered by a lack of money, changes in the law, and punitive attitudes on the part of politicians and the public. In the future, it may well be that an extended use of milieu therapy for adult psychopaths may register resounding successes.

At this point in history, however, the preponderance of evidence indicates that most experiments in changing the adult psychopath have either failed or been curtailed by circumstances beyond the control of the researchers. As a result, the focus of attention has shifted to the child defined as psychopathic (below the age of 15) and attempts to deflect the person from his or her psychopathic pattern early in life.

References

Abrahams, J., & McCorkle, L. Group psychotherapy at an Army rehabilitation center. *Diseases of the Nervous System*, 1947, *8:*50– 62.

Adatto, C. Observations on criminal patients during narcoanalysis. *Diseases of the Nervous System*, 1947, *8:*82– 92.

Agee, V. L. *Treatment of the violent incorrigible adolescent.* Lexington: Lexington, 1979.

Aichhorn, A. *Wayward youth.* New York: Viking, 1935.

Almansi, J., & Impastate, D. The use of electro-shock therapy in correctional institutions. In R. Lindner and R. Seliger (Eds.), *Handbook of correctional psychiatry.* New York: Philosophical Library, 1947.

Banay, R. S., & Davidoff, L. Apparent recovery of a sex psychopath after lobotomy. *Journal of Criminal Psychopathology*, 1942, *4:*59– 66.

Bauer, G., & Clark, J. Personality deviance and prison incarceration. *Journal of Clinical Psychology*, 1976, (April), 6, 118– 120.

Beck, J. L. An evaluation of federal community treatment centers. *Federal Probation*, 1979 (Sept.), *43:*118– 121.

Bilos, D. Crime and the use of prisons. *Federal Probation*, 1974 (June), *43:*311– 314.

Bishop, N. Nordic criticism of treatment ideologies. In *Nordic criminal policy and criminology.* Stockholm: Scandinavian Council for Criminology, 1975.

Bohnstedt, M. Answers to three questions about juvenile diversion. *Journal of Research in Crime and Delinquency*, 1978 (Jan.), *11:*410– 420.

Bromberg, W. Dynamic aspects of psychopathic personality. *Psychoanalytic Quarterly*, 1948, *17:*58– 70.

Carney, F. L. Inpatient treatment programs. In W. H. Reid (Ed.), *The psychopath.* New York: Brunner/Mazel, 1978.

Cleckly, H. *The mask of sanity.* St. Louis: Mosby, 1959.

Conrad, J. P. Curing the American disease. In E. Bitner and S. L. Messinger (Ed.), *Criminology review yearbook.* Beverly Hills: Sage, 1980.

Corsini, R. J. Psychodrama with a psychopath. *Group Psychotherapy*, 1958, *11:*33– 39.

Craft, M., Stephenson, G., & Granger, C. A controlled trial of authoritarian and self-governing regimes with adolescent psychopaths. *American Journal of Orthopsychiatry*, 1964, *34* (No. 3).

Craft, M. Mental disorder in the defective. *Mental Health*, 1958, *17:*95– 99.

Curran, D., & Mallinson, P. Psychopathic personality. *Journal of Mental Science*, 1944, *90:*266– 286.

Darling, H. F. Definition of psychopathic personality. *Journal of Nervous and Mental Disease*, 1945, *101:*121– 126. (a).

Darling, H. F. Shock treatment of the psychopath. *Journal of Nervous and Mental Disease*, 1945, *101:*247– 250. (b)

Darling, H. F., & Sandall, J. W. Treatment of the psychopath. *Journal of Clinical and Experimental Psychopathology.* 1953, *13*, Sept., 3.

Davidson, W., & Robinson, M. Community psychology and behavior modification. *Correctional and Social Psychiatry*, 1975 (June).

Doctor, A. M., & Polakow, R. L. A behavior modification program for adult probations. Mimeo, 1973.

Douds, A., Englesjord, M., & Collingwood, T. R. Behavior contracting with youthful offenders and their parents. *Child Welfare*, 1977 (June).

Dynes, T. P. Managing the causes of sociopathic felons. Ph.D. dissertation, Ohio State University, 1979.

7. Treatment of Adult Psychopaths

Falconer, M. A., & Shurr, P. Surgical treatment of mental illness. *Recent Progress in Psychiatry* (Vol. 3). New York: Grove Press, 1959.

Fishman, R. An evaluation of eighteen projects. In Sir Leon Radowicz and Marvin Wolfgang (Eds.), *Crime and justice* (Vol. III). New York: Basic Books, 1977.

Freeman, W., & Watts, J. W. Prefrontal lobotomy. *American Journal of Psychiatry*, 1945, *101:*739–748.

Freyhan, F. A. Psychopathology of personality functions in psychopathic personalities. *Psychiatric Quarterly*, 1951, *25:*458–471.

Gendrau, P., & Ross, B. Effective correctional treatment. *Crime and Delinquency*, 1979, *14:*100–115.

Gibbons, T. C. N., Pond, D. A., & Stafford-Clarke, D. A follow up study of criminal psychopaths. *British Journal of Delinquency*, 1955, *6:*6.

Glaser, D. *Crime in a changing society.* New York: Holt, Rinehart and Winston, 1978.

Glaser, E., & Chiles, D. An experiment in the treatment of youthful habitual offenders. *Journal of Clinical Psychopathology*, 1948, *3:*376–425.

Granick, A. Management of character disorders in a hospital setting. *American Journal of Psychotherapy*, 1977, *5:*318.

Green, E., Silverman, D., & Geil, G. Petit mal electro shock therapy of criminal psychopaths. *Journal of Criminal Psychopathology*, 1944, *5:*667–695.

Heaver, W. L. A study of 40 male psychopathic personalities. *American Journal of Psychiatry*, 1943, *100:*342–346.

Hill, D. F. Amphetamine in psychopathic states. *British Journal of Addiction*, 1947, *44:*50–54.

Hilsheimer, G. von Correcting the incorrigible. *American Laboratory*, 1977, *6:*180.

Hippchen, L. J. Biomedical approaches to offender rehabilitation. *Offender Rehabilitation*, 1976 (Fall),

Jenkins, W. *The post prison analysis of criminal behavior.* Montgomery, Alabama: Rehabilitation Research Foundation, 1974.

Jesness, C. F. Comparative effectiveness of behavior modification and transactional analysis programs for delinquents. *Journal of Consulting and Clinical Psychology*, 1975, *8:*411–415.

Jones, M. *Social psychiatry.* London: Tavistock, 1952.

Jones, M. The concept of the therapeutic community. *American Journal of Psychiatry*, 1956, *112:*647–650.

Kassenbaum, G., Ward, D., & Wilnet, D. *Prison treatment and parole survival.* New York: Wiley, 1971.

Kellner, R. Drug treatment of personality disorders and delinquents. In W. Reid (Ed.), *The psychopath.* New York: Brunner/Mazel, 1978.

Lefkowitz, M. Effects of diphenylhydantoin in disruptive behavior. *Archives of General Psychiatry*, 1969, *20:*418–421.

Liebman, M. D., & Hudlund, D. A. Therapeutic community and milieu therapy of personality disorders. In J. R. Lion (Ed.), *Personality disorders.* Baltimore: Williams and Wilkins, 1974.

Lindner, R. *Rebel without a cause.* New York: Grune and Stratton, 1944.

Lipton, H. The psychopath. *Journal of Criminal Law, Criminology and Police Science*, 1952, *40:*584–596.

McCann, W. H. The psychopath and the psychoneurotic in relation to crime and delinquency. *Journal of Clinical and Experimental Psychopathology*, 1948, *9:*551.

McCord, W., & McCord, J. *The psychopath.* Princeton: Van Nostrand, 1964.

McCreary, C. P., & Mensh, I. Personality factors associated with age in law offenders. *Journal of Gerontology*, 1977, *6:*405–410.

Martinson, R. What works. *The Public Interest*, 1974 (June), (No. 36), *9:*114–126.

Mitford, J. *Kind and usual punishment*. New York: Knopf, 1973.

Mohr, P. Die Forensiche Bedetung der Psychopathen. *Schweiz. Arch. Neurol Psychiat.*, 1947, *60:*

Morris, N. The failure of imprisonment: Toward a punitive philosophy. *Michigan Law Review*, 1974, *72:*305–315.

Newton, A. The effects of imprisonment. *Criminal Justice Abstracts*, 1980, *12* (No. 1), 405–411.

Nilson, L. Frontal lobotomy in Sweden. *Nursing Times* (London), 1949, *45, 22:*447–451.

O'Donnell, L. P. The problems of treating psychopaths. *Psychiatric Quarterly*, 1940, *14:*248–254.

Phillips, E. Behavior shaping works for delinquents. *Psychology Today*, 1973 (June),

Quay, H. C., & Love, C. T. The effect of a juvenile diversion program on rearrests. *Criminal Justice and Behavior*, 1977 (Dec.), 5, 410.

Rapport, J. A. Patuxent revisited. *Bulletin of the American Academy of Psychiatry and the Law*, 1975 (March), 4, 302–314.

Redl, F., & Wineman, D. *Controls from within*. Glencoe, Illinois: Free Press, 1954.

Reid, W., *The psychopath*. New York: Brunner/Mazel, 1978.

Robin, A. A. A controlled study of the effects of leucotomy. *Journal of Neurology, Neurosurgery and Psychiatry*, 1958, 21:51–57.

Robinson, J., & Kevotkian, M. Intensive treatment project. Research Report 27, California Department of Corrections, January, 1967.

Rosow, H. M. Some observations on group therapy with prison inmates. *Archives of Criminal Psychodynamics*, 1956, *1.*

Rotenberg, M. Psychopathy, insensitivity, and sensitization. *Professional Psychiatry*, 1975, *3:*97–99.

Rubin, S. New sentencing proposals and laws in the 1970's. *Federal Probation*, 1979, *2:*80–89.

Sarason, I. G., & Glaser, V. J. Modeling and group discussion in the rehabilitation of juvenile delinquents. *Journal of Consulting Psychology*, 1973, 200–205.

Scharback, H. The difficult problem of therapeutic responsibility. *Annales Medico-Psychologiques*, 1977, *5:*307–319.

Schenkenbach, A. F. START. Paper presented at Conference on Behavior Control in Total Institutions, New York, 1973.

Schmideberg, M. The analytic treatment of major criminals. *International Journal of Psychoanalysis*, 1949, *30:*197.

Schwitzgebel, R. K. *Development and legal regulation of coercive modification techniques with offenders.* Rockville, Maryland: National Institute of Mental Health, Center for Studies of Crime and Delinquency, 1971.

Shead, M. The effect of lithium on impulsive aggressive behavior in men. *American Journal of Psychiatry*, 1976, *133:*125–129.

Shostack, N. Treatment of prisoners at the California medical facility. *American Journal of Psychiatry.* 1956, *112:*821–824.

Shovron, J. J. Benzedrine in psychopathy and behavior disorders. *British Journal of Addiction*, 1947, *44:*58–63.

Silberman, C. *Criminal justice, criminal violence.* New York: Random House, 1978.

Silverman, D. E.E.G. and the treatment of criminal psychopaths. *Journal of Criminal Psychopathology*, 1944, *5:*439–466.

Stafford-Clarke, D., Pond, D., & Doust, J.W.L. The psychopath in prison. *British Journal of Delinquency*, 1951, *2:*117– 129.

Sykes, G. *Criminology.* New York: Harcourt Brace Jovanovich, 1978.

Templeman, T. L., & Wallersham, J. P. A cognitive-behavioral approach to the treatment of psychopathy. *Psychotherapy*, 1979, *16:*416– 421.

Toch, H. An interdisciplinary approach to criminal violence. *Journal of Criminal Law and Criminology*, 1980, *71:*216– 230.

Tong, J. Cited by M. Craft, in Psychopathic personalities. *British Journal of Criminology*, 1961 (Jan.) *1:*14.

Van Dine, S., Conrad, J. P., & Dinitz, S. *Restraining the wicked.* Lexington, Ma.: Heath, 1978.

Wade, T. C. A family crisis intervention approach to diversion from the criminal justice system. *Juvenile Justice Journal*, 1977, *7:*230– 325.

Watts, F., & Bennett, D. Social deviance in a day hospital. *British Journal of Psychiatry*, 1978, *6:*109– 125.

Wilson, J. Q. *Thinking about crime.* New York: Basic Books, 1975.

Wodarski, J. S., & Pedi, S. The empirical evaluation of the effects of different group treatment strategies. *Journal of Clinical Psychology*, 1978, *138:*415– 423.

Yochelson, S., & Samenow, S. The change process. *The criminal personality* (Vol. 2). New York: Jason Aronson, 1977.

8

Treatment of Child Psychopaths

Punishing teaches the child only how to punish; scolding teaches him how to scold. By showing him that we understand, we teach him to understand; by helping him, we teach him to help; by cooperating, we teach him to cooperate.

Ernst Papanek, late Director of the Wiltwyck School; Federal Probation, June 1953

In 1975, young people accounted for a disproportionate amount of American crime: 57% of those who were arrested were below the age of 25; 42% under 21; and 26% under age 18. Young children between 11 and 14 committed more crimes than adults aged 30–34 (FBI, 1976). Teenagers were arrested approximately 25 times more often than people over 65 (FBI, 1976). Juveniles under 18 made up 43.5% of all people arrested for serious crimes (FBI, 1976).

Clearly, juvenile delinquency presented a severe problem to the United States. Whether accounted for merely by the invention of the concept of juvenile delinquency—a relatively new idea— or the decline of the American family, the effects of the mass media, the impact of urbanization, less maturity and greater physical strength, or many other factors, there can be no doubt that juvenile crime had emerged as a major dimension of American life (Empey, 1978).

Moreover, during the 1960s and 1970s, the rate of juvenile arrests went up strikingly, particularly for violent crimes. Between the years 1960 and 1975 the rate of arrests for violent crimes by juveniles increased by 293% (FBI, 1976). Part of this increase can be attributed to the growth in the youth population during the same period. Nonetheless, when adjusted by census figures, the rate of arrest per 100,000 juveniles went up by 123% for violent crimes and 57% for all index crimes during the period 1960–1975 (Empey, 1978). This alarming increase (which included an unknown number of child psychopaths) prompted startling changes in the American approach to juvenile delinquency.

Convinced by evidence that labeling and incarceration perpetuate delinquent tendencies, some jurisdictions responded by attempting to protect young people from the more deleterious effects of the justice system. Massachusetts abolished all reform schools in the 1970s and attempted to provide "community treatment." New York and California innovated with a number of experiments that would "divert" young people from the criminal justice system and, indeed, offered them counseling, job training, and family therapy.

Most Americans, however, responded by calling for a more punitive approach (Rubin, 1979). Police forces increased. The age at which a juvenile could be tried as an adult generally went down. Critics attacked the entire juvenile court system and called for its severe modification, if not abolition. The concept of rehabilitation for delinquents went into decline while a philosophy of retributive justice gained adherents. Optimistic beliefs in the efficacy of rehabilitation were seriously tarnished.

This emphasis on the punitive treatment of delinquents gained its momentum from several sources. One impetus, of course, was the actual increase in violent juvenile crime, which in certain urban areas created an atmosphere of fear and loathing of youths. Some people formed vigilante groups; others stopped wearing gold chains or rings, and the majority carefully guarded their purses and watchfully eyed potential "crazies" on subways or in parks. To some degree this fear had a basis in fact. Often, however, the mass media inadvertently "brought coals to Newcastle" by publicizing a particularly vicious slashing, murder, or rape. (Thus, New York City gained a reputation as the crime capitol of the world, although in fact it ranked thirteenth from the top in violent crimes per capita committed in American cities in 1980.)

Various scholars in the 1970s also contributed to the punitive atmosphere by asserting that their well-publicized research suggested the impossibility of rehabilitating delinquents. Robert Martinson (1974) applied his doctrine that "nothing works" with equal vitriol to delinquents as well as adult criminals. James Q. Wilson's (1975) belief that all felons should be locked up by determinate sentences struck a response in the apprehensive public. Yochelson and Samenow (1977) gained publicity with their pronouncement that criminals are born, not made. In her review of the Cambridge–Somerville Study (a large-scale attempt to prevent delinquency), Joan McCord (1978) went so far as to claim that treatment programs actually increased the rate of crime, alcoholism, and other forms of deviance 30 years after the program had been in operation. "The message seems clear," she concluded, "intervention programs risk damaging the individuals they are assigned to assist [p. 209]."

These assertions have been attacked by a number of other scholars (Vosburgh & Alexander, 1980). Only 12 out of 650 of the Cambridge–Somerville subjects, for example, actually received the originally planned treatment, and they appeared to benefit from it (McCord, McCord, & Zola, 1959). Nonetheless, during the 1970s, various messengers of gloom prevailed over the opposition of moderate, more careful critics.

In the 1970s, 500,000 American children were put in jail each year while another 500,000 served time in detention facilities. In some areas, as many as 43% of such children had not committed any crime, but the courts regarded them as in need of supervision (Chavkin, 1978).

If the juvenile crime rate is actually increasing—as it seems to be—and if methods of reformation fail with ordinary delinquents—as some scholars purport—what is the fate of the child psychopath? Is he or she as unamenable to treatment as the adult counterpart? Here, we must turn to the best empirical evidence in order to reach even tentative conclusions.

Incarceration

Until the middle of the nineteenth century, juvenile criminals were whipped, branded, transported to another country, or hung for their crimes. As a humane, progressive step, America introduced "training schools" or reformatories during the 1840s. Whereas these reform schools enforced severe discipline, they also aimed at educating and rehabilitating the child. The first reformatory, the Lyman School of Massachusetts, was established in 1846; we have studied its effects between 1952 and 1980 (see Chapter 9). A program that began with immense optimism ended dismally in 1973 when Massachusetts closed the Lyman School as well as all other juvenile training schools. After more than a century of experiments with juvenile prisons, most authorities had concluded that they encouraged rather than cured the problem of crime. Jerome Miller, director of youth services in Massachusetts, had tried to correct the deficiencies of the schools (or jails) but concluded that it would be better to abolish them and place all juvenile delinquents in a network of community services (Ohlin, Miller, & Coates, 1977).

Concurrently, in 1974, a Texas court ordered two training schools closed because of their brutality (Morales vs. Turman, 1974). These schools primarily enrolled "status offenders" of a young age. An "unruly" child could be tear-gassed in his cell or "racked" (hit in the stomach while standing against a wall). If they behaved according to the schools' rules, they spent their time digging holes with pickaxes and refilling them. The boys were punched or kicked for such "offenses" as speaking Spanish. The Texas courts ended the brutality and dehumanization of these children.

Some juvenile institutions have tried to enforce conformity on child psychopaths. Unfortunately, we do not possess many well-documented reports of these experiments. The research that has appeared dealt only with a handful of cases at the Hawthorne Cedar-Knolls School and in the children's unit of a mental hospital (Slawson, 1943; Wolfe, 1942). In both cases, officials of the schools attempted to impose strict conformity on the children by forcing them to adhere to an unbending regimen. Wolfe examined 17 "psychopathic" cases and found that only 2 could be considered as fully recovered. Even these two were later redefined as nonpsychopathic (Wolfe, 1942).

Although not dealing solely with child psychopaths, Charles Murray and Louis Cox (1978) argued that incarceration can be useful, particularly with chronic offenders. They suggested that researchers should use a standard of "suppression"—a reduction in arrest rate—rather than measures of an absolute end to criminal behavior. Using a large sample from Illinois, Murray and Cox found that incarceration rather than probation effectively "suppressed" arrest rates, particularly when used early in life and with chronic offenders. (We can assume from prior evidence that many child psychopaths could be found in the ranks of chronic offenders.) Over a period of 2 years, the researchers noted that the rate of re-arrest for children on probation went down by 36.6% while it decreased by 68.4% among those sent to a reformatory.

Superficially, this study would appear to indicate the efficacy of incarceration and to contradict the great majority of findings. The work of Murray and Cox, however, has been severely criticized by such scholars as Richard McCleary and Michael Maltz who oppose it on statistical grounds. They also argue that extraneous factors, such as the age of the various groups, may have had an impact rather than the particular policy adopted (McCleary, 1980; Maltz, 1980).

On balance, then, most studies indicate that incarceration has no effect on the recidivism rate of child psychopaths or other types of juvenile delinquents (Bartollas, Miller, & Dinitz, 1976; Jessness, 1970; Kassenbaum, Ward, & Wilner, 1971; Lipton, Martinson, & Wilks, 1975). Whether due to a lack of resources or the nature of the institution itself, the typical reform school teaches a child new methods of crime, a greater hatred of authority, and an increased feeling of rejection (Empey, 1978). The cure, if any, for child psychopathy must be found in a different approach.

Group and Individual Psychotherapy

Early psychotherapists conducted long-term, and often heroic experiments on changing child psychopaths through the process of patient individual therapy. Acting on the assumption that child psychopaths lacked a loving environment (Levy, 1937), some therapists went so far as to take such children into their homes. One therapist assumed the role of a foster parent for a child psychopath (Stanley King, reported in Lippman, 1949). Guiltless and aggressive, the boy refused to talk to his psychotherapist–foster parent for a long period of time. Eventually, however, he sought affection, developed a conscience, and went on successfully to college. Other psychotherapists dealing with child psychopaths in a more conventional manner reported more limited success (Eisner, 1945; Friedlander, 1947; Slawson, 1943). A review of eight such studies showed that seven could report at least some improvement in these children and have attributed it to psychotherapy or other forms of counseling (Levine & Bornstein, 1972). These encouraging results were, however, often based upon only one or two subjects who had received particularly intensive attention.

More recent studies have provided little reason to believe that individual psychotherapy, psychoanalysis, counseling, or group therapy has a lasting effect on large numbers of child psychopaths.

Psychotherapy seems particularly futile in the treatment of child psychopaths (Cima, Montbarrio, & Venuti, 1968; Bender, 1947; Lippman, 1949; Morrison, 1978; Szurek, 1949; Whitaker, 1946). Szurek (1949) had long experience with child psychopaths in San Francisco and concluded that psychotherapy could not work because the psychopathic child has such meager loyalties to others. Dismayed by the children's total lack of love, Lauretta Bender (1947) tried to treat hundreds of cases in New York, but failed. Such children could not form emotional bonds. "Once the defect is created," Bender wrote, "It cannot be corrected [p. 367]."

PREVENTIVE COUNSELING

Large-scale attempts at sporadic counseling of delinquents have also failed. One of the most important of these programs, the Cambridge–Somerville Study, offers an example. Begun in 1935 as an experiment in the prevention of delinquency by Richard Clarke Cabot, the project aimed at providing counseling over a 10-year period for a group of lower-class boys. In addition, the program offered school, medical, and psychological services. The children were divided into a treatment group and a control group (which did not receive more than the usually available community services). Each group contained boys who had been predicted to become delinquent and those who were predicted to be nondelinquent.

The depression of the 1930s and the impact of World War II prevented the complete fulfillment of Cabot's goal. Very few children received the treatment he envisioned and a high rate of turnover among counselors often hindered a lasting relationship with the boys. After completion of the project, various analysts concluded that the project had no significant impact on the character or criminal rates of most of the treated subjects once they became adults (J. McCord, 1978; W. McCord, J. McCord, and J. Gudeman, 1960; W. McCord, J. McCord, and I. Zola, 1959; Powers and Witmer, 1951).

Edwin Powers and Helen Witmer (1951) noted that the project had little effect on children who were psychopaths. Typical of these boys was one whom Witmer described in this fashion: "He could not form a close relationship with anybody. He stole continuously . . . and lied about it with no sense of guilt [p. 140]." Such children, Witmer concluded, could not be helped by the intermittent counseling which the project provided: "The whole personality was organized against interpersonal relationships; to have been beneficial the counselors

would have had to effect a complete personality change in these boys
[p. 559]."

Ten years later, McCord, McCord, and Zola (1959) followed up the
Cambridge– Somerville Study and reached the same conclusion: The
treatment, such as it was, had little discernible effect on adult criminality, alcoholism, or mental disorder. A few children did, in fact,
receive long-term intensive counseling and they seemed to benefit,
particularly when the counseling began at an early age.

Thirty years after the termination of the project, J. McCord (1978)
conducted another follow-up study of the Cambridge– Somerville
group. Her results, as I have mentioned, were even bleaker: She
claimed that the treatment in fact might have harmed some boys.
Her conclusions were based on probation files, public records, and
mailed questionnaires. She located 95% of all subjects, and 54% of
the treatment group and 60% of the control group had mailed back
questionnaires. Critics have claimed that the researcher did not continue the original matching process, that the responses to mailed
questionnaires contradicted official records, and that the project did
not truly test the effects of treatment as only 12 boys received it
(Vosburgh & Alexander, 1980). Others have suggested that the control
group may have received some special type of treatment and that this
factor was not examined (Messinger & Bittner, 1979). Certainly, this
research does not establish that the Cambridge– Somerville project
damaged people. Taken in concert with earlier studies, however, it
offers no evidence that the Cambridge– Somerville project helped delinquents or aided in eliminating the problems of child psychopaths.

COUNSELING

With only a few tentative exceptions, other studies have failed to
demonstrate the effectiveness of counseling in reducing recidivism
rates or achieving other beneficial results. The California Department
of Corrections experimented with reducing the caseload of parole
officers so that they could expend more time on the counseling and
supervision of their prisoners. Lower caseloads did not produce lower
recidivism rates (Adams, 1970). The Los Angeles County Probation
Department found better results with lower caseloads, but both the
California Youth Authority and the Federal Department of Probation
failed to confirm these results (Empey, 1978; Lipton, Martinson, &
Wilks, 1975). None of these studies answered this question: What
would have happened if nothing had been done to these children?

Thus, counseling programs of one type or another have yet to establish their utility for ordinary delinquents. They have certainly not provided evidence that the young psychopath can be cured by such methods. As Helen Witmer (1951) remarked, alteration of the behavior of child psychopaths may require an extensive change in the child's total personality. Some attempts in this direction have been made by those who advocate behavior modification.

Behavior Modification

A handful of experiments in positive conditioning have been carried out on the average delinquent, but none on the child psychopath. Generally, the results have seemed hopeful, if marred by methodological faults in the various studies. Alvord (1971) reported training parents and children, using a "token economy," to teach the children to avoid delinquent behavior. He claimed a 75% rate of success, but based this report merely on what the parents said.

Schwitzgebel (1974) "shaped" delinquents by reinforcing them with money, food, or other rewards. In a 3-year follow-up study, he reported that the "shaped" delinquents spent less time in correctional institutions than a matched control group. His total sample was, however, composed of only 20 subjects and a comparison group of another 20. Other researchers have examined the impact of behavioral intervention in families and reported less recidivism within a period of 6–18 months (Alexander & Parsons, 1973). Child psychopaths were apparently not included in these studies.

Aversive conditioning has also been widely used on delinquents. SEED, a Florida institution for juvenile drug addicts, subjected its inmates to "rap" sessions that lasted from 10 A.M. to 10 P.M. Speaking over a microphone, a staff member addressed some 500 children at a time. In a bullying and humiliating way, he encouraged each child to confess his sins over the public address system. SEED rewarded children who informed on each other. Lasting effects have yet to be established (Chavkin, 1978).

The Farrall Company of Grand Island, Nebraska produces a variety of remote control shock instruments. The devices can be used on delinquents who are 300 ft away and convey a shock of up to 800 volts. If a staff member does not like the behavior of a delinquent, he can use his wireless shocker to "zap" the child. The child may not even realize what hit him, but the Farrall Company maintains that the instrument has a "correctional" aversive effect (Chavkin, 1978).

The company has produced no evidence to support its claims but they seem true enough—if one's goal is to produce temporary conformity.

In the increasingly repressive atmosphere of the late twentieth century, such aversive conditioning techniques have become popular. Whether they rehabilitate a child psychopath, convert him into a zombie, or simply make him more bitterly hostile, remains to be seen. One of the results is already clear: "This nation's traditionally compassionate approach to helping a youngster overcome some of her or his dilemmas is fast becoming a sentimental memory [Chavkin, 1978, p. 59]."

Various other programs—including those that granted cash to successful clients, "token economy" privileges, and behavioral "contracts"—all reduced recidivism (Douds, Englesford, & Collingwood, 1977; Stuart & Lott, 1976). As none of these programs were directed specifically at child psychopaths or were evaluated according to the children's diagnoses, we do not as yet know whether behavioral modification has a distinct impact on children, who are the central concern of this chapter.

Psychosurgery and Drug Therapy

Impressed by evidence that the limbic system affects a variety of human emotions—pain, pleasure, sex, and uncontrolled rage—some scientists have argued that child psychopaths require radical brain surgery. Specifically, they focus on the hypothalamus (the supposed center of inhibition) and the amygdala area (the region presumed to be responsible for aggression).

Experiments have been conducted to implant electrodes in the amygdala region to control behavior or even to excise parts of the brain. Through psychosurgery, some experts have contended that they could control violent behavior by electrically stimulating one part of the brain—the lateral amygdala that supposedly stops explosive rage and temper tantrums (Mark & Ervin, 1970). Psychosurgery has also been used to destroy parts of the amygdala and the hypothalamus (Mark & Ervin, 1970). Temporarily, if such surgery does not destroy the child, it reduces any obstreperous drives he may feel, subdues him, and leaves him emotionally flattened. Perhaps, in some sense, this represents a cure of child psychopathy—but only at the cost of the child's intellectual or creative potential. In fact, we do not yet possess the evidence to make any decisive conclusions. Using mainly black, Hispanic, and poor children, however, the surgeons have proceeded.

Physicians have also used a variety of drugs, sometimes in massive doses, to try to change child psychopaths. Generally, these efforts have failed, although it is clearly possible to sedate almost anyone into a condition of docility.

Fads for particular drugs in the treatment of young psychopaths have blossomed and disappeared. Phenobarbital reportedly had some effect on severely aggressive children in the 1940s, but later studies failed to confirm its effects (Cutts & Jasper, 1939; Lindsley & Henry, 1943). Early experiments with Benzedrine suggested that it might have a soothing effect on child psychopaths (Cutts & Jasper, 1941; Davidoff & Goodstone, 1942; Lindsley & Henry, 1943). Other research with child psychopaths indicated that the drug did not permanently change the person's character structure (Bender & Cottington, 1942; Korey, 1944). One study suggested that Benzedrine might have a calming effect on neurotic children but that it increased the anger and instability of psychopathic children (Bender & Cottington, 1942). All of these studies were done on small numbers of children, lacked long-term follow-up, and suggested that whatever effect the drugs had wore off as soon as the child stopped taking them.

Dilantin Sodium apparently soothes severely hyperactive children but its effects on child psychopaths have not yet been established (Lindsley & Henry, 1943; Walker & Kirpatrick, 1947). The children returned to their original behavior when removed from the drug.

The status of certain drugs remains in limbo. Some researchers have found that Neulepitl decreases impulsive behavior in adolescent psychopaths. Because of its side effects, however, it is not licensed for production in the United States (Gelina, 1967). Diphenylhydantoin (DPH) may reduce aggressive behavior (Resnick, 1967), but its ultimate effects have been questioned by other researchers using placebos (Eisenberg, 1963; Lefkowitz, 1969).

Some experimenters placed their faith in drugs that normally stimulate an average child, such as dextroamphetamine and methylphenidate. Used on hyperactive children, these drugs reduce highly impulsive activity. It may be that they increase inhibitory cortical control—a crucial deficiency in the psychopath (Satterfield & Cantwell, 1975). Their effects on child psychopaths are as yet unknown. A critical unanswered question in the use of similar compounds such as Ritalin or Dexedrine is whether these drugs produce just a temporary passivity and a kind of compliance. Is genuinely violent behavior modified on a lasting basis or do the children on such drugs merely become zombies (Chavkin, 1978)?

Minor tranquilizers have no proven effect on child psychopaths, but there is a possibility that a massive tranquilizer such as lithium may be beneficial (Klein, 1978).

As pharmacotherapy is still in its infancy as a discipline, it does not offer a magical cure for the young psychopath. In further attempts to alter the asocial behavior of children and adolescents, many researchers have turned to "community" treatment.

Community Treatment

Popular, humane, and inexpensive ways of dealing with delinquents achieved eminence in the 1960s and 1970s. Whether these techniques can work on child psychopaths remains to be seen.

Community treatment takes many forms: diversion programs aimed at preventing delinquency by keeping children out of reform schools, deinstitutionalization projects where children attend regular public schools, and "halfway" houses where delinquents live together in a home but have regular contacts in the community. In general, each of these approaches produces a similar or lower rate of recidivism than does total incarceration in the usual reformatory. The specific programs drastically differ (Empey, 1978).

Leaders of diversion projects hope to avoid stigmatizing children. They wish to release them from the usual criminal justice system. How this should be done remains problematic. Edwin Schur (1973), for example, would like to leave delinquent children totally alone on the assumption that they will grow out of their criminal pattern. Schur ignores the child psychopath and apparently believes that such children should be allowed to proceed down any path they choose. This unrealistic if kind approach would be condemned by those who have actually dealt with child psychopaths such as the murderer Mary Bell.

In contrast, other experimenters want to keep children out of reform schools but advocate intensive supervision and counseling of the more dangerous types (Klein & Talmann, 1976). Following this counsel, the Alternative Routes Program offered counseling to individuals and families (Carter & Gilbert, 1973). Sacramento delinquents received family crisis therapy (Baron, Feeney, & Thorton, 1973). Project Crossroads gave employment advice as well as counseling. All of these programs tried to reintegrate the delinquent into the community and spare the child from indignity, labeling, legal processing, and strict implementation of probation terms.

No studies of this type have dealt with serious, repeating offenders who would often be considered psychopathic (Klein & Talmann, 1976). Recidivism rates seem to be approximately the same for juveniles who went through diversion programs as opposed to those who were legally processed or simply let go (Gibbons & Blake, 1976; Klein, 1978). At this point in history, there is no reason to believe that diversion has succeeded better with ordinary delinquents—let alone child psychopaths—than other attempts to cure delinquency.

DEINSTITUTIONALIZATION

Deinstitutionalization of criminal offenders has been tried extensively. In these programs, the assumption has been that delinquents commit crimes because of their membership in certain groups, that their opportunities have been limited, and that they have not learned the appropriate means to achieve the American goal of "success." If these assumptions were true, it would make sense to remove the children from their original groups and to offer them new opportunities (Empey, 1978). Two important programs tested these assumptions.

The first, a program in Provo, Utah, allowed delinquent children to live at home, but required them to attend a daily counseling session. In addition, the experimenters hired the youngsters to work in a public program (Empey & Rabow, 1961; Empey & Erikson, 1972). A second program, the Silverlake Experiment, followed the same pattern (Empey & Lubeck, 1971). As the second project was conducted in the metropolitan area of Los Angeles, it was not physically possible for the boys to live at home. Instead, they were placed in a home in a middle-class residential section of Los Angeles. In addition, they received special tutorial help at a local high school.

Both programs were partially successful. While under direct supervision, children had a lower crime rate than boys who had been placed on probation. Later recidivism rates were approximately equal to those of institutionalized boys (Empey & Erikson, 1972). Lloyd Ohlin in Massachusetts found a similar result among boys who had been deinstitutionalized (Ohlin, Miller, & Coates, 1977).

In a comprehensive study of Massachusetts, Craig McEwen (1976) compared children in 10 training school cottages and 13 community-based centers. He found that the community programs, based on greater equality between staffs and inmates, diminished the power of inmate cultures. Nonetheless, as La Mar Empey has commented, "The best that can be said is that community programs do at least as well as training schools, but they are not superior [Empey, 1978, p.553]." The possible impact, if any, on child psychopaths is unknown.

Other studies offer more hopeful prospects for juvenile delinquents and child psychopaths, but we still do not know the exact results. A few examples: Jerome Miller has headed a project of the National Center on Institutions and Alternatives. His program offers ways that criminals may "pay back" the crimes they have committed by providing community services (*Newsweek*, August 4, 1981, p. 37). New York offers the same opportunities (*Rockland Sunday Journal News*, July 27, 1980, p. 13). Some criminal justice authorities have argued that delinquents should be placed in an entirely new environment within the community. The California Youth Authority, for example, has put delinquents in foster homes and assigned them to probation officers with a small load. The first reports indicated that the children were doing relatively well and had lower recidivism rates (Warren, 1967). Some critics have argued that parole officers for the children were unusually lenient (Martinson, 1974).

It is far too early to guess whether any of these programs has a genuine impact on young psychopaths. Discouraged scholars have concluded: "Researchers should expect future projects to be unsuccessful [Lindman & Scarpitti, 1980, p. 677]."

Incapacitation

Recognizing failure in some efforts to rehabilitate delinquents, various people have fallen back on the old solution of incarcerating all delinquents.

The concept of incapacitating delinquents—in an age with the idea of "cracking down" on young offenders—had immense appeal. If the police arrested more delinquents, juvenile courts imposed harsher sentences, and the offenders were stored away in reform schools, so the theory went, the crime rate would drop (Wilson, 1975). A national survey in 1972 suggested the public's desire for a "get tough" policy: 81% of Americans believed that the police "should be tougher in dealing with crime and lawlessness [Hindelang, 1975,

p. 60]." Twelve states adopted mandatory sentences for certain crimes (Sykes, 1977). Throughout the nation, movements have developed to reduce the discretionary power of juvenile courts (Empey, 1978).

As yet, no one knows what results such policies have had on young psychopaths convicted of delinquencies. The general effect on even the ordinary delinquents remains highly debatable. In 1954, the New York Police Department doubled the number of officers assigned to East Harlem in an effort to reduce the number of street crimes. The immediate impact was impressive: muggings, ordinarily committed by juveniles, dropped from 69 to 7 during a period of 4 months. As one result, the New York police force increased its size by 54% over the next 2 decades. The overall rate of delinquency, however, continued to soar (Wilson, 1975).

In 1972, the police of Kansas City conducted a similar experiment. Randomly assigned districts increased their police patrols by more than two times. When compared with districts where the police patrols were decreased or eliminated, George Kelling and his colleagues (1975) could find no impact on the crime rate—whether measured by official statistics, surveys, or participant observation.

Harsher sentencing procedures have also produced ambiguous results. Tougher laws in New York, for example, made drug possession a felony rather than a misdemeanor and imposed more severe penalties. Passed in 1973, the new laws primarily affected juveniles. When the effect of the stiffer penalties was studied in 1976, researchers found that "the risk of punishment facing offenders did not increase noticeably [*The New York Times*, 1976]."

All of the evidence concerning the custodial incarceration of delinquents indicates that it is correlated with increases in the rate of crime, particularly among young psychopaths. Further, the whole notion of incapacitation rests on the assumption that we can predict the future danger of delinquents and impose punishment on them before they have committed a particular act. Legally, this belief seems questionable; empirically, it remains to be tested. Fairly accurate prediction is plausible at this stage in history. Yet, the best studies indicate that for every truly dangerous person kept in confinement, two more people who would not commit a crime must also continue their imprisonment (Kozol, Boucher, & Garfalo, 1972; Wenk & Smith, 1972). As Norval Morris (1972) commented, "There is a seductive appeal to separating the dangerous and the nondangerous offenders and confining imprisonment principally to the former. . . . It would be such a neat trick if it were possible; prophylactic punishment—designed to save potential victims of future crimes [p. 1165]." The obvious difficulty, as Gresham Sykes (1978) noted, is that the idea "that dangerousness can be determined in advance—an idea that is fundamental to the justification of punishment as a method of incapacitation—is open to serious doubt [p. 490]."

What approach, then, is left? Some prominent criminologists have retained a cautious hope that milieu therapy—a complete change in a child's environment and a total mobilization of forces that would aid him or her—might well bring about alterations in certain types of delinquents, particularly child psychopaths.

Milieu Therapy

Milieu therapy is based on the premise that only a total transformation of the child's environment over an extended period of time can lead to a lasting change in the personality of child psychopaths. Its origins can be traced back to Austria in 1907 and the work of August Aichhorn, a Viennese psychoanalyst and educator. Appalled by the nation's attempt to establish military schools for all maladjusted boys, Aichhorn founded his own homes for children as an alternative. A disciple of Freud, Aichhorn advocated the use of psychoanalytic techniques with such children, a radical alteration in their original environment, and large doses of kindness that, he hoped, would lead the youths to form lasting emotional relationships. By 1918, he had founded a home specifically designed for delinquents, the famous *Oberhollabrunn*.

There, he treated two types of children: neurotic delinquents and psychopathic delinquents. Aichhorn noted that the psychopathic children were asocial, aggressive, and impulsive. Raised without affection and suffering from brutality, these children grew up without a well-developed social conscience. Over a period of time that sometimes extended into years, Aichhorn treated the psychopathic children with permissiveness and affection. This lack of brutality, he believed, sharply contrasted with their pasts. Then, if an affiliative relation had been established with someone on the staff, Aichhorn and his associates gradually imposed controls on the child and attempted to instill a sense of guilt and social responsibility. In capsule form, Aichhorn summarized the treatment: "First we had to compensate for this great lack of love and then gradually and with great caution begin to make demands upon the children. Severity would have failed completely [1935, p. 172]."

Aichhorn reported that all of the boys eventually developed consciences and successfully adopted to society. Although he provided no systematic proof for this assertion that everyone had been "cured," his work earned him the title of "father" of milieu therapy and inspired many followers. Fritz Redl established Pioneer House in Detroit (Redl & Wineman, 1954), Bruno Bettleheim created the Orthogenic School in Chicago (Bettleheim, 1950), Hawthorne– Cedar Knolls and Wiltwyck in New York also adopted the techniques developed by Aichhorn with some minor variations.

THE HIGHFIELDS PROJECT

One of the most significant of these experiments was the Highfields project. Lloyd McCorkle and his associates selected seriously delinquent children who had already failed on probation and placed them in a special group home, Highfields, on the old Lindberg estate in New Jersey (McCorkle, Bixby, Lovel, & Elias, 1958). The teenaged boys, who never numbered more than 20, lived with a small staff on unguarded grounds. The staff imposed few formal controls on the boys, but depended instead on the informal sanctions of the entire group. During the day, the boys worked in a local hospital; in the evening they broke up into discussion groups. The staff encouraged the boys to develop forms of self-government and to help each other.

Original reports on the Highfields project were most encouraging. When researchers compared the Highfields boys to a somewhat similar group committed to a regular reformatory at Annandale, they found that only 37% of the Highfields sample versus 53% of the Annandale boys had a subsequent criminal record (Weeks, 1958). Later critics contended that the two groups may not have been strictly similar; the Annandale boys tended to be older, more experienced delinquents who would be more likely to continue their delinquent careers. Nonetheless, as one criminologist has concluded, the findings seemed to indicate that "Highfields was able to do just as well as total incarceration but at much less expense to the state and at much less personal cost to the delinquents involved [Empey, 1978, p. 512]."

McCorkle, Redl, and Bettleheim all reported enthusiastically on their results in treating aggressive and psychopathic children.

HAWTHORNE-CEDAR KNOLLS

In contrast, a research team at Hawthorne-Cedar Knolls was faced with extraordinary problems in trying to treat 81 girls who were strikingly psychopathic (Powdermaker, Lewi, & Touraine, 1937).

They described the girls as "asocial but not obviously neurotic. . . .
It became clear that the feature common to them was an inability to
make a real transference to any member of the staff. . . . They acted
largely, some of them seemingly exclusively, on impulse and apparently had no . . . real conflict or sense of guilt [p. 196]." The
Hawthorne–Cedar Knolls staff had no success in dealing with this
type of girl by using the Aichhorn method or any other.

By the 1950s, despite its failures at Hawthorne and the ambiguous
results at Highfields, milieu therapy appeared to be an eminently
promising approach with child psychopaths. Aichhorn, Redl, and
Bettleheim had advocated the approach with enthusiasm. Yet, no one
had checked their results or followed up their children in later life.

Conclusions

Research on the treatment of young psychopaths—the Mary Bells
of this world—has unfortunately been meager and inconclusive.
Some promising experiments apparently dealt with less serious delinquents than child psychopaths; others, aimed specifically at child
psychopaths, reported contradictory and often impressionistic results. Awaiting further knowledge, we are left with only a few solid
generalizations:

- Rates of juvenile crime in America increased during the 1960s
  and 1970s. Some psychiatrists, sociologists, and political scientists publicized their view that any attempt to change this
  pattern—except by stern repression—was hopeless or even
  damaging.
- Incarceration has no positive effect on recidivism rates of delinquents in general or child psychopaths in particular. Controversial evidence suggests that incarceration may possibly suppress
  (somewhat reduce) the rate of juvenile delinquency.
- Whether within a reformatory or in the community, programs
  aimed at increasing the individual awareness of delinquents—
  psychotherapy, psychoanalysis, group therapy, counseling—
  have yet to prove effective. It seems particularly doubtful that
  child psychopaths would respond to this approach.
- Behavioral modification apparently has some effect on ordinary

delinquents in reducing their rate of crime. The impact of positive reinforcement on child psychopaths, however, is as yet unknown. Negative reinforcement remains, at best, an inconclusive but sometimes brutal approach.

- Drug therapy of young psychopaths is in limbo. Most experiments with a variety of drugs indicate that they might have a passing effect on child psychopaths. Psychosurgery induces placidity but no other confirmed results.
- "Community treatments"—diversion, deinstitutionalization, or similar attempts—have yet to indicate their superior worth over other approaches. Child psychopaths have not been included in the usual experiments. While more humane and less costly than other programs, the danger remains that such experiments may free child psychopaths to continue their depredations within the community.
- Incapacitation of delinquents through more comprehensive policing, harsher sentences, and the imposition of punishment at earlier ages has a doubtful effect, if any, on child psychopaths.
- Milieu therapy, a total effort at restructuring the life of the child psychopath, seems to offer the best hope of rehabilitating such children. Experiments with this approach, however, have produced contradictory results that have too often been based on meager, unsubstantiated reports.

Impressed by the tentative evidence that milieu therapy might be the best approach to helping young psychopaths, I initiated a series of studies in 1952 to assess its impact. I chose the Wiltwyck School of New York as one important example of Aichhorn's therapy.

Under the leadership of Ernst Papanek, a follower of both Alfred Adler and August Aichhorn, Wiltwyck had emerged as the most prominent example in America of attempts to treat child psychopaths in a warm, permissive environment. The school provided extensive psychiatric, psychological, and social work care for delinquents who had often been rejected by their families, the courts, and the public reformatory system as uncontrollable.

As a contrast, I also studied the Lyman School in Massachusetts—the oldest reform school in America and a representative of a repressive, vocationally oriented approach to delinquents—for purposes of comparison. In the next chapter, I present the results of a series of studies aimed at evaluating the long-term effect of this uniquely promising experiment on child psychopaths and other types of delinquents.

References

Aichhorn, A. *Wayward youth*. New York: Viking, 1935.

Alexander, J., & Parsons, B. Short term behavioral intervention with delinquent families. *Journal of Abnormal Psychology*, 1973, *81*:71– 80.

Alvord, J. The home token economy. *Correctional Psychology*, 1971.

Barron, R., Feeney, F., & Thorton, W. Preventing delinquency through diversion. *Federal Probation*, 1973, *6*:118– 130.

Bartollas, C., Miller, S., & Dinitz, S. *Juvenile victimization*. New York: Wiley, 1973.

Bender, L. Psychopathic behavior disorders in children. In *Handbook of correctional psychology*, Robert Lindner (ed.). New York: Philosophical Library, 1947.

Bender, L., & Cottington, F. The use of amphetamine sulphate in child psychiatry. *American Journal of Psychiatry*, 1942, *99*:116– 121.

Bettleheim, B. *Love is not enough*. Glencoe, Illinois: Free Press, 1950.

Carter, R., & Gilbert J. *Alternate routes*. Sacramento, California: Youth Authority, 1973.

Chavkin, S. *The mind stealers*. Westport, Connecticut: Laurence Hill, 1978.

Cima, E., Montbarrio, E., & Venuti, G. Psychotherapeutic experiments in subjects with abnormal behavior of a character disorder nature. *Revista di Psychiatria*, 1968, *3*:158– 161.

Cutts, K., & Jasper, H. Effects of benzedrine sulphate and phenobarbital on behavior problem children with abnormal E.E.G.'s. *Archives of Neurology and Psychiatry*, 1939, *4*:1138– 1145.

Davidoff, E., & Goodstone, G. Amphetamine-barbituate therapy in psychiatric conditions. *Psychiatric Quarterly*, 1942, *16*:541– 548.

Delbat, D., & Blanchard, F. An impact study of two diversion projects. Paper presented at the American Psychological Association, 1975.

Dowds, A., Englesford, M., & Collingwood, T. Behavior of youthful offenders and their parents. *Child Welfare*, 1977, *14*:200– 209.

Eisenberg, L. Psychopharmacologic experiment in a training school for delinquent boys. *American Journal of Orthopsychiatry*, 1963, *33*:212– 230.

Eisner, E. A. Relationships formed by a sexually delinquent adolescent girl. *American Journal of Orthopsychiatry*, 1945 *15*:301– 308.

Empey, L. *American delinquency*. Homewood, Illinois: Dorsey Press, 1978.

Empey, L., & Erikson, M. *The provo experiment*. Lexington, Kentucky: Heath, 1972.

Empey, L., & Lubeck, S. *The silverlake experiment*. Chicago: Aldine, 1971.

Empey, L., & Rabow, J. The provo experiment in delinquency rehabilitation. *American Sociology Review*, 1961, *26*:300– 311.

Federal Bureau of Investigation. *Uniform crime reports*. U.S. Government Printing Office, Washington, D.C., 1976.

Friedlander, K. *The psychoanalytic approach to juvenile delinquency*. London: Kegan, Paul, Trench, and Tribner, 1947.

Gelina, L. A trial application of neulepitl in the practice of child psychiatry. *Zhurnal Nevropatologi i Psikatri*, 1967, *67*:270– 275.

Gibbons, D., & Blake, F. Evaluating the impact of juvenile diversion programs. Paper presented at the Pacific Sociological Association, 1976.

Hindelang, M. *Public opinion regarding crime*. Washington, D.C.: U.S. Government Printing Office, 1975.

Jessness, K. The Preston typology study. *Youth Authority Quarterly*, 1970, *9*:273– 276.

Kassebaum, G., Ward, D., & Wilner, D. *Prison treatment and its outcome*. New York: Wiley, 1971.

Kelling, G., Pate, T., Dreckman, D., & Brown, C. The Kansas City preventive patrol experiment. In S. Halleck (Ed.), *The Aldine crime and Justice Annual*, Chicago: Aldine, 1975.

Klein, M. Alternative dispositions for juvenile offenders. Social Science Research Institute. Los Angeles: University of Southern California, 1975.

Klein, M., & Talman, K. Pivotal ingredients of police juvenile diversion programs. Washington: National Institute for Juvenile Justice and Delinquency Prevention, 1976.

Klein, R. Drug treatment of personality disorders and delinquents. In W. H. Reid (Ed.), *The Psychopath*. New York: Brunner/Mazel, 1978.

Korey, S. The effects of benzedrine sulfate on the behavior of psychopathic and neurotic delinquents. *Psychiatric Quarterly*, 1944, *18:*127–137.

Kozol, H., Boucher, R., & Garfalo, R. The diagnosis and treatment of dangerousness. *Crime and Delinquency*, 1972, *18:*173–180.

Lefkowitz, M. Effects of diphenylhydantoin on disruptive behavior. *Archives of General Psychiatry*, 1969, *20:*418–425.

Levine, W., & Bornstein, P. Is the psychopath treatable? *Washington University Law Quarterly*, 1972, *5:*673.

Levy, D. Primary affect hunger. *American Journal of Psychiatry*, 1937, *94:*643–652.

Lindman, R., & Scarpitti, F. Delinquency prevention. In L. Messinger and E. Bittner (Eds.), *Criminology review yearbook*. Beverly Hills: Sage, 1980.

Lindsley, D., & Henry, C. The effect of drugs on behavior and the E.E.G. of children with behavior disorders. *Psychosomatic Medicine*, 1943, *4:*140–149.

Lippman, H. Difficulties encountered in the psychiatric treatment of chronic juvenile delinquents. In K. R. Eissler (Eds.), *Searchlights on Delinquency*, New York: International Universities Press, 1949.

Lipton, D., Martinson, R., & Wilks, J. *The effectiveness of correctional treatment*. New York: Praeger, 1975.

McCleary, R. Review of beyond probation. In *Crime and delinquency*, July, 1980.

McCord, J. A thirty-year follow-up of treatment effects. *American Psychologist*, 1978 (March), *33*(3):284–289.

McCord, W., McCord, J., & Gudeman, J. *Origins of alcoholism*. Stanford: Stanford University Press, 1960.

McCord, W., McCord, J., & Zola, I. *The origins of crime*. New York: Columbia University Press, 1959.

McCorkle, L., Bixby, W., Lovel, F., & Elias, A. *The Highfields story*. New York: Holt, 1958.

McEwen, C. *Designing correctional organizations for youth*. Cambridge, Massachusetts: Ballinger, 1976.

Maltz, M. Review of beyond probation. In *Crime and delinquency*. July, 1980.

Mark, V., & Ervin, F. *Violence and the brain*. New York: Harper, 1970.

Martinson, R. What works. *The Public Interest*, 1974, *9:*114–126.

Messinger, S., & Bittner, E. *Criminology review yearbook*. Beverly Hills, Calif.: Sage Publications, 1979.

Morales *vs.* Turman, 383 F. Supp. 53, 1974.

Morris, N. The future of imprisonment. *Michigan Law Review*, 1972, *6:*18–27.

Morrison, H. The asocial child: A destiny of sociopathy? In W. H. Reid, (Ed.), *The psychopath*. New York: Brunner/Mazel, 1978.

Murray, C., & Cox, L. *Beyond probation*. Beverly Hills: Sage, 1978.

The New York Times. Drug law effectiveness questioned in U.S. study. September 5, 1976.

Newsweek, Aug. 4, 1981, p. 28.

Nordquist, C. Return from Moriah. Unpublished paper, 1973.

Ohlin, L., Miller, A., & Coates, R. *Juvenile correctional reform in Massachusetts*. Washington, D.C.: U.S. Government Printing Office, 1977.

Powdermaker, F., Lewi, H., & Touraine, G. Psychopathology and treatment of delinquent girls. *American Journal of Orthopsychiatry*, 1937, 7:61.

Powers, E., & Witmer, H. *An experiment in the prevention of delinquency*. New York: Columbia University Press, 1951.

Redl, F., & Wineman, D. *Controls from within*. Glencoe, Illinois: Free Press, 1954.

Resnick, O. The psychoactive properties of diphenylhydantoin. *International Journal of Neuropsychiatry*, 1967, 3:107–113.

Rockland Sunday Journal News, July 27, 1980.

Rubin, S. New sentencing proposals and laws in the 1970s. *Federal Probation*, 1979, 43:25–30.

Satterfield, J., & Cantwell, D. Psychopharmacology in the prevention of anti-social and delinquent behavior. *British Journal of Mental Health*, 1975, 9:217–225.

Schur, E. *Radical nonintervention*. Englewood Cliffs, New Jersey: Prentice-Hall, 1973.

Schwitzgebel, R. *Streetcorner research*. Cambridge, Massachusetts: Harvard University Press, 1974.

Slawson, J. Treatment of aggression in a specialized environment. *American Journal of Orthopsychiatry*, 1943, *13*:384–441.

Stuart, R., & Lott, L. Behavioral contracting with delinquents. In C. Franks and G. Wilson (Eds.), *Annual review of behavior therapy and practices*. New York: Brunner/Mazel, 1973.

Sykes, G. *Criminology*. New York: Harcourt Brace Jovanovich, 1978.

Szurek, S. Some impressions from clinical experiences with delinquents. In K. Eissler (Ed.), *Searchlights on delinquency*. New York: International Universities Press, 1949.

Vosburgh, W., & Alexander, L. Long term follow-up as program evaluation. *American Journal of Orthopsychiatry*, 1980 (Jan.), *50* (1).

Walker, C., & Kirkpatrick, B. Dilatin treatment for behavior problem children with abnormal E.E.G. *American Journal of Psychiatry*, 1947, *103*:484–492.

Warren, M. Community treatment project. Report #8, California Youth Authority, 1967.

Weeks, H. A. *Youthful offenders at Highfields*. Ann Arbor: University of Michigan Press, 1958.

Wenck, E., & Smith, G. Can violence be predicted? *Crime and Delinquency*, 1972, *18*:75–82.

Whitaker, C. Ormsby village. *Psychiatry*, 1946, *19*:239–250.

Wilson, J. *Thinking about crime*. New York: Basic Books, 1975.

Wolfe, B. The later adjustment of sixteen children diagnosed as psychopathic personality. *Smith College Studies in Social Work*, 1942, *13*:156–157.

Yochelson, S., & Samenow, S. *The change process. The criminal personality* (Vol. 2). New York: Jason Aronson, 1977.

9

The Wiltwyck–Lyman Project: A Twenty-Five-Year Follow-Up Study of Milieu Therapy

WILLIAM McCORD
JOSÉ SANCHEZ

My goal was to see to it that these children who had been brutalized in so many ways not only survived but survived whole.
[Ernst Papanek, late Director of the Wiltwyck School]

In 1938, Dr. Ernst Papanek—a small, rotund, balding, bespectacled man—became the leader of one of the greatest refugee efforts of our time. He had already achieved distinction as a child psychologist, educator, and leader of the Austrian Social Democratic Party. Hitler's virulent anti-semitism obliterated Papanek's normal life in Vienna and swept him into a poignant movement to save children from Nazi persecution.

After the "Night of Broken Crystal," when Nazi thugs terrorized the Jews of Germany, it became clear to some prescient people such as Leon Blum in France and Marshall Field in America that a massive refugee effort had to be mounted. An organization of compassionate Russian and Polish doctors took the initiative in trying to save Jewish children and other opponents to Hitler. All too often, however, the politicians of France, England, and the United States—including Franklin Roosevelt—ignored their pleas for help.

Acting privately, the doctors' organization bought castles in Montmorency near Paris and in other areas of Southern France. They asked Papanek to direct these homes for desperate children. He had escaped from Austria, reached France, and held a precious visa to the United States. For him, it must have been a wrenching decision. He had already led Social Democrats in the streets of Vienna against the Nazis. Although a pacifist by conviction, he had ordered his men to fire on the stormtroopers. He knew very well the fate that awaited him and his family if the Nazis caught him; he also recognized military realities: An enfeebled France would soon fall victim to Hitler's rule. Despite all this, he returned his coveted steamship tickets and visa in order to stay with the refugee children.

Soon, hundreds of youngsters fled to his care. The Nazis had already killed or interned many of their parents. The children came from a variety of backgrounds. Orthodox Jewish children presented a special problem for Papanek; he did not even know much about the special dietary laws they observed. Another group, called the "Cubans," arrived from the doomed ship St. Louis. They had been on the last vessel to sail from Germany, headed for Cuba and supposed freedom. Cuban officials and then American bureaucrats refused to allow the ship to dock because the passengers lacked "proper" documents. The Nazis celebrated this incident as it proved that "nobody" wanted the tainted Jews. After wandering the seas, the ship finally landed in Antwerp where the parents were separated from their children. The Nazis eventually eliminated the parents while the children—some babies, some teenagers—escaped to Papanek's sanctuary by way of the underground.

At Montmorency and the other schools, Papanek treated the children with compassion, humor, and warmth. He encouraged traditional teaching but also created new democratic institutions within the schools. The schools taught the usual subjects—geography, reading, arithmetic, science—but centered the teachings on a single weekly theme such as the German invasion of France which had immediate relevance for the children. Papanek tried to reassure the children about the future, assuage their guilt about leaving their parents, and prepare them in practical tasks such as building bomb shelters.

One of his great problems was securing financial support. Initially, for example, the Baroness de Rothschild gave 40,000 francs to the schools but assured Papanek that she could not afford another *sou*. Within 1 month, after seeing the work of the schools, she contributed an additional 1 million francs.

When the Nazis invaded, Papanek tried desperately to save the children. At times, he failed. At other times, he and his comrades succeeded. Once the *Maquis* blew up a Nazi train transporting children to Auschwitz and saved the children. Due to Papanek's courageous efforts, a few hundred eventually reached America. His account of this epoch "is, without question, one of the great stories of our time," Donald Harrington has written, "and Dr. Papanek one of the great heroes [Papanek & Linn, 1975, p. ii]." Papanek himself eventually escaped to the United States where he applied his methods of milieu therapy to the re-education of juvenile delinquents at the Wiltwyck School.

Although dealing with children from quite different social backgrounds, Papanek at Wiltwyck applied essentially the same principles as he had developed in France. Whether dealing with refugees or emotionally disturbed delinquents, Papanek realized that they came from brutal environments and needed compassionate rather than punitive treatment. In both groups, he demanded complete truthfulness: "You can't be dishonest with children at any time. To take the odor of dishonesty upon oneself . . . can be fatal [1975, p. 90]." He was deeply aware of the psychic damage that both sets of children had suffered and did everything to exorcize it. In France, Papanek had created a permissive educational system. He did so because his charges were "Jewish children who had come to us instilled with the Jewish respect for education." At Wiltwyck, he found that most of the delinquents did not share these values. "To a great extent, they had to be taught how to read and write. No value had been placed on education in their homes. They were at Wiltwyck because very little attention of any kind had been paid to them [1975, p. 122]." Yet, he found that the same methods worked at Wiltwyck: "Children enjoy working too hard. What they don't enjoy is being told to study when they would rather be doing anything but [1975, p. 123]."

Aided by the generosity of Eleanor Roosevelt, Papanek became a lionized hero among the delinquent children at Wiltwyck, just as he had been among the refugees of Montmorency. Although he died in 1973, Papanek left behind a significant heritage. As his son later wrote, "As long as a man's name is remembered with love anywhere in the world, that man is not dead. . . . By the tokens in which mankind measures out its time, Ernst Papanek will live for a long time [George Papanek, in E. Papanek, 1975, preface]."

9. The Wiltwyck–Lyman Project

Milieu Therapy at Wiltwyck: The 1950s

Founded in 1937, Wiltwyck originally served as a summer camp for children and then as a rather strict residential center for maladjusted and delinquent children. Ernst Papanek arrived in 1950 as the director and transformed the school (then in Esopus, New York) into an outstanding center for the treatment of child psychopaths and other types of delinquent boys.

Claude Brown, a "streetwise" delinquent from Harlem and later the author of *Manchild in the Promised Land,* recalled Ernst Papanek's arrival at Wiltwyck. "At first, most of the cats up at Wiltwyck thought Papanek was kind of crazy. . . . But Papanek wasn't anything like crazy. He was probably the smartest and the deepest cat I had ever met [1965, p. 85]." Papanek radically altered Wiltwyck and, in the process, the life of Claude Brown: "In a little while, with just talk, he had won every living ass in the place—just took everything over with a few words that we couldn't even understand too well [1965, p. 86]." Claude Brown soon respected him. "Papanek brought a whole new way of doing things to Wiltwyck. He made a rule that boys were not to be beaten or even slapped by counselors any more. . . . I had never met anybody before who never got mad, and he would never hit anybody [1965, p. 87]."

Papanek sought particularly to help psychopaths, the most recalcitrant of delinquents. His milieu therapy offered them a combination of friendliness, nonpunishment, and a policy that each boy must somehow pay for the consequences of his action. The auxiliary services—educational, psychiatric, psychological—played an important but not paramount role in the whole mosaic of milieu therapy at Wiltwyck.

The Wiltwyck experiment soon gained public attention through the efforts of Eleanor Roosevelt and such graduates as Claude Brown and Heavyweight Champion Floyd Patterson. When I first went to the school in 1952, it rested on a forested meadow of some 200 acres near the Hudson River. Clustered in an unwalled quadrangle were cottages, a classroom building, a gymnasium, a craft shop, an art room, and a dining hall. Psychopathic, neurotic, emotionally disturbed, and confused children occupied the buildings. At that time, the boys ranged in age from 9 to 13. New York courts had referred all of the boys to the institution, largely because their parents or public reform schools could not handle them. The courts had adjudged all of the boys to be "incorrigible" delinquents or highly neglected. Many had previously spent time in other institutions.

Under Papanek, Wiltwyck emphasized individual and group therapy for every child. Four social workers and two psychotherapists treated the boys in a formal fashion, but Papanek encouraged everyone—from psychiatrist to maintenance man—to establish a warm environment for the children. Indeed, in his opinion, the most successful therapist of all was the fat, smiling, ever-generous cook. He encouraged child–staff as well as interracial recreational activities. A male and female counselor, pseudo-parents, supervised 10 youths in each cottage. (The fatiguing task of allowing them to maintain a friendly, nonpunitive environment for their children necessitated the cottage masters needing 3 days off per week.) An elected student council, a food committee, job committee, canteen committee, and sports committee cooperated with the staff in the discussion of problems. Papanek did not believe in true self-government for boys of this age and temperament, but he attempted to introduce them to democratic principles.

In 1953, Papanek summarized the school's therapeutic orientation:

> Children who have never known understanding, social acceptance, prestige, friendship or love, or who have misinterpreted or misused them when offered in an ever-protective and unchallenging way, would find in Wiltwyck a community of understanding grown-ups and children among whom they can gain security and status by social experience [p. 76].

Papanek mobilized the whole Wiltwyck environment in an attempt to reassure such children. He based his efforts on the tenet of nonpunishment. The children were allowed to express their antagonism, *but* they could never hurt another person and they had to make up for the consequences of their explosions. For example, an aggressive newcomer to Wiltwyck broke 32 windows in the school dining room. After waiting for the boy to "cool off," the staff explained that some money would be deducted from the boy's weekly allowance to help pay for the damage. Three weeks later, the staff called the boy to the office and quietly reinstated the full allowance.

Although most of its boys were toughened delinquents and many exhibited psychopathic or pre-schizophrenic traits, Wiltwyck ran smoothly along a course that eschewed the brutal punitiveness that so many of the boys had experienced. The basic principle in 1953 was to avoid brutality, punishment, and authoritarianism.

The staff consisted entirely of college graduates who had been screened for their ability to tolerate abusive behavior. Many had master's degrees in the behavioral sciences. All participated in weekly in-service training. The staff as did the students represented a mixture of ethnic groups.

An initial follow-up study indicated that 29% of the boys had a serious criminal record after 5 years of freedom (Wiley, 1941). This research occurred before Papanek's arrival but during a time when a strong minority of the staff were urging the type of milieu therapy that Papanek advocated. These researchers did not follow the boys into maturity, or use records other than those of the New York Social Service exchange, or compare the success rate of the school to those of other schools.

After Papanek's arrival, the school changed in atmosphere and instituted an after-care program. After an average residence of 18 months, a boy returned to New York and Wiltwyck's after-care center. There, psychiatric social workers counselled parents and the boy.

Papanek argued that delinquent behavior, particularly that of child psychopaths, stems from psychic problems and particularly an unrequited need for love. Following August Aichhorn and Alfred Adler, Papanek believed that a regime of "disciplined love" would establish emotional relationships between the children and adults. In adopting this position, Papanek stood in opposition to the prevailing practices of training schools of the 1950s. Yet, Papanek's techniques remained empirically untested.

As an initial step in determining whether the Wiltwyck approach achieved more beneficial results than a punitively oriented attack on the problem, I compared the Wiltwyck School with the Lyman School of Massachusetts (1953). As the oldest reform school in America, Lyman provided a crucial contrast in philosophy and methods.

The Lyman Training School: The 1950s

Originally founded as a somewhat daring innovation in the nineteenth century, the Lyman School had evolved into a typical public reformatory by the 1950s. By 1952, the school took in hundreds of children referred by the courts. Basically, the children resembled the Wiltwyck boys: Overwhelmingly, they came from lower-class urban areas and from families disrupted by divorce or desertion. They were in their early adolescence in 1952 and most had developed a delinquent record. Some, as at Wiltwyck, had been sent to the school for so-called "status offenses": parental neglect, habitual truancy, and the inability of the parents to cope with the child. In intelligence (average score on the Stanford-Binet: 91.5) and school performance, they also resembled the Wiltwyck boys. They differed in only one potentially salient respect: more of the Lyman boys came from French Canadian, Irish, or Italian extraction than at Wiltwyck; in contrast, more of the Wiltwyck boys came from the black and Hispanic ethnic groups.[1] Both sets of boys suffered from severe economic and social deprivation and a similarly high proportion in each group exhibited psychopathic or pre-psychotic tendencies.

The boys at Lyman encountered a vastly different environment from Wiltwyck's. Many boys stayed for only a few days, placed there temporarily until transferred to other schools or social agencies.[2] Those who remained at Lyman for 18 months or more were submitted to a discipline-oriented environment. The school emphasized strict adherence to its rules, formal education, and agricultural work. On arrival, the child automatically received a sentence of 3000 credits that he had to work off by good behavior.

The pattern could be altered by the slightest infraction of discipline: talking when not allowed, smoking, "stubbornness and disobedience" or any other minor deviation. Upon violating a rule, the boy was sentenced to a disciplinary cottage where all privileges — attending school, seeing movies, playing games, swimming, or even talking — were suspended. The cottage master maintained silence at all times and automatically imposed an extra sentence of 1000 credits. Children who tried to escape received an additional sentence of 3000 credits. During residence in the disciplinary cottage, the boy could not work off his credits. Normally, he spent his time shovelling manure on the farm that the school maintained.

If a boy escaped direct punishment, he was educated in a strict classroom. The principal of the school expressed his philosophy of education in this manner: "I don't know whether you agree and I don't care. The real cause of juvenile delinquency is all the fol-de-rol of progressive education. Modern kids need firm discipline. Their social relations can take care of themselves [McCord & McCord, 1953, p. 416]."

As a publicly financed, often overcrowded school, Lyman could not afford the sophisticated psychological therapy offered by Wiltwyck. One trained psychologist had to limit her efforts to administering Stanford–Binet IQ tests to the hundreds of children who streamed

---

[1] We will discuss the effects of this difference later in the chapter. At this point, however, it should be noted that the ethnicity of the Wiltwyck and Lyman boys did not correlate with their original crimes or other early forms of deviance.

[2] Such boys were omitted from the follow-up study. Only those who remained for 18 months or more were included.

through Lyman. The more permanent residents received a diagnosis, but little or no treatment. The masters of the various cell blocks (usually two men for every 35 boys) were underpaid, had no education beyond the high school level, and generally regarded their wards as "punks." A popular theory among the guards at the time was that movements of the moon—and nothing else—determined delinquent behavior.

Lacking any treatment program, Lyman offered religious services and a rudimentary vocational education. Basically, the children maintained the school. Lyman gave no in-service training to its staff and, unlike Wiltwyck, made no attempt to establish student governments. "We don't give the boys authority," one teacher told me, "It especially goes to the heads of the colored boys." The reformative philosophy of the school was summed up to me by the school librarian who said, "All these boys need is a father with a good strong razor strap!"

The Lyman school, neither better nor worse than the average American reformatory of the 1950s—and, indeed, the 1980s—tried to remold children through discipline and rudimentary education. The Lyman officials ruled the inmates without any effort at self-government, counseling, or attempts to improve human relations.

On release, the boys usually returned to their original environments; many served time as attendants at state police barracks or were urged to join the army. (In later life, three boys in our sample even made a career out of being military policemen.)

In 1947, an early study of the school occurred because of accusations of brutality. The researchers traced 228 boys through a 3-year parole period (Boston Citizen's Committee, 1947). They found that 48.3% of the boys had been honorably discharged from parole but that 35.3% were already serving sentences in other institutions within the state.

The contrasts between Wiltwyck and Lyman in philosophy and practice—despite the basic comparability of their populations—offer an unusual opportunity to estimate the success of two approaches to the correction of delinquents.

The Effects of Wiltwyck and Lyman: 1952–1953

In an effort to gauge the impact of the Wiltwyck School and the Lyman School on their inmates, researchers selected 35 boys from each school to undergo a variety of psychological tests and questionnaires about attitudes (McCord & McCord, 1953). The boys represented relatively similar comparison groups in age (9–13), ethnic origin, original offense, intelligence, and socioeconomic background. All came from urban areas.[3]

Privately interviewed, each of the children went through a battery of tests. These included the Adult–Child Interaction Test (developed by Henry Murray), a word association test, a questionnaire on authoritarianism and prejudice (constructed by Theodore Adorno and his colleagues), a set of projective personality questions (e.g. "What desires do you have difficulty controlling?"), and a values questionnaire (e.g. "Do you think that cheating is sometimes a good thing?").[4]

Some highly suggestive differences appeared between the two schools:

- Wiltwyck boys generally chose a nonaggressive person as their best friend at the school. Lyman boys clustered around a hostile, possibly psychopathic boy as their leader.
- When asked to describe the best type of cottage master, a majority of the Wiltwyck boys talked about a loving, understanding person. In contrast, a majority of the Lyman subjects chose a "disciplinarian" (a person who "hits you when you need it" or "who makes you obey").
- When divided by the number of months they had spent in each school, the Wiltwyck boys showed a decided decrease in insecurity. Although they exhibited less insecurity upon entry at the school, the Lyman boys did not basically change.
- Extreme aggressiveness, a characteristic of some child psychopaths, did not appear to change at either Wiltwyck or Lyman.
- A majority of the Wiltwyck boys viewed the world as essentially "good" while a majority of the Lyman children portrayed the world as threatening, dangerous, and evil.
- The Wiltwyck boys exhibited a higher level of self-esteem than did the Lyman inmates.
- When asked, "What are good parents like?" 55% of the Wiltwyck boys replied with a loving ideal ("They respect you") whereas a majority of Lyman boys answered with a disciplinary ideal ("Mother doesn't baby you when father hits you").

[3] We excluded boys who had resided at the schools for only a short period and, for fear that they would misinterpret the questions, those who scored lower than 80 on the Stanford–Binet IQ test.

[4] The reliability and validity of these instruments have been previously described (McCord, 1953).

In general, it appeared that the boys reflected the schools' environments—at least for a time. The Wiltwyck treatment may have decreased anxiety, effected a reduction in prejudice, fostered a more positive view of the world, and allowed for more friendly relationships between the boys and staff. There was no evidence, however, that the school reduced the aggressive tendencies of the boys. These results could not be attributed to the family backgrounds of the boys (as they were essentially comparable) or to the fact of sheer incarceration itself (as both groups had spent equal lengths of time in their institutions). Age, original offenses, ethnic group, or other possible variables did not affect the results at that time.

The 1952–1953 comparison of Wiltwyck and Lyman seemed tentatively encouraging, for it suggested that the Wiltwyck environment had affected some of the basic personality traits and attitudes of the boys. Yet, a number of unanswered questions remained: Why did aggression not decrease in the Wiltwyck environment? What might have happened if nothing had been done to either group of boys? How does each environment affect children with different problems? And, most critically, could either school positively affect child psychopaths?

In an effort to answer some of these questions, a second study was initiated between 1954 and 1955 that focused on the impact of the Wiltwyck school and its specific results with child psychopaths.

The Impact of the Wiltwyck School: 1954–1955

Because of the hopeful results of the first study, it seemed valuable to trace the impact of Wiltwyck on different types of children: psychopaths, "behavior disorders," neurotics, and pre-psychotics. In 1954, we administered a variety of tests to the entire population (107 boys) of the school. These included the Adult–Child Interaction Test, a questionnaire on values, and measures of actual behavior. The original sample included 15 child psychopaths. My interest focused specifically on these children who had not managed to internalize the morality of their particular society or even subsociety (McCord & McCord, 1956).

A typical example of these "rebels without a cause" was John, a 10-year-old, scowling, bitter child:

> John had been "peculiar" since birth. Instead of crying, for
> example, he would hit his head against the wall in a demand for

food. His parents did not care. In fact, the mother had undergone four abortions before his birth. Only physical reasons prevented her from aborting the birth of John.

The parents loved to play bridge and would often lock John in a closet for the night while they went out for a game. Because of his aggressiveness, the parents took John to a child psychiatrist when the boy was three. The psychiatrist agreed that the boy suffered from a serious maladjustment and he asked the parents to enter psycho-therapy. They refused.

John began school at age six but he lasted for only one day. He tore down the curtains in the school room, over-turned desks, attacked little girls with a knife—and ended the day by setting fire to the teacher. The school suspended him. The parents hired 44 tutors over the next three years in an attempt to teach him to read and write. They failed.

At age nine, John bashed in the head of a nightwatchman in a ware-house he had attempted to burglarize. The man died. A court sent John to the New York detention home where he revolted the other children by cutting out the intestines of gold-fish and forcing the other children to eat them. As a last resort, the court remanded him to Wiltwyck. He spent his time in the school boxing, hitting fish out of a stream with a stick, and threatening other children.

During the original research interview, John evinced no guilt, and announced that he hated everyone. He attacked another child who was in the office and hid under a couch as he tore up the results of other interviews. Only the patience of an Ernst Papanek gave this boy some hope in life.

John, along with all of the other children in the school, finally underwent a series of projective and objective tests (see McCord & McCord, 1956). Among other measures, the researchers included the so-called "Rover" test. This was composed of a set of pictures of "Rover," a dog, faced with a variety of frustrating experiences. Rover would look into the mirror and see an ugly reflection, or he would find that his girlfriend went out with another dog, or he would encounter a threatening policeman on the beat. With each picture, the child was asked, "What does Rover want to do?" The boy then chose one of three pictures. One alternative portrayed an aggressive response, another a withdrawn one, and the third, a neutral reaction to the frustration.

Among other tests, the boys underwent an actual frustrating experience when they had to clean up their cottages during recreation time. They also took a series of tests aimed at measuring their feelings of guilt about violations of conventional American morality, their attitudes toward authority, their self-perception, and their hopes for the future. The various measures—projective tests, behavioral observations, open-ended questionnaires, etc.—were designed to reveal various levels of personality and behavior.

Divided over the time of residence they had spent in the school, both the psychopathic boys and those suffering from a "behavior disorder" showed:

- a marked decrease in actual and fantasy aggression
- an increase in internal controls and guilt
- a less hostile view of authority
- more positive self-perceptions
- and a more realistic response to frustration.

Neurotic and borderline psychotic boys did *not*, however, evince any great changes in behavior or attitudes.

In a thoughtful critique of this study, Roger Brown (1965) pointed out that the results could not necessarily be attributed to Wiltwyck's brand of milieu therapy. "Suppose", he wrote, "that the school had been changing its admissions policy in such a fashion that the boys admitted each consecutive month were more severely aggressive than those admitted the previous month [p. 393]?"

Brown rejected this hypothesis as 25 boys were tested again 8 months after their arrival. The results were the same: on a variety of measures, aggression decreased and the strength of conscience of psychopathic boys increased.

Yet, as Brown pointed out, these results should not go unquestioned. Perhaps the boys would have changed if nothing had been done for them. "Perhaps anyone taking the tests a second time would have changed his answers so as to appear to be less aggressive . . . perhaps it was just age that changed them [1965, p. 393]." Brown discarded these objections as it was clear that psychopathic boys had changed whereas neurotic or pre-psychotic children had not. As Brown added: "Apparently, a second administration of the tests does not inevitably lower scores and apparently eight months of additional age does not do it either [1965, p. 394]."

Strictly, the controls were not perfect. It would have been ideal to compare psychopathic boys raised in an environment different from Wiltwyck's with those who underwent the experience. "In any case," as Brown commented, "I think Freud would have been surprised to find consciences developing at Wiltwyck without the aid of the Oedipus Complex and at an average age of eleven years [1965, p. 394]."

However hopeful, the original Wiltwyck research obviously required a comparison with psychopathic boys who had not received the treatment and a follow-up study to discern whether the effects were lasting. Some later studies and changes at Wiltwyck and Lyman underscored the importance of these issues.

Changes at Wiltwyck and Lyman: 1955–1980

WILTWYCK

Despite all of his virtues, Ernst Papanek lacked accounting abilities. Concerned with financial difficulties, the board of trustees dismissed him. A series of other executive directors at Wiltwyck followed in his path, and he continued to advise the school until his death. The subsequent directors maintained the general guidelines of Papanek's policy. The most recent, Dr. Barry Fireman, adhered as strictly as he could to the policies of milieu therapy.

Lacking Papanek's charismatic leadership, the school inevitably changed. The trustees ordained that the school should change location. It was moved from the bucolic setting on the Hudson River to a new campus in Yorktown Heights, New York. In 1965, the children took up residence in the new location.

Meanwhile, graduates of the Wiltwyck School founded halfway houses in New York City to provide further residential care for children who could not return to their families. In 1962, Floyd Patterson House, a comfortable brownstown in Gramercy Park, New York, opened its doors for the boys. Attended by social workers, the boys lived in the home and went to local public schools. Psychiatrists and psychologists helped in the process of relocation.

In 1967, Howard Weiner and Nina Engel (1967) conducted a modest follow-up study of Wiltwyck. They chose 12 children from the files and later added 70 other boys who had lived at Wiltwyck between 1952 and 1967.[5] The researchers secured information from the Department of Social Services concerning whether the boy was currently under treatment, in a correctional institution, or living at home.

Weiner and Engel defined a boy as "successful" if he lived at home, worked, and had not gotten into serious trouble with the law. An

---

[5] The dates are highly approximate as the authors did not exactly specify them. The authors also did not explain how their subjects were chosen.

"unsuccessful" boy was classified as one who had a criminal record or a mental hospital commitment. The authors well understood the pitfalls in their categorization: "We recognize the grossness of our measuring techniques . . . and their somewhat arbitrary nature [1966, p. v]."

Nonetheless, of the boys whom they could trace, 35% could be considered "trouble-free." Most of the "unsuccessful" boys were involved in minor ways with the law: petty stealing, school disruption, or were considered to be "out of parental control." None had committed truly serious crimes. In this particular study, only one variable seemed to affect the later destiny of the child: 77% of the boys who returned to homes where only the mother was present developed some type of criminal record. Where only the father was present, 32% appeared before a court. This particular study did not compare the Wiltwyck children to any other group. "It is evident," the authors commented, "that more refined efforts of measuring changes and also the all important problem of control groups is necessary to truly evaluate the impact of Wiltwyck treatment on its patients [1966, p. vii]."

LYMAN

The Lyman School changed radically during the intervening years and was, in fact, abolished in 1972. Children who would have gone there are now scattered in regional centers, foster homes, forestry camps, and a few (10%) in secure detention centers.

This dramatic change in policy began in 1969 when the director of the Division of Youth Services resigned his job after numerous investigations of Massachusetts' training schools revealed serious shortcomings, if not outright brutality. At this point, 70% of Lyman children had a recidivist record after 1 year of release.

Dr. Jerome Miller assumed the directorship and attempted to humanize the schools. Old staff members, often well connected with state legislators, complained of his policies. Miller gave up hope of gradual changes in the schools and quietly ordered their dismemberment. In 1973, after he had set the process of abolition in motion, Miller resigned during a period of chaos.

Anticipating a series of major changes, Lloyd Ohlin and his associates at Harvard (Coates, Miller, and Ohlin, 1978) began a series of important studies concerning the process and effects of reform in Massachusetts. Virtually total deinstitutionalization of a state's delinquent population had not been tried before. The researchers attempted to measure the impact of this change by using combined measures of the child's perception of himself and the community, the organization of the new centers for delinquents, self-reports of delinquency, and official measures of recidivism as the new "community-based" program went into action (Coates, Miller, & Ohlin, 1978).

The researchers found that the former inmates of the school perceived that the quality of their life had improved once they were placed in community residences. The delinquents believed that they had more control over their futures, fitted in better with others, and had more links to the community (Coates, Miller, & Ohlin, 1978). These were, of course, subjective responses.

Sophisticated statistical analysis revealed that many of the short-run gains were lost when the boys eventually returned in freedom to their original environments. Interviewed some 6–9 months after placement in the community, the youths had generally re-entered their old patterns. It became abundantly clear to the researchers that the youths' original environment (particularly whether the mother worked or not), rather than their experience in any type of program, was the most potent force in shaping their future.

The actual recidivism rates of the boys *increased* after the community program began. Further, in the 1974 follow-up study, 10% of the population had been charged with serious crimes against the person versus 2% who had been institutionalized and then released in 1968. The increase in serious offenders could well have been due to various changes in the American social climate during that period or to the fact that the average age of boys indicted in 1974 had increased. Seventy-four percent of boys in 1974 had reappeared in court after a period of 1 year as opposed to 66% in 1968.

Seventy-one percent of boys who received a jail sentence were further committed, as were 67% of children who had been sentenced to a "secure care" unit. These results should be expected as presumably such boys represented the most severe cases. The lowest rate of recidivism (41%) was achieved by boys who were sent to foster homes. Again, however, we may reasonably assume that these children differed substantially from the others and represented the "less dangerous" offenders (Coates et al., 1978).

A surprising result was, however, that 84% of boys who received *no* treatment reappeared in court and 55% were recommitted. Thus, the hypothesis of Edwin Schur and others was not confirmed: simply letting delinquents mature, avoiding labeling them, and waiting for them to grow up does not work. "It seems clear," the researchers concluded, "that leaving these youngsters alone did not result in their staying out of trouble and in fact seemed to make matters worse [Coates *et al.*, 1978, p. 155]."

One other result casts doubt on reports about "self-reported" delinquency. Of children who were actually in a training school and had been convicted of delinquency, 23% said that they had *not* been in trouble with the law. By definition, they had, but chose to lie.

The Harvard researchers did not follow up specifically on child psychopaths who were incarcerated at Lyman. They found, however, that children who had been exposed to court processing were most likely to commit other crimes, that "status offenders" were less likely to recidivate, and the "hard-core, aggressive offenders" (many of whom *may* have been psychopaths) needed special treatment. "To focus only on the youths who can be easily handled in the open community and ignore the needs of the more difficult individual is irresponsible [Coates *et al.*, 1978, p. 190]." Clearly, the researchers viewed incarceration in maximum security institutions as a very last resort.

Thus, the dramatic changes at Lyman and the important, but less chaotic alterations of Wiltwyck left open the question of whether milieu therapy—or any other form of relatively humane treatment—could affect the fate of child psychopaths. After 25 years of waiting for the original sample of boys to mature, we set out to find the answer to this problem in 1980. The rising crime rate, the increase in violence, the cynical claims of some scholars that no treatment works or that it even harms people, the vitriolic debate between those who wanted to "lock them up and throw away the key" versus those who wanted society to divest itself entirely of reform schools, jails, and prisons as well as growing public fears and an increasing clamor for capital punishment—all of these factors lent particular urgency and significance to this research.

Wiltwyck versus Lyman: Twenty-Five Years Later

By 1980, the graduates of Lyman and Wiltwyck during the 1952–1955 period were in their late thirties or early forties. They had either reformed or become "hardened criminals." The effects, if any, of the two schools on comparable populations should have become evident. Fortunately, we possessed records that indicated the subjects' original diagnoses, intelligence, home background, special treatment, and many other facts about their early situation in life. Thus, we were in a position to differentiate between child psychopaths and other people who had been convicted of delinquent acts or status offenses.

Independently, without using our knowledge about the subjects' original diagnoses or backgrounds, we developed a fund of information about their later lives: criminal records, mental health information, health statistics, and—in a minority of cases—self-reports about their later lives. This information offered a classic opportunity to trace the subjects over a long period of time and to compare the possible effects of the two schools with each other (as well as national rates and similar children in Massachusetts who had experienced "community treatment").

This research seemed particularly important as the Lyman School (although it no longer existed) had remained a model for the typical reform school in America and public opinion demanded the building of ever more "Lymans." In contrast, the Wiltwyck model had been adopted by only a few private agencies in America. Frustrated by financial difficulties, similar experiments in "milieu therapy" such as Detroit's Pioneer House, had gone out of existence. Simultaneously, however, correctional administrators and scholars in other nations—particularly England, Denmark, and Sweden—had paid attention to the original Wiltwyck research and increasingly called for the establishment of more "Wiltwycks" in their own countries.

In some circles, the Massachusetts experiment in closing all residential centers—laudable in its objectives and humanity—gained increasing popularity. Nonetheless, the Harvard research indicated that the closing of all training schools resulted, at least in the very short run, in an increase in recidivism, particularly of violent crimes. The research further suggested that child psychopaths—who, as new research has demonstrated, may be suffering from neurological problems as well as social deprivation—should not be automatically sent back to their communities.

Therefore, lacking truly long-term studies of different approaches to juvenile correction, both experts and the public were still left with the unanswered question of "what works?"

DESIGN OF THE 1980 STUDY

Information on the early life of the Wiltwyck and Lyman boys was gathered at the Wiltwyck School and at the Massachusetts Department of Youth Services. Information on the later life of the subjects was gathered with the assistance of a variety of social agencies, departments of correction, departments of mental health, bureaus of vital statistics, and the military services in New York, Massachusetts, Florida, Colorado, California, Connecticut, Maine, New Hampshire, and Alabama. It proved possible to trace the entire population at Wiltwyck (175 men) who had resided at the school for more than 18 months between 1952 and 1955. In addition, we traced 165 men who had resided at the Lyman School for 18 months or more during the same period of time.[6] Seventy percent of Wiltwyck's population had permanently stayed in New York and 80% of Lyman's population remained in Massachusetts. By telephone, address, commitment to another institution, or death records, it was possible to definitely locate 81% of the Lyman group and 75% of the Wiltwyck ex-inmates.[7] From the men who remained alive, we selected randomly 12 cases who were extensively interviewed about their marital, educational, and employment histories. In addition, each person gave his own version of his life history and noted some of his attitudes about life. We avoided the use of written or mailed questionnaires because of their obvious unreliability and the impossibility of getting former delinquents to respond. Instead, we depended on face-to-face interviews. Each person granted his permission before the interview and was guaranteed anonymity. No mention was made of a prior criminal or mental hospital record unless the individual brought the subject to the surface.[8] Because the interviews required at least 3 hours for each subject, the respondents were paid for their time.[9]

During the interviews, it became apparent that some people had committed various crimes for which they had not been convicted. Usually, however, the person freely admitted his criminal record—although he was not specifically questioned about it. Those diagnosed as psychopaths, in fact, tended to brag about crimes that may have been imaginary or inflated in importance. Although the confidentiality of the interviews precluded prosecution, we did not find a high rate of "hidden" crimes among the self-reported criminals. This fits well with Charles Silberman's (1978) contention that serious criminals who repeat their crimes five or more times stand little chance of

[6] It proved impossible to secure a total sample of the Lyman men for an odd technical reason: the display machines at the Massachusetts Department of Youth Services broke down because of mechanical malfunction.

[7] No statistically significant differences in criminal, death, alcoholism, mental health, or original background records differentiated those who had left the states from those who remained or between those who had been definitely located and those who had not.

[8] Massachusetts law prohibited interviews in that state with current or ex-mental patients.

[9] All records containing the name or other identifying information of the individual were burned in August, 1981. The privacy of the individual was maintained at all times.

escaping detection. Naturally, as the respondents were paid for their interviews, the possibility remains that we as well as all of the various community authorities involved could have been fooled by "normal" psychopaths.

The criminal records of the subjects secured from various states and the armed services were based *solely* on felonies that resulted in jail or prison sentences, omitting minor infractions of the law. People were recorded as alcoholic or psychotic only if they had been committed to a mental agency on the basis of these diagnoses. Causes of death were ascertained from death certificates in various states.

A person's diagnosis as a psychopath was made on the basis of his original childhood record. The researchers did not have access to later information about the psychopaths when these diagnoses were recorded and could not, therefore, be influenced by knowledge of a later criminal record. This information was supplemented by military service records of the nature and type of discharge.[10]

As noted, we also possessed information gathered on Massachusetts children who had undergone community treatment (Coates *et al.*, 1978) and FBI Uniform Crime Reports (1978) that provided information on the national pattern by age of the commission of crimes. Thus, it was possible to trace the careers of Wiltwyck and Lyman boys up to the age of 40 and to compare these data to the short-run effects of deinstitutionalization, as well as the national pattern of officially recorded crime.

Armed with these data, we are in a position to gauge the possible long- and short-run effects of Wiltwyck and Lyman on their graduates who had now reached middle age.

RESULTS: 1980

The basic results of the research proved initially confusing and posed an intellectual puzzle. Measured in terms of prison and mental hospital commitments for serious offenses, Wiltwyck graduates had a much *lower* recidivism rate than did Lyman graduates up until age 25. The recidivism rates of Lyman graduates were originally quite high, but the rate *dropped* as they grew older. The Wiltwyck rates of criminal activity, however, *increased* steadily with age. Only a minority of *both* groups were still involved with the law between ages 35

[10] At least one-third of the Lyman men had spent time in the armed services; very few of the Wiltwyck men did. Lyman actively encouraged its graduates to enlist, although supposedly the armed services reject volunteers with serious delinquent records. All remained in the lower ranks of enlisted men.

TABLE 1
Recidivism[a]

Age	Wiltwyck (N = 175)	Lyman (N = 165)
15–19	9%	67%
20–24	16%	22%
25–29	24%	20%
30–34	29%	11%
35–40	32%	8%

[a] This table includes those who were convicted of felonies and omits those incarcerated in jails and prisons or mental hospitals, and those who had died at each age level.

and 40. Nonetheless, the proportion of active criminals in the Wiltwyck group exceeded that of the Lyman group by this period of relatively quiescent middle age (Table 1).

In fact, as the lines criss-crossed by age 25, the facts lent themselves to two simplistic explanations:[11]

1. The treatment at Wiltwyck worked for at least 5 years (during a period of high criminality) in changing the boys' attitudes and behavior but dissipated in effect as the men grew older. Indeed, by a stretch of the imagination and by ignoring any significant events that may have taken place in the intervening years, one *could* argue that the Wiltwyck treatment adversely affected recidivism in middle age.

2. The harsh discipline at Lyman failed to change young offenders but, complemented by further punishment up to the age of 25, eventually had a deterrent effect. This argument would, of course, lend some credence to the position of those who would like to incapacitate offenders during the ages when they are most likely to commit crimes.

Because data on deinstitutionalized children in Massachusetts were limited to crimes and had been collected only up to age 24, it was necessary to limit our samples. Similarly, the FBI national statistics reflect only the commission of crimes.

The comparative pattern of crime is as follows (Table 2).

[11] All results presented in this chapter are statistically significant at the .05 level or better.

TABLE 2
Four Crime Rates

Percentage	Age	
	15–19	20–24

80

70   Deinstitutionalized children (Mass.)

60

50   Lyman School

40

30

            FBI Uniform Crime Reports
20

10   Wiltwyck School

0

The FBI reports (1978) indicate that by middle age only 6% of men are still committing crimes. The peak for all men in America occurs between 15 to 19, stays fairly high until 25, and then sharply drops.

In youth and early manhood, when most crimes are committed, it would appear that Wiltwyck's policies were most significantly effective. In contrast, the practices currently followed in Massachusetts seem the least useful way of stopping common crimes—although the policy is less expensive and more humane than the previous procedures followed by Lyman with similar boys. The crime rate of Lyman graduates also dropped by age 25 to approximately the national average. (Interviewees from Lyman indicated that they had changed their way of life not because of Lyman, or a happy marriage, or other positive events in their early life but merely because they were sick of repeated arrests.)

An anomaly still exists: As Wiltwyck men grew older they more often reverted to a criminal pattern than did Lyman men or the national sample recorded by FBI statisticians.

As the interviews with the men suggested, however, the reasons for this strange finding are extremely complicated. Wiltwyck men generally recognized their experience at the school as highly constructive.

They thought of Wiltwyck as a "country club" and many expressed a desire to return there. As one example, a Wiltwyck man who was a psychopath responded to the interview in this fashion:

"Robert" is a 34-year-old male, approximately 5'7" in height and effeminate in appearance. He has been classified by criminal justice records as black but he considers himself white. One of his parents was white, the other black. This was a constant source of problems for him as a child. While attending a predominantly white school, he was hated as a black. When in a predominantly black school, Robert was treated as white. He has never married and considers himself a homosexual since the age of 9. His first homosexual experience occurred at Wiltwyck.

Early in his life, at age 9, Robert became involved in theft, shoplifting, and constant truancy. He was apprehended and sent to Wiltwyck where he lived for approximately 2 years. There, he was diagnosed as a "psychopathic personality."

Robert speaks of Wiltwyck as if he were on vacation. He remembers riding horses, swimming, and enjoying himself with students and staff. His relationships with these people are remembered as "O.K." For Robert, his encounters with social workers and psychiatrists meant very little; they were "only interviews." His intelligence was tested yeilding a superior IQ. Every reference he made to Wiltwyck is of a pleasant nature, and the notion that Wiltwyck was a vacation was repeatedly stated. This view of Wiltwyck is held not only by Robert but by every Wiltwyck graduate we interviewed.

After being released from Wiltwyck, he returned home to his mother and his step-father (whom Robert did not like). He was enrolled in public school, but continued to be truant. "The kids," he said "used to make fun of me because I looked effeminate, so I didn't want to go to school—I preferred being out running the streets." His truancy led to placement in a special "600" school which he hated. Again, the other children made fun of him, called him names, "ass-grabbed" him and harrassed him in general. As Robert put it, "Everybody hated the 600 school. But I hated it the most. I was feminine so the boys would always call me names like 'queer' and 'faggot.' So I stopped going to school. They put me in another 600 school and the same stuff started happening again. Everybody was always feeling my ass, so I stopped going there too. So I started running the streets."

At age 17, Robert was arrested for stealing and was placed on probation, which he violated. He was then sent to Elmira prison where he spent 3 years. There he was placed with older prisoners who saw him, sexually, as "choice." At Elmira, he met an inmate who became his "steady" lover and protector. Contrary to the usual pattern of psychopaths, Robert still resides with him.

Robert's later criminal record demonstrates a high incidence of recidivism in a surprisingly consistent pattern. Between 1970 and 1981, he has been arrested approximately three times every year for larceny, carrying dangerous weapons, possession of stolen property, assault, harrassment, and more recently, drug dealing.

Intermittently he was employed as a hairdresser and described himself as "highly creative." When out of jail, he used heroin and cocaine. He knew that heroin was "bad for the body" but he felt that the "high" was worth it.

In responding to questions about his attitudes, Robert revealed a classic psychopathic pattern. He could not define good or evil. He felt that "everyone was out for themselves" and agrees completely that "you only live once, so you'd better get and do what you can now." "One must be willing," he stated, "to lie about something if it will get you out of trouble," as well as to "step on a few people in order to make it." He regarded his own life as "fucked up" but thinks he could have been a great actor if he had attended acting school. He values "shrewdness" as the key to survival.

Despite his "hustling ability" and his "calculations," Robert—a drug dependent, homosexual mulatto—has failed to cope with the world outside of Wiltwyck. He thinks he has gotten smarter and "more devious" after his release from Wiltwyck. Yet, in his own words, he is "smart, but stupid. I know what to do, but I don't do it."

In contrast to the Wiltwyck group, many of the men from Lyman found it relatively easy to deal with life on the outside. One retired policeman from Lyman commented:

I fooled around a lot when I was a kid—all kids do. But then I got an uncle on the force. When I was twenty, he straightened me out. He got me my first job as a traffic man. And look at me now, sitting on this porch and enjoying life! It helps to have the Irish connection.

Another ex-Lyman man, originally diagnosed as a psychopath, but later engaged in a career as a restaurant supplier, expressed the same theme in a different fashion. This man was reputed to be connected with the Mafia and came from Italian extraction. He did not have an official criminal record in later life.

> I hated that place [Lyman] but it made connections for me. I done
> learned how to get along in the world, made the right friends. They
> started me out in a little market and I met more friends. Today, well
> . . . look at the cigars I smoke, my clothes, my shoes. Pretty ex-
> pensive, huh? Yep, my friends done right by me.

Lyman men viewed their incarceration in the school (and subsequent imprisonments in early manhood) as horrifying, except for contacts that they may have made.

One ex-inmate from Lyman—originally identified as a psychopath
who seemed in middle age to border on psychosis—said:

> It killed me. I done my time there but still they put me in the
> discipline unit. Any time I even moved they got me. Later I done a
> few little things—and what do they do? They sent me up to Con-
> cord, Norfolk, then Walpole and Bridgewater. There ain't nothing
> wrong with my mind! And they took all that money from me just so
> I could get out—but they never paid off. Why did they treat me that
> way?
> Sure, I tried to get away from each place but they caught me.
> Sure, I did a few things that people done think I was wrong. But I
> got to live. Right?

Suddenly, this man's tone changed and he started to sob. "I want you
to find my Mommy and Daddy. Get me out of here! You got the
release forms?"

This man had been incarcerated for life. He had been convicted of
murder, larceny, auto larceny, assault and battery, as well as other
crimes. His parents, who had rejected him, died years before the
interview. Because the state considered him a habitual criminal, he
had been incapacitated for life. As a young French Canadian, he recalled, he had faced a bleak future outside the prison walls. In the
1980s as much as the 1950s, many Bostonians considered French
Canadians as "lazy, shiftless, and violent [Allport, 1954; interviews
with prison officials, 1981]." This stereotype and his record would
have prevented him from getting a job.

We explored several possibilities—intelligence, original home
background, special treatment in the schools, placement after release, education, etc.—which might have explained the difference between the two schools in the later behavior of the released inmates.
None did. One factor, however, stood out: the person's original ethnic
background.

TABLE 3
Recidivism (Lyman)[a]

Percentage convicted of felonies	Age	
	15–24	25–40

Blacks and French Canadians (N = 26)

Irish and Italians (N = 35)

Other Whites (N = 39)

[a] This table omits those who had died, were incarcerated, or who had not been affixed with a definite ethnic label.

ETHNIC BACKGROUND AND CRIMINAL BEHAVIOR

We found that ethnicity had a powerful effect upon the behavior of the men, particularly after age 25.[12]

At Lyman, all ethnic groups declined in crime rate as age advanced. The pattern differed, however, by ethnic origin:

• Whites, without a particular ethnic label, declined most significantly after age 25.
• People who identified themselves as Irish or Italian also had a lower crime rate as age advanced.
• Blacks and French Canadians declined in recidivism, but relatively remained at a rather high level after age 25 (see Table 3).

The general opportunity structure open to whites, Irish, and Italians in Boston society seems to account for this phenomenon.

[12] We chose as a cutoff age the periods below and above 25 as the previous materials have indicated that this is the critical point at which the crimes of Lyman graduates began to drop and those of Wiltwyck graduates rose slightly.

Irishmen, for example, controlled the police, Italians dominated the food business and other sectors of the economy, and the various other whites had many opportunities opened to them. Moreover, members of these groups could often return from Lyman (or other places where they had been incarcerated in early manhood) to established communities with a high degree of social control as well as links to the larger society.

In contrast, blacks returned to a society that promised little opportunity and lots of prejudice. Although some blacks had resided in Boston since pre-Revolutionary times, most of those who became involved with Lyman were first generation immigrants from the South who knew little or nothing about the Boston black community.

In a somewhat similar fashion, Boston had precluded French Canadians from entering all but the lowliest of occupations. Like the Irish of the 1850s, they were regarded as indolent thieves and drunkards. Most of the men in our sample were first generation immigrants and suffered from linguistic as well as cultural problems. Their families had not yet had the time or opportunity to establish their own communities or to win dominance in politics, the police, or other occupations.

Wiltwyck had a different mixture of ethnic groups: Blacks and Hispanics predominated over whites. People who identified themselves as specifically French Canadians, Italians, or Irish were very rare. Nonetheless, a similar pattern emerged: *the more deprived ethnic groups were more likely to commit crimes in later life* (Table 4).

Clearly, as age increased, the recidivism rates of blacks and Hispanics went up, whereas those of other whites declined. The interviews suggested that all of the men remembered Wiltwyck fondly — perhaps, in a sense, too fondly. Their life in childhood had been spent in brutal or neglecting environments. The sojourn at Wiltwyck, lasting up to 4 years, offered a welcome relief from "real" society. Upon re-entering the world of New York, they had high expectations, a memory of kindness, and a new sense of self-esteem. Therefore, in early manhood, they were able to try a life other than crime.

Yet, as the years passed, their experiences at Wiltwyck became largely irrelevant. The blacks and the Hispanics encountered discrimination in education, jobs, and housing. A feeling of frustration and dashed hopes may have engulfed them. The blacks and Hispanics often returned to a life of crime as thieves, dope peddlers, or armed robbers. As Wiltwyck had provided a dream that they could not fulfill, the less privileged ethnic groups returned to their "normal" activities.

TABLE 4
Recidivism (Wiltwyck)[a]

Percentage who commit felonies	Age	
	15– 24	25– 40

```
60
          Blacks (N = 48)
50

40              Hispanics (N = 15)

30

                            Other whites (N = 38)
20

10

0
```

[a] This table omits those who had died, were incarcerated, or who had not been affixed with a definite ethnic label.

As the Wiltwyck and Lyman populations did not differ in various other possible respects, it would appear that the differences in ethnicity largely accounted for crime rates after the age of 25. Wiltwyck had a higher proportion of members of minority groups. Thus, its graduates eventually had a higher crime rate in later life.

This is a sad commentary on our society. *Wiltwyck, in fact, rehabilitated most of its boys. Lyman did not.* Some 10 years later, however, the men faced the all too tangible barriers of prejudice and lost the advantages given them by the treatment at Wiltwyck. Increasingly, they resembled their colleagues at Lyman—some of whom had to cope with similar burdens in later life.

This finding suggests that effective treatment in childhood must be accompanied by a virtual revolution in our society: an elimination of unequal opportunity for blacks, Hispanics, French Canadians, or any other group. However desirable such a drastic change would be, it seems unlikely to occur in the foreseeable future. Perhaps the French Canadians and Hispanics will gradually meld in the melange of ethnic groups in America and the barriers of prejudice will fall—as they did for the Irish and the Italians. Except for the possibility of intermarriage or a major shift in economic status, however, blacks are likely to remain a visible target of bigotry.

The central concern of this book is, of course, the impact of treatment on child psychopaths. How did they fare in later life?

IMPACT ON PSYCHOPATHS

Psychopaths composed approximately the same percentages at both schools: 35% of the Wiltwyck population and 31% of the Lyman sample.[13]

It should be noted that diagnoses of the children on their original admittance to the schools were kept confidential. Psychologists, psychiatrists, or others made the diagnoses but they were kept in private files that were not accessible to the staff. Counselors at Wiltwyck discussed specific cases and their family background, but not their diagnoses. The staff at Lyman discussed nothing about the boys except their misbehavior in the school. Thus, *the psychopathic children did not suffer from biases or self-fulfilling prophecies attributable to their diagnoses than did other children at the schools.* Society and their families had defined every child as "bad" by the sheer act of incarceration.

Nonetheless, psychopaths—as one would predict—came from more emotionally barren, deviant environments than did other types of children who were imprisoned:

- Father and son relationships were particularly disturbed in the psychopathic group (Table 5).[14]

TABLE 5

Father's Relationship and Psychopathy

Nature of father's relationship to son	Psychopaths ($N = 99$)	Others ($N = 191$)
Supportive	6%	45%
Abandoned/Dead	40%	25%
Rejecting	19%	15%
Neglecting	35%	15%

- Whether present or absent, the father hardly offered the son a good role model. In cases where records could be obtained, the

[13] Naturally, these figures omit any estimates of "normal psychopaths" as both populations were incarcerated. An ideal study would include a random sample of the entire American population at birth who are then followed up thoroughly in later stages of life.

[14] Children who were not diagnosed were omitted.

majority of psychopaths' fathers were criminal, alcoholic, or psychiatrically disturbed.[15]
- Mothers also offered little support to the psychopaths. Like the fathers, they were either absent or dead. If present, they tended to neglect or reject their children (Table 6).[16]

TABLE 6
Mother's Relationship and Psychopathy

Mother's relation- ship to son	Psychopaths (N = 81)	Others (N = 103)
Supportive	19%	95%
Abandoned/Dead	14%	1%
Rejecting	25%	2%
Neglecting	22%	2%

Confirming prior research, psychopaths much more often suffered from maternal neglect, abandonment, or rejection than did other types of delinquents. Although at a lesser rate than the fathers, the mothers of psychopaths also exhibited significantly higher rates of criminality, alcoholism, mental disorder, and sexual promiscuity. Unfortunately, because the proper neurological and psychological tests were not administered in the 1950s, it was impossible to discern the physiological states of the psychopaths.

The Wiltwyck and Lyman Schools had significantly different effects on psychopaths after their incarceration. The following pattern emerged as the subjects entered middle age (Table 7).[17]

Clearly, at both schools, psychopaths exceed other types of inmates in the commitment of felonies at virtually every age level. The one exception was the age span of 20–24 where the two groups were virtually equal. Wiltwyck apparently had its greatest impact on psychopaths during the first 5 years after release.

If one compares the various populations of both schools, however, an interesting pattern emerges:

[15] Children who were not diagnosed and cases where the father's record was missing have been omitted. People listed under alcoholic or psychotic had records only for these problems. Criminal fathers, in some cases, also had records that incorporated alcoholism and psychiatric disturbance.

[16] Cases where the mother's relationship with the child or the child's diagnosis were missing have been omitted.

[17] Subjects who were not diagnosed or were incapacitated or who had died at each age level are omitted.

TABLE 7
Recidivism

Age	Psychopaths		Others	
	Wiltwyck	Lyman	Wiltwyck	Lyman
	($N = 42$)	($N = 37$)	($N = 71$)	($N = 81$)
15–19	11%	79%	8%	55%
20–24	12%	14%	17%	24%
25–29	46%	39%	20%	14%
30–34	36%	29%	15%	6%
35–40	33%	19%	19%	3%

- *Non*psychopaths released from Lyman more often were convicted of felonies than were psychopaths from Wiltwyck up to the age of 25. Thus, *Wiltwyck appears to have been particularly — perhaps uniquely — helpful in preventing further crime during the years immediately following the boys' release.* After that early age, however, psychopaths at Wiltwyck and Lyman had approximately the same recidivism rate.
- Except for the age group of 15– 19 who had been released from Lyman, a *minority* of psychopaths at both schools were convicted of felonies. This fact undermines the prevailing opinion that psychopaths continue in a life of crime forever.
- Psychopaths from either school committed the *majority* of all crimes (56% to 70%) at all age levels. They were highly versatile, ranging from crimes against the person, to forgery, to drug dealing, to acting as a "fence."

These phenomena could be explained in a variety of possible ways:

- One could argue that psychopaths more often died or were killed at early ages and that fate had removed them from the pool of possible criminals. Psychopaths and other types of ex-inmates from both schools did not differ significantly from each other in their rate of mortality at any age. Psychopaths did, however, die more often during crime-related activities as either the offender or the victim.
- A related argument would be that young psychopaths at Wiltwyck were more often incapacitated by incarceration in another reform school, jail, prison, or mental hospital than Lyman psychopaths, and this factor prevented the Wiltwyck graduates from committing as many crimes in early age.

In fact, no general pattern emerged. Psychopaths from both schools usually, but not always, had a higher rate of incarceration than did other groups. Comparing psychopaths in the critical 15–19 year range, more of the Wiltwyck group (37%) than the Lyman group (17%) almost immediately underwent further incarceration. Yet, other types of ex-inmates at this age exceeded both groups of psychopaths in their rate of incarceration. Even adding together psychopaths at both schools who were either dead or incapacitated does *not* explain the great gap in recidivism rates between Wiltwyck and Lyman during the ages of 15–19.

The nature of further incarceration differed. Ex-Wiltwyck children between 15 and 19 were often sent on to Children's Village or other un-walled institutions that basically resembled Wiltwyck; a few were transferred to adolescent units in psychiatric settings, such as Rockland State Hospital. In contrast, further incarceration for Lyman boys of that age usually meant transfer to state police barracks or sentencing to even more severe disciplinary units such as the Shirley Industrial Training School or the Bridgewater unit for the criminally insane.

There are, of course, many other alternative explanations of the initial success of the Wiltwyck psychopaths and their later relative equality with Lyman:

• The original success of Wiltwyck might be explained by the special psychiatric or medical treatment that some boys received in the school. Yet, we did not find any differences either at Wiltwyck or at Lyman in the eventual pattern followed by those who did or did not receive such unique help.

• Wiltwyck's early success with psychopaths might have had something to do with their placement after they left the school. We did not discover any significant differences at either school between the ages 15 and 24 between boys who returned to their original home, went to a foster home, or received special care after their release.

• Surprisingly, however, *after* age 24 when one would presume that parental influence was waning, the original disposition of the boys seemed to make a slight difference among Wiltwyck graduates. If they had been returned to the immediate family—which was usually highly disturbed—Wiltwyck men after the age of 24 more often committed recorded felonies: 24% of those who had gone back to their families continued to commit crimes after age 24 as opposed to 10% of those who went to other environments. At the Lyman school, the immediate disposition of the child made no difference at any age.

- For the Wiltwyck psychopaths, sending them home to a family where both parents had a criminal record made a significant difference in later recidivism *after* age 24. Thirty-three percent of psychopaths who had returned from Wiltwyck to a highly deviant home recidivated as opposed to 8% who returned home to a family where neither parent had an official criminal record.

- Intelligence might have played a slight role. One could reasonably argue that the more intelligent psychopaths would learn at an earlier age to avoid committing crimes where they might easily be caught. The staff at both schools had administered the Stanford–Binet IQ test to most of the children. Up to the age of 24, no differences in recidivism based on intelligence appeared among psychopaths at either Lyman or Wiltwyck. Therefore, intelligence could not account for the initial advantage of the Wiltwyck children. Strangely, after age 25, more psychopaths of *superior* intelligence from both schools were convicted of felonies than were those of average or below average intelligence. Conversely, people of low intelligence who had been diagnosed as nonpsychopathic committed *more* crime at both schools as time passed.

- Conceivably, the prognosis given at the school at the time of the boy's release could have affected his recidivism rate—even though the child himself was unaware of the prognosis. Following labeling theory, it would be possible to argue that psychopaths who received a "negative" prognosis would be more likely to continue in a deviant career. The label could have followed them throughout life. This did not prove true. No significant differences appeared between psychopaths (or others) at either school who had been labeled "positively" or "negatively."

- Perhaps the original diagnoses were wrong or biased. At this point in history, there is no way to prove or disprove this hypothesis. Status offenders who had committed no actual crimes were as often diagnosed as psychopaths as children who had a long record of previous crimes. The diagnosis of psychopathy did concur with reports in the literature that psychopaths came from seriously disturbed environments. Later information showed that psychopaths from both schools continued to commit crimes more frequently in later life—but this obviously could not have been known when the children entered the school. In any case, any argument about the biased nature of the diagnosis would not explain the disparity in recidivism rates between Wiltwyck and Lyman in the age group 15–19 or their similarity in later life.

TABLE 8
Mental Hospitalization

Age	Wiltwyck (N = 175)	Lyman (N = 165)
15–19	16%	15%
20–24	7%	9%
25–29	16%	14%
30–34	14%	12%
35–40	14%	5%

• Psychopaths might have come more often from ethnic groups that suffered from discrimination. As psychopaths came equally from various ethnic groups, this factor does not explain the initial advantage which the Wiltwyck graduates enjoyed.

It would have been delightful to report that Wiltwyck had a lasting effect on psychopaths or other delinquents. The pattern of our results is, however, much more ambiguous. It is apparent that the treatment at Wiltwyck significantly changed the attitudes and criminal behavior of the boys for a period of 5–10 years. After that, it would seem that the lasting effect of such a benevolent environment was eroded by other influences or events.

MENTAL DISORDER AND ALCOHOLISM

Rates of mental disorder—measured by commitment to a mental hospital on a diagnosis of psychosis—were basically similar between the populations of the two schools up to age 34. From age 35 onward, slightly more Wiltwyck men than those from Lyman manifested overt psychotic symptoms that led to mental hospital treatment (see Table 8).

This finding is consonant with the original Wiltwyck–Lyman research that found that neither school had a major effect on the behavior and attitudes of children who were first diagnosed as severely neurotic or pre-psychotic. Apparently, Wiltwyck's intense psychiatric and psychological treatment did not deter hospitalization in later life—perhaps because the roots of psychoses are too deeply embedded or events in later life were more potent than exposure in childhood to a psychiatrically oriented environment. Another important factor may have been that Wiltwyck took in more boys with severe emotional disorders than did Lyman.

The two schools also had basically similar patterns of alcoholism, as measured by arrests for alcoholic offenses or commitment to a mental hospital on a diagnosis of alcoholism. Less than 1% of each group at each age level could be considered as alcoholic in later life, a remarkably low incidence for a population of deviant children (Robins, 1966). As neither school actively sought to prevent alcoholism, however, this finding should not be surprising.

Conclusions

The Wiltwyck School—a highly progressive, psychiatrically oriented environment for adolescent boys—dramatically changed the attitudes, self-esteem, moral values, and behavior of its children between 1952 and 1955. Its most potent effect was on psychopathic children who developed consciences, absorbed new codes of ethics, and identified with helpful adults.

In contrast, the Lyman School in Massachusetts brought about no changes in its wards. Oriented to vocational training and strict discipline, the Lyman school typified the public reformatory system of the late twentieth century in America.

Because of the popular belief that treatment does not work or actually harms people—and the complementary notion that criminals should be incapacitated rather than rehabilitated—it seemed of great importance to trace the lives of boys who had undergone quite different experiences in early adolescence. The boys closely resembled each other in age, family backgrounds, intelligence, school records, urban residence, and socioeconomic level. They differed only in that they came from diverse ethnic backgrounds: Irish, Italian, French Canadian, and other whites predominated at Lyman. Black and Hispanic boys formed a majority at Wiltwyck.

With the cooperation of a variety of social agencies in many states, it was possible to secure various records on the boys that reflected their later recidivism rates for felonies, mental hospital commitments, military service, alcoholism, and mortality rates. In addition, we conducted personal interviews with a sample of the men to see if suggestive patterns appeared in later life. In addition, we possessed the original information on the boys' families, diagnoses, dispositions, and many other aspects of their early life. The basic results were:

1. Wiltwyck graduates up to the age of 24—and particularly during the 15–19 age bracket—had a lower recidivism rate than did Lyman graduates. After age 24, recidivism dropped at Lyman and slightly increased at Wiltwyck. Only a minority of each group was committing felonies by the time they had reached their late thirties.

2. Until age 24, Wiltwyck ex-inmates had a lower recidivism rate than deinstitutionalized children in Massachusetts or national rates for men of the same age.

3. Ethnicity had a powerful effect on both Wiltwyck and Lyman graduates. From an originally low level, the crime rate of blacks and Hispanics at Wiltwyck gradually climbed to a higher rate than in their youth. Presumably, the Wiltwyck men had undergone a beneficent, pleasant experience in early adolescence. Once faced with the discrimination of general society and a lack of opportunities, they tended more often to revert to a criminal pattern. In a somewhat different form, the same pattern held true at Lyman: the rate for Irish, Italian, and other whites dropped as age progressed. Excluded by prejudice from participation in the larger society, the rates for French Canadians and blacks remained relatively high.

4. Wiltwyck had a highly significant effect on psychopathic children immediately during the first 5 years after their release; Lyman's psychopaths exhibited a high rate of serious crime during the same period. After age 24, however, relatively equal proportions of psychopaths from both schools engaged in a criminal fashion and were responsible for the majority of crimes committed.

4. Although psychopaths as a group came from more highly deprived emotional backgrounds than did other delinquents, this fact alone did not account for the initial differences between the schools.

5. Mortality rates, incapacitation, special treatment received in the schools, original disposition on release, prognosis, intelligence, possible faults in diagnosis, and ethnic origins did not explain the initial difference between psychopaths at Wiltwyck and those at Lyman.

Therefore, it would appear that the general Wiltwyck environment had a positive effect on psychopaths during the first 5 years after their release. In later life, a majority of ex-inmates from both schools were not convicted for later crimes—undermining the belief that psychopaths continue forever as incorrigible criminals.

It is, of course, quite possible that some psychopaths continued their criminal pattern and were not caught or entered normal, if shady enterprises. Our interviews indicated that ex-psychopaths admitted—or bragged about—crimes for which they had not been sentenced. Both groups of psychopaths might have become increasingly streetwise, but this would not explain the initial 5-year gap in recidivism between the two schools at exactly the period when the national crime rate reaches its peak. The fact that Wiltwyck can help child psychopaths at an early age and that most psychopaths stop committing officially recorded crimes in later life suggests some major changes in both the law and public policy.

References

Allport, G. *The nature of prejudice*. Cambridge: Addison-Wesley, 1954.

Boston Citizen's Committee. Lyman investigation. Mimeo, 1947.

Brown, C. *Manchild in the promised land*. New York: Macmillan, 1965.

Brown, R. *Social psychology*. New York: Free Press, 1965.

Coates, R., Miller, A., & Ohlin, L. *Diversity in a youth correctional system*. Cambridge: Ballinger, 1978.

Federal Bureau of Investigation. *Uniform crime reports*. Washington, D.C.: U.S. Government Printing Office, 1978.

McCord, W., & McCord, J. Two approaches to the cure of delinquents. *Journal of Criminal Law, Criminology and Police Science*. 1953 (Nov.–Dec.), *44* (No 4):442–467.

McCord, W., & McCord, J. *Psychopathy and delinquency*. New York: Grune and Stratton, 1956.

Papanek, E. Training school: Program and leadership. *Federal Probation*, 1953, *6*:219–223.

Papanek, E., & Linn, E. *Out of the fire*. New York: William Morrow, 1975.

Silberman, C. *Criminal violence, criminal justice*. New York: Random House, 1978.

Weiner, H., & Engel, N. A longitudinal study of 103 Wiltwyck boys. Mimeo, 1967, Wiltwyck School.

Wiley, L. Report on Wiltwyck. Mimeo, New York School of Social Work, Jan., 1941.

10

The Lonely Stranger, the Law, and Public Policy

This action is a confession of social and legal failure.
[Judge Joseph Ullman, sentencing Herman Duker, "to be hung by the neck until dead."]
Joseph Ullman, *A Judge Takes the Stand* (New York: Knopf, 1933).

• In 1971, an Englishman, George Fish, was found guilty of killing and eating children. Under the M'Naghten or "diminished responsibility" rules that prevail in England the court found Fish sane and responsible for his acts. Fish's intellectual and perceptual capacities were not impaired. "When he ate children . . . he knew what he was doing, and he knew . . . that what he was doing was contrary to law and public morality [Finagrette, 1972, p. 177]."

• In 1981, two Los Angeles teenagers walked the streets one night. They tried to rob one man, but he had no money; they stopped a couple who handed over $8 and their wristwatches; then they came across two elderly women and killed them. As they walked, they encountered a Frenchman, visiting Los Angeles for the first time. They killed him after a few words. Finally, they encountered an old man; they took his money and then killed him (*Newsweek*, 1981, p. 40). What should be done with these young men who were later found to be psychopathic?

• Herman Webb Duker had been diagnosed as a psychopath in early childhood and committed to a New York City reformatory. After his mandatory release, he migrated to Maryland where he robbed apartments and served time in a Maryland school. Psychiatrists had diagnosed him as a psychopath but under Maryland law he could not receive psychiatric treatment or be isolated from society. He escaped from jail and returned to New York. He committed more crimes and served a term at the Elmira Reformatory where he was handled like any other criminal. After release, he killed a man while robbing him. He appeared before the court of Judge Joseph Ullman who found the defendant guilty. Five psychiatrists, for both the prosecution and defense, declared Duker to be psychopathic. "To paraphrase the views expressed by every expert witness in this case," Judge Ullman (1933) said, "the psychopathic personality is emotionally unbalanced. . . . He knows the consequences of wrong-doing, but impulses beyond his control sway his actions. . . . Every witness in this case agreed that Duker had not the normal emotional moral impulses and controls [p. 217]."

Nonetheless, under current law, Judge Ullman had two choices: life imprisonment or execution. Ullman decided that the man was "legally sane, medically of abnormal psychology, and socially extremely dangerous [p. 218]." Judge Ullman added: "Duker is a mentally abnormal person, and I knew him to be so when I sentenced him to hang. There is something very ugly about that bald statement. . . . I do not believe in capital punishment . . . society confesses its own failure every time it exacts a life for a life [p. 229]."

Judge Ullman recognized that society had had the chance of changing Duker in New York schools, at Elmira, and in Maryland but had failed. Other organizations, such as Wiltwyck, might have altered Duker's pattern and saved the life of the man whom he eventually killed. Very reluctantly, knowing that society had failed to save an individual or to protect itself, Judge Ullman sentenced Duker to hang.

These cases and others like them raised a series of grave questions that have dismayed social scientists, judges, and philosophers. Is the psychopath legally and morally responsible for his or her actions? Is the psychopath mentally diseased? Can we—as judge, psychiatrist, or sociologist—predict the ultimate danger that a person may present? Assuming that an individual is convicted of vicious crimes, what social policy should be followed?

Are Psychopaths "Responsible" for Their Actions?

Throughout the Western world and much of the rest of the globe, judges have applied four tests (or some combination of them) to estimate the degree of responsibility of a person for his or her criminal actions:

1. The M'Naghten Rule: In 1843, M'Naghten, an Englishman, killed the secretary of Sir Robert Peel. He believed that Peel headed a conspiracy to persecute him and, equally mistakenly, mistook the secretary for Peel himself. Over the objections of the House of Lords, the courts adjudged M'Naghten as mentally irresponsible for his admitted murder. The judges argued that a plea of insanity depended on showing that "at the time of committing the act, the party accused was labouring under such a defect of reason, from disease of the mind, as not to know the nature and quality of the act he was doing, or, if he did know it, that he did not know he was doing what was wrong [M'Naghten, 1843]." In England, this test replaced the old custom (1724) that held a person irresponsible if "he doth not know what he is doing, no more than . . . a wild beast." America, Canada, Australia, and India followed the example of the M'Naghten rule and adopted it in most jurisdictions, particularly emphasizing whether the defendant knew the difference between right and wrong.

Critics in the twentieth century have attacked the M'Naghten rule as unrealistic, impossible to apply in particular cases, and potentially dangerous to society as it could provide for the acquittal of vicious people. They have argued that the M'Naghten rule was based on an outmoded theory of nineteenth century psychology. Such a rule ignores the interaction between a person's cognitive faculties, consciousness, emotions, and the inseparable link between rational and irrational impulses. As one judge remarked, "The modern science of psychology . . . does not conceive that there is a separate little man in the top of one's head called reason whose function it is to guide another unruly little man called instinct, emotion, or impulse in the way he should go [Durham, 1954, p. 196]."

The M'Naghten rule, as Herbert Finagrette (1972) pointed out, provides no exact interpretation of "wrong." Is it that the person's *knowledge of the meaning of wrong* is intellectually defective—as it clearly is *not* with most psychopaths—or is it that he or she is *incapable of acting* in accord with society's moral standards? What should be the plausible definition of "to know"? Should this be interpreted as cognitive awareness or the internalization of society's standards?

Many philosophers have also elaborated on the issue of how one should define "wrong" itself under the M'Naghten rule. If the phrase strictly means "legally" wrong, then the psychopath should be held responsible as he or she knows the rules as well as all of us. If one broadens the interpretation to include "morally" wrong, the standard becomes more ambiguous. The psychopath lacks emotional attachments, as most of us experience them, to others. If he or she harms another person, they subjectively feel no guilt. Should he or she be held responsible for this action? "Why is the affectless person [the psychopath] irrational if others really do not matter to him? If they do not matter, is not the conduct perfectly rational? [Finagrette, 1972, p. 84]." By this standard, the psychopath would have acted "rationally" and should be held responsible—even though, by other standards, he or she would be considered either immoral or legally irresponsible.

Similar issues have emerged concerning "innocence" as it is defined under the M'Naghten rule. Finagrette provided an example: "Imagine Adam and Eve commanded by God not to eat of the tree of life and imagine them then disobeying. They would no longer be innocent of wrong-doing. . . . Young children are, of course, often precisely in this condition . . . while still retaining their innocence [p. 141]."

Yet, are not psychopaths in the same position as young children? Perhaps they have been told the rule, but they disobey. They remain in a "state of innocence" as they have neither internalized the rules nor learned the wisdom of obeying them.

Because of the ambiguities in the M'Naghten rule, 15 states in America and in other areas have adopted the "irresistible impulse" rule.

2. The Irresistible Impulse Rule. Used in conjunction with the M'Naghten rule, the irresistible impulse test probably originated in Ohio in 1834 (State *vs.* Thompson, 1843). England and Canada have rejected it in its pristine form. Essentially the test says that a defendant may well know the difference between right and wrong but is irresistibly driven to commit the act. Usually, courts have added that the person suffers from some mental compulsion.

This standard has failed to gain wide acceptance among judges as it does not clearly define the term "irresistible." As Frank Hartung (1966) pointed out, "The crucial problem of the concept of irresistible impulse is to find empirical evidence of its existence, *other than the act itself* [p. 93]."

In addition, the word "impulse" connotes spontaneity. Yet, many psychopaths and other criminals have long contemplated their crimes before committing them. In one crucial case, for example, a man named Pollard admitted his guilt to three charges of attempted armed robbery of banks. His attorney pleaded the irresistible impulse defense as Pollard had witnessed the murder of his wife and daughter and—supposedly because of the trauma—felt compelled to obtain money for his second wife. Pollard himself argued that he was sane. Judge Theodore Levin found him guilty and argued cogently against the irresistible impulse rule: "The uncritical adoption of this point of view would completely do away with the concept of criminal responsibility [United States vs. Pollard, 1964]." Pollard was sentenced to prison.

Without using exactly the same wording, England has adopted a rule of "diminished responsibility." Children such as Mary Bell have been exempted from full responsibility on the basis that they were too young to inhibit their murderous impulses. On the adult level, some psychopaths, such as the killer of 13 prostitutes, have successfully used the diminished responsibility plea on grounds that they had temporarily gone insane.

As this standard has done little to clarify the status of psychopaths, most jurisdictions in the Western world have not adopted it.

3. *The Durham Decision.* In 1954, Judge David Bazelon heard the appeal of Monte Durham, a felon who had been in and out of mental hospitals and jails. The Navy had discharged him at age 17 with the appended opinion that he suffered from a profound personality disorder. Returned to civilian society, Durham engaged in car theft and forgery. Medical examiners declared him a psychopath. Psychiatrists noted that "If the question of right and wrong were propounded to him, he could give you the right answer." Nonetheless, by any other standard, Durham seemed mentally aberrant (Durham, 1954, p. 862).

The court proposed another standard of criminal responsibility: "An accused is not criminally responsible if his unlawful act was the product of mental disease or mental defect [Durham vs. United States, 1954, p. 862]." The new decision specifically included psychopaths under this rubric. The rule seemed revolutionary as it did away with issues such as whether the person had a cognitive knowledge of right and wrong, whether he was impulsive, and whether he was outwardly rational.

Actually, the Durham decision had long precedents. The Greenstein Act in Pennsylvania (Pennsylvania Public Law, 1933), Connecticut, and Maryland had already led to the adoption of laws that provided that mental disorder should serve as an acceptable defense. The various rulings, repealed later, suffered from similar problems. Their defect was that the earlier laws usually depended on the demonstration of consistent "antisocial" behavior. This standard posed two basic difficulties : (a) A mentally disordered person may never have acted in a criminal way before, and (b) repeated antisocial conduct did not equal psychopathy or encompass mental disorder. The previous laws could have provided for preventive detention of people, violated their constitutional liberties, and ignored the actual offenses that they may have committed (Brakel & Rock, 1971).

The Durham rule, however, seemed to provide new grounds for considering the issue of psychopathic responsibility. Although slightly modified by the McDonald decision in 1962 and the Washington decision of 1967 (McDonald vs. United States, 1962; Washington vs. United States, 1967), few jurisdictions have accepted the Durham rule. Several difficulties have arisen.

First, what is a "product"? This issue involves jurists in complicated questions of causality for which few have an answer. Second, what is "mental disease or defect"? Most judges hesitate to base a verdict on this issue for the obvious reason that even experts in the field have trouble defining the terms.

The Model Penal Code of 1962, offered by the American Law Institute, attempted to resolve these problems.

4. *The Model Penal Code.* Although not mandatory, the American Law Institute's Model Penal Code has been adopted by many states and the majority of Federal jurisdictions. In essence, the code specifies that a "person is not responsible for criminal conduct if at the time of such conduct as a result of mental disease or defect he lacks substantial capacity either to appreciate the criminality of his conduct or to conform his conduct to the requirements of the law "(see Brakel & Rock, 1971, p. 383). The English Homicide Act of 1957 partially inspired the American model code. It specifies that a person who kills should be convicted of manslaughter rather than murder if his act resulted from "such abnormality of mind . . . as substantially impaired his mental responsibility for acts."

The new codes combine the M'Naghten and irresistible impulse rules and take account of volitional as well as cognitive capacities. The drafters of the code, however, rejected the Durham decision because it did not outline a concept of causality. The Model Code overruled previous formulations on several grounds. The authors felt that both M'Naghten and the irresistible impulse rules required a complete impairment of all judgment—a condition that seldom, if ever, occurs. In addition, the authors of the code rejected the irresistible impulse rule on grounds that it excluded the brooding, planning criminal who might be mentally ill. The Model Code did not include the psychopathic personality on the reasonable grounds that many psychopaths have been defined *only* in terms of their recidivism. (Our research has demonstrated that repeated criminality should not be considered in the diagnosis of psychopath.)

In general, however, the Code had broadened the definitions of irresponsibility "in an effort to reflect some of the shades in the spectrum between complete mental collapse and complete understanding [Brakel & Rock, 1971, p. 383]."

Various nations have adopted formulations that, to some degree, resemble the Model Penal Code. France does not find guilt in the case of "le caràctere délicteux." Belgian jurists consider the person's ability to control his actions. Cuba, Sweden, and England all recognize irrationality as an excuse for criminal actions—and charge the prosecution with proving the opposite. Russia and most of Eastern Europe decide issues of responsibility primarily in terms of the person's "social danger"—an ambiguous standard that has, at times, been used to hospitalize political dissenters. Virtually every nation, in one form or another, uses the concept of mental disorder as a standard of irresponsibility.

Like all of the other attempts at conceptualizing the idea of responsibility, the Model Code suffers from several deficiencies. First, by ignoring the psychopath under the definition, the drafters of the code ignore evidence that psychopaths suffer from traumatic familial experiences and possibly neural deficiencies. Should a person be held responsible for his family background or damage to his brain? Second, the Code fails to define the crucial words "substantial capacity." How, then, can an ordinary court establish whether a person can "appreciate" the criminality of his actions or "conform his conduct to the requirements of the law"? Third, and most importantly, the Code—like all other rules concerning responsibility—fails to define "mental disease or defect." This is critically important in the case of the psychopath as—however rational or irrational, however impulsive or deliberate his actions may be—distinguished experts on both sides have failed to decide whether he is "mentally diseased" or, indeed, have been unable to define "mental illness" itself.

Is the Psychopath "Mentally Diseased"?

All existing concepts of responsibility or irresponsibility rest on the assumption that a "normal" criminal has, by his own free choice, assumed a mantle of guilt or blame. "The single constant element," Abraham Goldstein (1970) commented, "is the concept of blame. . . . Because it is widely assumed that 'blame' plays a critical role in maintaining individual responsibility and social order, the insanity defense continues to be regarded as exceptional [1970, p. 15]."

Except under the Durham rule, psychopaths are generally considered as responsible because they do not suffer from a psychosis. I agree that one should not be adjudged a psychopath on the basis of psychotic symptoms or repeated antisocial actions. As the Canadian Royal Commission on Insanity (see Brakel and Rock, 1971) concluded, "The act must necessarily involve more than mere knowledge that the act is being committed; there must be an appreciation of the factors involved in the act and a mental capacity to measure and foresee the consequences of violent conduct." This standard may or may not include the psychopath. Can any of the standards provide a measurable definition of "to know." or a "product of mental disease" or "impulsivity" as applied to the psychopath or other criminals? Probably not. Yet, 93% of the members of the Group for the Advancement of Psychiatry said that there are cases in which criminals were "incapable of controlling . . . the impulse to commit harm [Goldstein, 1970, p. 100]." Surely, this standard would fit the majority of psychopaths.

It is eminently clear, however, that most experts cannot agree on the concept of "incapability" or "mental disease." Therefore, we are left with the question of what constitutes mental disease and whether the psychopath fits it.

Psychiatrist Thomas Szasz would do away with the concept of mental disease and irresponsibility altogether. From his point of view, the only mental disease appears to be one caused by a physical condition (e.g., general paresis caused by advanced syphilis). Otherwise, he believes it is merely a semantic label placed on persons for reasons of social control.

Szasz (1961) argued that psychiatrists themselves cannot distinguish between "mental health" and "mental illness." He has also contended that psychiatric considerations might well undermine Western standards of civilization. He believes that putting the good of the individual above that of responsibility may well subvert the social order. Thus, Szasz has concluded, "Treating offenders as responsible human beings, even though sometimes they may not be individually 'blameworthy,' offers them the only chance . . . of remaining 'human' and possibly becoming more so [1961, p. 118]." Essentially, Szasz suggests that courts should consider all human beings *as if* they were responsible for their actions.

He does, however, leave open potentially ambiguous interpretations of his position by suggesting that jurists should consider all of the "human circumstances" that prompt an individual to commit crime and that these "scientific" considerations should be included in any judgment about the disposition of the person.

Szasz's attempt to alter the concept of mental illness has encountered formidable opposition. Herbert Morris (1976), a distinguished philosopher, argued that "If it is an injustice to punish an innocent person, it is no less an injustice, and a far more significant one in our day, to fail to promote as best we can through adequate facilities and medical care the treatment of those who are ill [p. 57]." Yet, Morris appears to contradict himself when he comments, "When we treat an illness we normally treat a condition that the person is not responsible for. . . . When we begin treating persons for actions that have been chosen with his normal functioning but we change the person so that he functions in a way regarded as normal by the current therapeutic community, we have to change him and his judgments of value. In doing this, we display a lack of respect for the moral status of individuals [p. 57]."

At points, Morris appears to agree with Szasz. Yet, Morris criticizes Szasz's belief that there are no mental illnesses except those caused by physical forces. Morris argues: "Szasz places on all those whom we might classify as mentally ill the burden of discovering their condition and taking steps to correct it [p. 69]." Could we expect this from a person suffering from hallucinations, paranoid delusions, a moron — or a psychopath? "Surely," Morris comments, "there are people whose extraordinary habits of thought and feeling of long standing and pervasive effect have impaired their capacity to view accurately either themselves or the world around them [p. 69]." This broad definition would certainly seem to encompass the psychopath and yet, Morris does not seem willing to accept this opinion.

Morris ends his discourse with the conclusion that mental illness is real and that certain human beings, exempt from mental illness, should be held responsible for their actions. As he comments, "Szasz has so extended the boundaries of responsibility that he partially destroys the very thing he wishes to preserve, a meaningful concept of human responsibility."

Finagrette attempted to infuse the concept of mental health and mental disorder with some meaning. Finagrette has defined insanity as (a) irrational conduct; (b) produced by a grave defect in the person's capacity for rational conduct; and (c) an inherent part of the person's nature.

Finagrette argues that insanity is failure to respond relevantly to what is essentially relevant. Therefore, criminal irresponsibility resides in the fact that the criminal "substantially lacked capacity to act rationally [1972, p. 11]." This standard leaves open the questions of what is "relevant" and who is "rational." A psychopath cares nothing about other human beings; if he demolishes them in the act of getting some gain, he could be acting rationally as human beings have no relevance to him.

Finagrette specifically indicts those whose standards of irrational conduct exclude psychopaths. Rightly, he suggests that irrational conduct—if that be the standard—should include psychopaths who are "incapable of responding to the relevant emotional–moral aspects of the situation and their conduct. He is emotionally flat and does not respond to the relevance of human suffering [p. 141]."

In a somewhat different form, Frank E. Hartung (1966) believes that the concept of reason should underlie most judicial opinions in Western society. He argues that the element of reason must be upheld to protect the central values of our society. Hartung envisions latent threats to the idea of moral responsibility in legal formulations using the concept of mental disorder. It is Hartung's opinion that "this development has been accompanied by violent attacks on the concept of reason and by attempts to eliminate the concept of culpability and to replace it with the concept of exculpation [p. 167]."

Hartung particularly objects to the juvenile court system and beliefs in rehabilitation: "One of the important consequences of this, in the United States, is the abrogation in the juvenile court of practically all of the constitutional procedural safeguards of the penal code [p. 230]." He cites wide departures from the traditional conception of due process and the inclusion of irrelevant, prejudicial, and hearsay testimony in juvenile courts.

Although he does not charge judges with consciously malicious behavior, Hartung raises the question of how the individual with problems can be saved from the potentially ravaging benefactions of his saviors. For these reasons, Hartung regards all violent criminals as responsible and as "normal" as other people. Legally and morally, he believes that they should be prosecuted. He attacks psychiatry and ignores the psychopath in a wide-ranging attack on the whole belief in "mental disorder."

To a lesser degree, Finagrette agrees. He correctly points out that no comprehensive definition of mental illness has ever existed. Even before the M'Naghten rule, a Royal committee announced that "upon the subject all definitions are unsatisfactory [Shetford, 1833, p. xxxvi]." More than a century later, Abraham Goldstein (1970) wrote, "It is now apparent that a precise definition of insanity is impossible [p. 87]."

While unable to agree on a definition of mental disease, however, many lawyers, psychiatrists, and social scientists believe that some sort of standard of rationality and responsibility should be maintained. As Finagrette argues, the criminal law "embodies a fundamental and characteristic resolution of the community that normally the state shall deal with all members of the community as responsible under law. . . . It is a central value . . . that socialization of conduct in our society shall normally be *through* responsibility under the law . . . the institution is itself an essential end for the society [1972, p. 57]."

Because he wished to uphold the value of reason in Western society, Finagrette established a standard that implicitly includes a consideration of mental disease. He argues that a criminally insane person must be not merely incapable of rational conduct (1972). The final test is that "the defendant's mental makeup at the time of the offending act substantially lacked capacity to act rationally [p. 211]."

This standard raised again the same questions: What is the meaning of "insane"? And what is the meaning of "rationality"? Finagrette responds to these issues in a circular fashion: Insanity involves the inability to act rationally specifically in respect to a crime; irrationality, in regard to the specific crime, indicates a lack of sanity. Thus, irrationality is insanity. What should happen, however, if the person fakes his answers? He may be perfectly rational but, for one reason or another, may put on a facade of irrationality. This is hardly an uncommon occurrence as the case of "Son of Sam" and the research of Rosenhan (1973) have illustrated.

"Son of Sam," a brutal New York murderer, originally claimed that he was obeying the orders of a dog named "Sam" while committing crimes. Later, he claimed that story was false and that he was really a member of a Satanic cult. No one knows which story was true or whether the man should be regarded as rational.

In a similar way—but for scientific purposes—Rosenhan and his colleagues faked mental illness to see if they could be detected. Rosenhan put himself and eight other psuedo-patients into 13 different mental hospitals. Each had been instructed to say the same words: that they were hearing voices saying that their lives were "empty and hollow." The pseudo-patients behaved "normally" within the mental hospitals and were all eventually released. Rosenhan concluded, however, that mental hospitals depersonalized, ignored, and humiliated their patients. Most importantly, he argued, "It is clear that we cannot distinguish the sane from the insane in psychiatric hospitals. The hospital itself imposes a special environment in which the meanings of behavior can easily be misunderstood [1973, p. 257]."

Rosenhan's intriguing experiment has been used as support for the position of Szasz and Erving Goffman. Sociologist Goffman has tried to distinguish physical causes from environmental factors in the creation of mental illness, as did Szasz. The position of Rosenhan, Szasz, and Goffman—which would exclude 80% of all mental patients, as well as psychopaths from treatment—has met with justified opposition.

Peter Sedgwick, for one, has argued, "There are no illnesses or diseases in nature [1972, p. 201]." Contrary to Goffman, Sedgwick argued that mankind assigns meaning to both mental *and* physical stigma. The Rockefeller Sanitary Commission on hookworm found in 1911 that many groups in North America regarded this disease as normal and as part of ordinary health. And in one South American Indian tribe, the disease of dyschromic spirochetosis, marked by the appearance of colored spots on the skin, was so "normal" that those who did not suffer from the disease were barred as pathological and excluded from marriage.

"In my own judgment," Sedgwick concluded, "mental disease can be conceptualized just as easily within the disease framework as physical maladies such as lumbago or TB [p. 19]." As physical diseases resemble mental diseases in social labeling, Sedgwick contends, Goffman's position falls into pieces.

Writing from a radical perspective, however, Sedgwick argues that the concept of psychopathy represents no more than "an attempt at social labeling, for control purposes, by psychiatrists working in tandem with the judicial authorities [p. 211]." Sedgwick did not concern himself with the type of evidence that indicates that psychopaths differ from others in both environmental and neurological backgrounds as well as eventual criminal records. In addition, he presented no evidence that psychiatrists were somehow in a conspiracy with jurists to preserve the status quo. Indeed, in our research, this could not possibly be the case as the diagnoses were held in private files.

Robert L. Spiter (1976) further attacked the position that diagnoses are merely arbitrary judgments. In considering Rosenhan's evidence, Spiter pointed out that auditory hallucinations and a desire to enter a mental hospital are a definite clinical portrait. Without a full-scale lie detection test (and perhaps not even then), it would be impossible to know that Rosenhan and his colleagues were lying and merely pretended to present these symptoms.

Spiter has pointed out that diagnoses are helpful to patients since specific antidotes—tranquilizers for schizophrenics, shock treatment for unipolar depression, lithium carbonate for manic depression—help those with particular symptoms but may harm those in other diagnostic categories. Spiter further criticizes Rosenhan's ambiguity in the diagnoses attached to his pseudo-patients and his refusal to name the various hospitals involved. Clearly, Spiter acknowledges, there is no universal definition of insanity, but he contends that this should not void particular diagnoses—especially when the subjects were consciously lying in an attempt to exhibit schizophrenic symptoms.

Steven Reiss (1972) further criticized the positions of Rosenhan, Szasz, and Goffman by opposing their views on philosophical grounds. He disposes, as did Sedgwick, with the argument of Szasz and Goffman that some sort of sharp distinction can be drawn between mental and physical disease. He further argues against a view that Szasz specifically offers: that the entire mental health movement resembles the Inquisition in that both involve an invasion of individual liberty justified by hypothetical constructs such as "mental disease" or "witchcraft" (see Szasz, 1961, 1970). Any treatment, according to Szasz, is viewed as immoral, because it violates the patient's basic right to autonomy. Yet psychotherapists try to relieve suffering, while inquisitors imposed only punishment or death. Therefore, Reiss argues, a patient—either psychopathic or suffering from some other malady—should be helped. If he or she is not, it is a violation of both law and medicine. There can be no justification of the law in any sense unless it is a barrier between the society and an individual's harmful actions. As no society exists without some type of law, we may legitimately assume that it is a protection against anarchy.

Similarly in the case of medicine, we may assume again that intervention may be necessary for the welfare of the individual or the larger society. At times—when a patient is in a coma and cannot give his permission, or has measles and needs to be secluded from the community (even though he may be ignorant of this fact), or in the case of psychopaths who have not been socialized to accept the moral beliefs of the community—medical intervention may be necessary. As citizens, each of us must formulate our own decisions on these matters. As this review of the literature indicates, one may reasonably conclude:

First, immense confusion has pervaded the legal, medical, and scientific communities over the question of responsibility. By some standards, the experts have considered the psychopath as responsible for his or her crimes. By others, he has been excluded. For nearly 150 years, lawyers, sociologists, psychiatrists, and philosophers have failed to agree on a definition of responsibility. They cannot even agree on a definition of such crucial terms as "knowledge," "wrong," "impulsivity," or "blame." Further, as Berel Ceasar (1979) argued, "Our criminal law is permeated with requirements of free will [p. 7]." Yet, no one has provided a satisfactory or universally accepted definition of "free will."

In this atmosphere of uncertainty and contention, it is my belief that both the protection of society and of the individual require us to hold that *adult psychopaths and all other criminals should be held legally responsible if found guilty of their crimes, regardless of the circumstances that prompted their actions.*

Medical and social scientists—while often able to agree on a specific diagnosis—are unable to reach a consensus on the nature of mental disease. Such an entity may not exist at all since disease in *any* form is a social label. Fine distinctions made by some scholars on the physical versus the environmental causes of mental disease have raised widespread disputes. As the very definition of "illness" remains in debate, *I believe that the term mental illness should not be included in a definition of the psychopath's responsibility or that of any other criminal.* I recognize all too well that some people do suffer from hallucinations, delusions, or even—to call upon a quaint, outdated phrase—"moral idiocy." In a court of law, however, I must also acknowledge that the concepts of "responsibility" and "mental disease" have become so nebulous as to be rendered unusable. In essence, it is my belief that questions involving "incompetency to stand trial," "responsibility" and "mental disorder" should not be considered. The judge and the jury's decision should depend on only one criteria: Did the person in fact commit the crime?

This would not, however, end the court's duties. A decision would still have to be made on the disposition of the individual, within statutory limits, if he or she is found guilty. It seems equitable to separate decisions concerning guilt from those concerning sentencing. It would be unwise and unfair to commit a person to a prison for a set number of years, forgetting their human situation and condition, if he or she were not given the best opportunities for treatment that society provides.

In 1945, lawyer–social scientist Sheldon Glueck suggested what he called a treatment tribunal to separate the two legal functions of deciding on guilt and deciding on sentencing. Some states (California, Maryland, and Wisconsin) had essentially adopted this point of view. Some 35 years later, however, these same states had abandoned their positions as various legislators have called for longer and mandatory sentences. Some jurists worried that Glueck's original proposition did not provide for sufficient constitutional guarantees for the convicted.

The Merits and Limitations of a Sentencing Panel

After a determination of guilt, a defendant would appear before a board of people composed of his judge, responsible probation and parole officers, some social scientists and psychiatrists, and perhaps representatives of the general public. Governed by legislative dictates, such a panel would consider the status of the convicted, bring various points of view to bear on the question of what sentence would be appropriate both for him and the protection of society, and would prescribe effective treatments for the person rather than an arbitrary punishment.

Such a panel would relieve judges of the sole responsibility for dictating a sentence. This is important for several reasons. First, it has been demonstrated that particular judges vary erratically in the sentences they impose for the *same* crime (Glueck, 1945). They may be influenced by prejudice, by lack of knowledge, or by their basic character. Second, the judge would not have to rely ultimately on his or her own personal judgment of the responsibility or mentally disordered state of the individual. Instead, he or she could benefit by the accumulated knowledge of specialists in particular fields rather than adjudicating a "battle of experts" in the court.

In essence, a sentencing panel would provide a more balanced view of the nature of the defendant and his or her relation to society. It would also allow for a further system of "checks and balances" to ensure that the personal biases or ignorance of a particular member of the panel could be moderated by the advice of others.

One could, of course, argue that the decisions of an exceptionally wise judge might have more merit than that of a panel of experts. Granted. Yet, who in this age of specialization can reasonably expect the law schools of this nation to turn out "philosopher kings" who are equally knowledgeable about law, psychiatry, the social sciences, and corrections. It is more reasonable to expect that a balanced panel— while hardly perfect—could reach decisions that would better protect society. This has been shown in the cases already cited where a judge has overruled the decision of a panel of experts and allowed a potentially violent criminal to go free [Monahan, 1981].

Would such a sentencing panel be just to the individuals involved? I believe that there are protections for convicted defendants that could be built into a system of sentencing panels. Among the more important of these protections for individual liberty, I would include:

1. The sentencing panel would have to be governed by the broad sentences for each crime that the public in a particular state or nation democratically demanded.
2. A free and obligatory psychiatric, medical, physical, and social examination should be completed by the board for every convicted criminal. Prisoners without means should not be expected to pay for this examination. The defendant should, however, be allowed to introduce his own experts, at no cost to the defendant, to refute condemnatory sentences.
3. If the panel finds that the person is in need of treatment, his or her behavior should be subjected to annual reviews by the panel. The person should have substantially the same rights as a civil patient, including the right to bring his or her case before an appellate panel. Thus, "a right to judicial review and a right to treatment by judicial review are paramount [Brackel & Rock, 1971, p. 423]."

Clearly, such a panel would have to make a judgment on the potential violence of the person and his or her danger to others—as do judges today. At the moment, American practices on this subject differ wildly: some states require automatic hospitalization of a dangerous person, some demand that the person should be held until "sane," and still others merely apply a thirty-day statute. Each society defines "dangerousness" in a different manner and the whole issue raises the spector of "preventive detection," Nazi concentration camps, and the "relocation centers" maintained for Japanese–American citizens during World War II.

"Dangerousness" and Sentencing Panels

The entire issue of "danger" of convicted criminals stirs debate in judicial, scholarly, and medical communities.

Some, such as Sheldon Glueck, contended that future delinquency could be predicted in early childhood. In the 1950s, there seemed great hope that delinquency—and especially psychopathy—could be predicted by actuarial tables based on the child's social background. The weighted scores included paternal discipline, maternal discipline, the affection of each parent for the child, and family unity. A series of studies suggested that the tests could actually predict delinquency (Black & Glick, 1952; Glueck, 1945; Thompson, 1952). Subsequent evidence, definitively summarized by John Monahan (1981), failed to provide evidence that any measures—the Glueck scale, the MMPI, the Rorschach, etc.—can accurately assess the possibilities of delinquency. Monahan clearly demonstrated that there was no relationship between mental illness and the commission of street crimes (murder, mugging, and rape).

Some commentators have jumped to the conclusion that "predictions of dangerous behavior are wrong about 95 percent of the time. . . . Mental health professionals almost always error by overpredicting, rather than by underpredicting, dangerous behavior [Taylor, 1981, p. 4E]."

Such observers have also cited obvious dangers to civil liberties. As Stuart Taylor (1981) maintained, "Any effort to identify and confine potentially dangerous people would trample on constitutional liberties [p. 4E]." The courts have been increasingly wary of depriving liberty (on the basis of predictions) and they have mandated that patients should be treated in the least restrictive atmosphere.

Monahan summarized the arguments against predicting dangerous behavior. The three basic criticisms, he noted, are "(1) that it is empirically impossible to predict violent behavior; (2) that, even if such activity could be forecast and averted, it would, as a matter of policy, violate the civil liberties of those being predicted; and (3) that even if accurate prediction were possible without violating civil liberties, psychiatrists and psychologists should decline to do it, since it is a social control activity at variance with their professional helping role [1981, p. 6]." Monahan recognizes, of course, that judges have always been involved in predicting behavior and that "it is likely that some forms of preventive confinement will continue to be practiced in every society [p. 1]."

The issue is empirically, ethically, and legally more complicated than many have recognized. On a legal level, the 1976 *Tarasoff* decision in California requires that psychiatrists and psychologists may be liable for the violent acts of patients they predict, or *should* predict, to be violent. As Monahan has noted, this decision has affected therapists in different ways; some focus more on violence, others more often consult with their colleagues; and still others have avoided asking questions or keeping records that would indicate a person's dangerousness. If a therapist decides that a person will not harm society, he can be sued if that person commits a violent action.

Empirically, the prediction of *violent* behavior—as opposed to some nebulous concept of dangerousness—is not as vague a science as some have argued. As Monahan noted, actuarial tables that include such factors as age, sex, ethnic group, prior record, employment stability, and family history can be remarkably accurate. Predictions made after a person has been convicted of a violent crime have proven to be reasonably accurate. In general, after thorough psychiatric and social examinations of convicted prisoners, a Massachusetts panel reported a 10-year follow-up study that indicated that 92% of prisoners predicted as nonviolent did not commit a violent crime within 5 years after release while 35% of prisoners predicted as violent (*who were, nonetheless, released by court judgment*) did commit a violent action (Kozol, Broche, & Garafolo, 1973). Yet the fact remains that approximately two people who are convicted felons would be detained for every one who subsequently commits further crimes—a penalty that perhaps most legislatures would not wish to propose.

Predictions of potentially violent behavior during the period from childhood to adulthood have proven more accurate. The often-maligned Glueck (1969) research in the prediction of delinquency errored generally on the side of overpredicting delinquency. Yet, if one took the *extreme* ends of a scale—which applied to only a handful of boys—the predictions were remarkably accurate: approximately 95% of eventually violent delinquents were at the upper end of the scale whereas 95% of nonviolent boys fell at the bottom end of the scale. Similarly, predictions made privately in early childhood by Cambridge–Somerville counselors concerning the eventual violent behavior of their subjects hit the mark almost exactly in adolescence—although the boys did not know what predictions had been made. Sixteen out of 17 who had been predicted as potentially violent did, in fact, commit violent crimes in later life. Only one person who had been predicted as nonviolent committed a violent crime; put differently, the predictions of violent behavior from childhood to adolescence were highly accurate in a sample of 1000 boys.

Ethically, the question of whether professionals should make predictions at all remains in question. On the one hand, it could be argued that prediction violates canons of confidentiality. On the other hand, clinicians who fail to predict an oubreak of typhoid, accurately diagnose cancer, or fail to report a carrier of an infectious disease would be regarded as derelict in their duty. Indeed, under the *Tarasoff* decision, they would be held liable for *not* predicting violent behavior. On the whole, it would appear that responsible professionals have a duty to predict violence.

Using criteria of age, race, and sex, however, would open up courts to charges of discrimination. In addition, a person who had been deemed to have served his time and is due for release should automatically be given another chance. Furthermore, no one can exactly judge the chance factors or the circumstances that might prompt a person to commit a violent act: entering a particular bar on a night when a long-standing enemy was there might trigger a violent response that otherwise might have lain dormant. Thus, some authors totally oppose prediction of crime (Shah, 1978).

Is it correct to allow judges and juries to make decisions on this matter? Monahan (1981) posed the problem, as it now exists, as a bleak dilemma: "Since we cannot be sure who would do us harm, we should detain no one. . . . Since we cannot be sure which ones will be safe, we should keep them all in [p. 90]." I think that the average judge or jury should not be left with such momentous decisions. A balanced panel of experts, however imperfect, could achieve a higher level of accuracy—although it is probable that they would make "false positive" judgments.

This danger, however, exists in a magnified form under the current system as the voting public has virtually surrendered decisions on sentencing to judges who may be arbitrary, incompetent, corrupt, ignorant, or biased. Even if they are totally honest and well qualified and they employed the services of psychiatrists or other social scientists, their judgment will be influenced by psychological processes. Fisher (1976), for example, found that more dogmatic psychiatrists and psychologists, as measured by the Rokeach scale, are more likely to predict that a particular prisoner would act in a dangerous fashion. A balanced sentencing panel would partially reduce such personal prejudices.

Clearly, however, such a sentencing panel should have exact limitations placed on its powers. In addition to the restrictions that have been noted—the imposition of mandatory (although broadly indeterminate) sentences by the legislators, annual judicial review, free examinations—there should be further protections for the individual:

1. The sentencing panel should be charged specifically with predicting violent behavior, instead of "dangerousness." At the moment, no state in America follows this rule.

2. The limit of mandatory sentences should be dictated by an elected legislature, eventually responsible to the voting public. We must ask legislators to make difficult decisions concerning the line they want to draw between individual liberty and the protection of others. It is indeed a dangerous path between the requirements of social order and the expression of individual freedom. To balance order against liberty should be done by society's courts and legislatures.

Therefore, *with reasonable protections, it seems wise that all jurisdictions should use a sentencing panel, controlled by legislative rulings, and bound by various limitations on its powers.* Such a system, however imperfect, would be better than allowing judges the power that they now possess.

Changes in the legal system, of course, will not in themselves solve the problem of psychopathy. Grave decisions on public policy persist: Should psychopaths, if they are accurately diagnosed, be executed for a vicious crime? If not, should they be restrained for life? What type of punishment or rehabilitation should be enforced? Should society intervene early in the life of a potential psychopath?

Public Policy and the Psychopath

CAPITAL PUNISHMENT

An easy solution to the problem of psychopaths, "habitual criminals," or other troublesome deviants condemned by their societies was to execute them. Up until the end of the nineteenth century, execution was a popular policy. Beginning in England, however, public opinion gradually shifted to the point of view that execution was inhumane and often unjust.

Nonetheless, some distinguished commentators in the twentieth century continued to advocate capital punishment—and some psychopaths, like Gary Gilmore, sought it. Perhaps the most brilliant defender of execution was George Bernard Shaw (1946). He contended that execution was more humane than possible imprisonment for life. This solution offered society certain protection, served as a deterrent, and would save the lives of guards and inmates locked up with the more violent criminals. Shaw did not condone revenge *per se* but, after reviewing the cases of some psychopaths, concluded: "At present you torment them for a fixed period, at the end of which they are set free to resume their operations with a savage grudge against society. That is stupid. . . . Releasing them is like releasing the tigers from the Zoo to find their next meal in the nearest children's playing ground. . . . Is it any wonder that some of us are driven to prescribe the lethal chamber as the solution for the hard cases [1946, pp. 50–51]?"

Shaw had a humane intent behind his advocacy of capital punishment: He wished to contrast the relatively civilized method of quick execution to the barbarous conditions of the British prisons of his day. In somewhat modified forms, these same conditions exist in many areas of the world in the late twentieth century.

Other proponents of capital punishment have based their arguments on spurious grounds of deterrence or sheer vengefulness. Indeed, 65% of the American public favored capital punishment in 1981 (Newsweek, 1980). Such is not the position supported by the evidence that has been presented. As our research has shown, many who have been diagnosed as psychopaths stopped committing crimes as they aged. They apparently were not immutable monsters. Moreover, errors in diagnosis can easily be made.

Capital punishment is irrevocable. Once the person is dead, you cannot bring him back to life. Changes in the individual or, indeed, errors of fact in his original trial can no longer be considered or corrected.

As I have noted, capital punishment based on predictions of danger would, at this time in history, involve the killing of two harmless people for every one who is actually dangerous. With even such mass slaughter by the State, there is no evidence that capital punishment has ever deterred crime. In fact, as Tobias argued (1972), capital punishment may increase the rate of violence because the state itself offers an example of brutality. Using highly sophisticated techniques, one economist, Isaac Ehrlich (1979), argued that capital punishment of violent crime might deter such acts, but fellow economists have vigorously disagreed with this analysis (Friedman, 1979).

As a tool for exacting vengeance, capital punishment seems unexcelled—even though many innocent people would also die. As a method of deterring crime, treating psychopaths in a humane manner, protecting society, or ensuring the rights of individuals, the evidence indicates that capital punishment is worse than useless.

INCAPACITATION AND THE PSYCHOPATH

Simply locking psychopaths up for a long period of time poses similar dangers. As our research indicates, psychopaths who have been subjected to relatively humane treatment as children can be radically changed. One problem would appear to be that society does not provide support for the changes that are effected or offer opportunity or even further treatment facilities for them once they are released.

Incarcerating psychopaths (or other criminals) for extended periods in our current system of prisons does not offer a viable alternative. Despite a public outcry in the 1980s that all criminals should receive their "just deserts" and that all violent criminals should undergo long mandatory sentences, formidable obstacles hinder such a policy:

• Our current prisons and reform schools are so drastically overcrowded that many courts have decreed that they represent cruel and unusual punishment, particularly for those persons who reside in jail even before they have been found guilty. The courts have ordered the penal facilities to remedy their problems.

• Such decisions put an impossible burden on prison administrators and legislators. Implementation of even a mandatory 5-year sentence for all felons would require the expenditure of billions of dollars for new facilities that will be antiquated by the time the population of the recent "baby boom" reaches the 1990s. As Norman Carlson, the Director of the Federal Bureau of Prisons, commented, "The 'knee-jerk' response of many legislatures in passing harsher sentencing statutes threatens to totally overwhelm our correctional systems. Unfortunately, in considering such legislation, few elected representatives realize the long-run consequences of their actions [Quoted in Leiber, 1981, p. 108]."

• The current sentencing process provides harsher sentences for the poor, minorities, and the uneducated (Leiber, 1981). Thus, for the same crimes, courts have arbitrarily pronounced lighter sentences on such groups as white, middle-class people. As our research indicates that psychopaths are sprinkled evenly among various ethnic groups, this discrimination may well give a special advantage to those who are white.

• Habitual offenders acts, which particularly affect psychopaths, have come under scrutiny. These acts represent the ultimate in incapacitation, except for capital punishment. In Texas, for example, a law passed in 1856 provides that any person convicted of three felonies should be automatically imprisoned for life. After extensive debate on the *Rummel* case, the Supreme Court ruled that the length of a prison stay is a matter of legislative prerogative. John Rummel had been convicted of using a stolen credit card, forging a check, and cashing another check that had been advanced as credit for work he never did. These three felonies netted him $229.11 and life imprisonment. As a result of the *Rummel* case, the Texas legislature and others are now reconsidering "habitual criminal" laws and replacing them with laws concerning only violent crimes. Such a change will, however, not affect the fate of John Rummel. He will continue to vegetate in the Angleton, Texas prison because of his relatively minor and nonviolent crimes.

Thus, our current system of incapacitation is unfair, uneconomical, unjust to those who are already disadvantaged, and, as pointed out earlier, ineffective.

JUVENILE JUSTICE AND THE PSYCHOPATH

Seventeenth-century England treated children as adults. They were tried before a court and then punished according to whether they were "rogues" or "idle" children. The colonies followed suit and punished children with up to 10 lashes for any deviation from the law. By the nineteenth century, America had altered its view and youths were regarded as immature until the age of 14, but children as young as 6 years of age could be punished if it could be demonstrated that they knew the difference between right and wrong.

By 1826, however, the New York Society for the Reform of Juvenile Delinquents argued that delinquents "were returned destitute to the same haunts of vice from which they had been taken [Kaufman, 1979, p. 17]." The Society recommended the establishment of special institutions for children. The Lyman School, as we have noted, became the first American establishment of this kind as a result of the movement. These new reform schools were to be benign and rehabilitative.

It was not until 1899, however, that children were completely removed from the jurisdiction of adult courts. Illinois established the first juvenile court system addressed to the special problems of the young. The courts were designed to serve a parental function and to protect the anonymity of the child. Simultaneously, such courts did away with many of the trappings of an adult criminal trial—confronting witnesses, a reading of specific charges, and trial by jury.

By the 1980s, the pendulum had swung back around. Some scholars advocated the complete abolition of juvenile courts (see Rubin, 1979). Their arguments varied.

As a result of various decisions—*In re Gault* (1967), *In re Winship* (1970), and Breed *vs.* Jones (1978)—the judiciary placed various restraints on the juvenile court, including protection against double jeopardy and the demand that a crime committed by a child should meet standards of "reasonable" doubt as applied to adults. Conservatives welcomed these opinions and contended that juveniles should be punished just as adults.

The push to abolish the juvenile court as an institution reached its height in New York. In 1978, the state passed a new juvenile offender law that required that all children of 13 indicted for second-degree murder should be tried in an adult court. If convicted, the youth could serve a prison sentence for life. The young convicts would first enter a juvenile center and then be transferred to an adult prison. Proponents of this measure argued that the new policy would result in stiffer penalties and thus serve as a deterrent to juvenile crime. They did not, of course, have any evidence for their position or realize that they had returned to the policies that prevailed in America until 1899. The legislature could not predict that the harsher law resulted in fewer and shorter sentences for violent juveniles. The "toughness" of the 1978 law resulted in fewer convictions because both judges and juries hesitated to expose a child to life imprisonment in an adult prison.

Advocates of civil rights also attacked the juvenile court system, but on quite different grounds. They argued that juveniles should have a right to a jury, that constitutional protections afforded to adults should apply to juveniles, and that defense attorneys should be allowed to act in an adversarial role in juvenile cases. Their goal was to protect the individual child.

Both conservatives and liberals argued that there should be determinate sentences for juveniles and that their sentences should be directly proportional to the seriousness of the crime. Such a position directly contravened the original idea behind a separate system of juvenile justice: that the delinquent should be treated, not punished for his original crime.

Most advocates of the abolition of juvenile courts also argued that "status offenders"—children who had been labeled habitual truants, incorrigible, or runaways—should also be removed from the jurisdiction of the court. Some cases—severely neglected and abused children—have been brought to court by child welfare officials. Supposedly, the argument went, such children should not be exposed to the presumably harmful influence of delinquents. Those who welcomed this position often forgot that the parents themselves, wishing to be rid of their own child, had brought him or her to court. Such a relatively innocuous suggestion has run into problems.

Should a court, for example, intervene in a situation where the ancestors have for three generations served as role models of thieves, prostitutes, and drug peddlers? This question arose in Pasadena, California, where a "Mrs. Wilson" lives and shares her space with nine children, some grandchildren, and assorted nephews (Newsweek, 1981). Police have arrested members of the family some 400 times. In 1981, a court decided that the family served as bad role models for the children. This was an unprecedented charge. The Wilson family had amassed 40 pounds of criminal records in California courts and some authorities sought to separate the children from the adults. Yet, the belief that families should remain intact at any cost bothered the California court. The two sides reached a compromise. The prosecution argued that three of the Wilson daughters had spent so much time in jail for prostitution that their absence had disrupted and damaged their children. The Wilsons pleaded no contest. Yet, California had to drop its petition to remove the youngest of Grandmother Wilson's children, ages 12 to 17, from the home as no one would adopt them. The "Wilson" case left open the issue of whether neglected, rejected children, or children who may be loved but are exposed to criminal models should be removed to an institution or a foster home.

Thus, opponents of the current system of juvenile justice made odd bedfellows. Some argue, in the "Wilson" case, that courts are too severe—particularly with status offenders. Others contend that the system is too soft on young offenders. The people who follow the hardest line are those who believe that all individualized treatment or sentences should be abolished. They think that "set sentences would serve as a deterrent to criminal behavior by minors and would remove dangerous minors from the community. They see delinquents not as wayward children but as sophisticated criminals [Wald, 1980, p. 47]."

Pleas for the abolition of juvenile courts are, in my opinion, harmful and mistaken. Any court, if it has no choice, as is now the case in

TABLE 1
Recidivism[a]

| | Wiltwyck | | Lyman | |
Age	Status ($N = 40$)	Delinquent ($N = 44$)	Status ($N = 19$)	Delinquent ($N = 65$)
15–19	34%	23%	47%	67%
20–24	17%	15%	31%	28%
25–29	34%	27%	11%	22%
30–34	18%	16%	11%	12%
35–40	17%	10%	6%	7%

[a] Excluding those who were dead, incapacitated, and originally subject to several charges at each age level.

Massachusetts, can send a child back to his original environment. Perhaps that action, such as a return of the family to "Mrs. Wilson," can have an even more pernicious effect than, say, a sentence to Lyman. A commitment to a place like Wiltwyck, on the other hand, where the children receive warmth and even love, perhaps for the first time in their lives, would appear to have a beneficial effect. Leaving options open to a juvenile court seems the wisest course.

"STATUS" AND DELINQUENCY

According to our research, the handling of "status offenders" remains an unanswered question. *In later life (15–40), children who were status offenders did not differ generally from juvenile delinquents in recidivism rates.* In many age groups, the rates of the children originally sent to one of the schools as a status offender slightly exceeded the rates of the juvenile delinquents (Table 1).

One could argue, of course, that reform schools breed and teach crime. Status inmates may have picked up new patterns of criminal behavior at both schools. But why did not the rate of later crime for actual delinquents exceed that of the status offenders? They, too, should have learned new techniques—perhaps more easily than status offenders.

One plausible explanation is that status offenders—who had often been committed by their own parents or had been repudiated by them—may have felt that incarceration was an especially bitter experience. As one Lyman boy recalled, "That bitch (his mother) done thrown me out. The folks at Lyman sent me back to her. She didn't want me. What was I to do but go out on the streets?" A possible indicator of their disturbance (or their rational choice to seek psychiatric treatment) was that approximately 17% of status offenders required commitment to a mental hospital at some point in their later lives as opposed to less than 1% of juvenile delinquents from both schools.

The currently popular opinion that status offenders should be diverted from the juvenile court system does not receive support from our research. Although children who suffer from neglect and brutality may be subject to arbitrary decisions and their disposition may well be left to court clerks (Sosin, 1981), the system should be reformed, not abolished. Judges should be aided by treatment panels in making decisions about status offenders, as well as regular criminals. Humane institutions, such as Wiltwyck, should be expanded, as neither deinstitutionalization nor commitment to a more punitive reformatory like Lyman protects society or offers equity to the young individual. This seems particularly true for child psychopaths who overwhelmingly (82%) come from neglecting, deviant, or brutal homes.

Even the most humane and equitable juvenile court system cannot, however, protect either society or the psychopathic child unless it is strongly reinforced by an institutional system that offers treatment and not punishment to young people.

Implications for Social Policy

Although certain changes in the legal system—such as the establishment of sentencing panels, further protections for civil liberties, abolition of habitual criminal laws, the use of judicial review for all sentencing decisions, and the strengthening of the juvenile court system—are both desirable and possible, they would be futile without other basic, more difficult alterations in public attitudes and public policy.

First, through patient education, the public's attitudes toward criminals and particularly psychopaths must change. In the last half of the twentieth century, the public has cried out for increasingly harsh measures. The average person knows nothing about the social and physiological factors that produce such "depraved monsters" as psychopaths. The vindictive attitude of the public has been faithfully reflected in the press. As one prominent columnist commented on two psychopathic murderers: "You would just have to say that these punks are plain bad, poison mean, inhuman little animals who deserve no consideration, no clemency. Society didn't make them that way, either. The rottenness must dwell within a man who kills strangers for fun when the killer himself is not insane [McCord & McCord, 1965, p. 194]." With bitter savagery, the columnist, like the public, demanded capital punishment.

This vindictive attitude ignores the facts that have been presented here concerning the causes and treatment of psychopathic behavior. A return to capital punishment would define the state as an instrument for the mass murder of often innocent people. Total incapacitation for long periods of time would jail two harmless people for every one person who was potentially dangerous. Criminals, even psychopaths, can be changed with proper treatment. Ignoring the causes of psychopathic behavior serves no purpose except for satisfying an inflamed public's desire for vengeance (and granting the wishes of some psychopaths to escape a destiny of life imprisonment). Vindictiveness does not deter, prevent, or control crime. Swifter, more certain entrapment of those who are repeated criminals might well accomplish these goals but, as yet, we have meager evidence that such policies as increasing the police force will have an impact.

Second, the public must recognize that therapeutic measures— such as those used at Wiltwyck—can effectively reduce the crime rate of psychopaths and other criminals during the period of their greatest danger: early manhood. After that age—regardless of society's actions—the majority of delinquents either "mature," "burn out," or have been so battered by prior incarceration that they cease criminal activity.

In essence, *the findings presented in the previous chapter suggest that the creation of more therapeutic communities such as Wiltwyck could perceptibly decrease the crime rate of younger people who are at the peak of violent tendencies between 15 and 24.* Such a policy would, of course, require adequate financing, particularly for the training of psychologists, social workers, psychiatrists, and other professionals in the difficult art of helping—not punishing—psychopaths and other types of children. Accompanied by Massachusetts' policy of deinstitutionalizing nonpsychopathic, less violent delinquents, existing physical facilities might well be adequate. The amount of money and lives saved for the entire community is incalculable.

Support for this point of view also comes from the work of Paul Gendrau and Bob Ross (1979) who reviewed 95 programs aimed at treating antisocial behavior. They concluded that programs that involved a combination of approaches, supplemented deinstitutionalization with community services, and that fitted the treatment to the individual character of the offender had a high rate of success. Thus, our research and that of others hardly supports the prevailing mood of cynicism in the general public.

Assuming the validity of current research, many psychopaths suffer from physical or neurological defects that are not readily curable by current medical practice. Nonetheless, the Wiltwyck–Lyman research has demonstrated that proper environmental treatment can overcome these problems that nature (or nurture) imposes. Clearly, it would be practical and humane to foster the growth of milieu therapy as an effective way of controlling youthful crime.

Third, our research suggests that habitually neglected, abandoned, or rejected children—possibly psychopathic—would benefit equally from milieu therapy as do youngsters who commit crimes early in life. It seems wise, then, that such children should be removed from their families, at their parents' request, or on charges of brutality, neglect, or delinquency and sent to live in special therapeutic environments. The mere abandonment of status offenders to their original families leads, as we have noted, to equal or higher crime rates than arrested delinquents and to higher rates of mental disorder.

Fourth, although milieu therapy has a definite impact on young men and their recidivism rates, this effect wears off for many. Adult psychopaths who continue to commit crimes of violence are in need of further treatment. Sentencing them to a therapeutic adult environment such as those created at Patuxent in Maryland or Herstead-vester in Denmark offers a viable alternative to perpetual imprisonment or death (Carney, 1978). Such adult institutions continue the type of milieu therapy offered at Wiltwyck. We have shown that a minority of psychopaths commit the majority of crimes at every age level. Thus, when adult institutions such as Patuxent report a recidivism rate of only 7% (even for released offenders originally sentenced to double or triple life sentences), the relevance of milieu therapy becomes apparent. Although such institutions must release their inmates at the end of the obligatory sentence, it is possible for a recovered inmate to be paroled under supervision at an earlier date. In the long run, such a policy would save society a great deal of pain—and money.

Two perhaps intractable issues remain. What can be done about the "normal" psychopath—the overtly noncriminal, often suave and intelligent person who is psychopathic but manages to escape legal condemnation? The danger of these individuals, particularly in the political realm, are evident in the histories of people such as Herman Goering. At times, such individuals may come to the attention of mental health experts but, as yet, there is little evidence that they change as a result of psychotherapy. Vigilance in the political realm, stricter law enforcement against white collar criminals, and a greater attention in the business, legal, and academic world to questionable practices may well result in greater protection for society. It must be admitted, however, that society has no ultimate defense against the "normal" psychopath.

A further complication, as our Wiltwyck research has indicated, is that milieu therapy appears useful in early manhood but—as the more deprived ethnic groups run into prejudice and discrimination—the psychopaths and others apparently become disillusioned as their originally high expectations are frustrated.

In the light of this finding, some might call for a social revolution—a magical restructuring of our society that would abolish prejudice, discrimination, and gross inequality as both the causes and perpetuators of criminal behavior. If such a revolution should occur and if milieu therapy spreads as a reform movement, I have little doubt that the toll of the psychopath could be significantly reduced.

Alas, this hope seems a chimera. No society in history—capitalist, socialist, communist, communitarian—has permanently abolished prejudices, inequities, and privilege (McCord & McCord, 1977). As Gordon Allport (1954) wisely commented on the problem of prejudice: "Since the problem is many-sided, there can be no sovereign formula. The wisest thing to do is to attack on all fronts simultaneously. No single attack has a large effect, yet many small attacks from many directions can have large cumulative results [p. 507]."

Similarly, in attacking the problem of psychopathy, reality condemns us to take small, interdependent, yet significant steps: improvements in the law, changes in reform school and community practices, implementation of research discoveries, and further experimentation in the treatment of adult psychopaths. If writers like Norman Mailer, Robert Smith, and Alan Harrington are indeed correct—that the psychopath is the wave of the future because he or she is better equipped to dominate our society—then the time has come to take effective measures to counteract this malevolent influence.

We have the means to diagnose psychopaths; we have a fund of knowledge about the causes of the disorder, and, through research such as the comparison of the Wiltwyck and Lyman environments, we know that psychopaths can be reached at a young age. If the public provides support, we can protect ourselves against the depredations of the lonely stranger.

References

Allport, G. *The nature of prejudice.* Cambridge, Addison Wesley, 1954.
Black, B. J., & Glick, S. Recidivism at the Hawthorne–Cedar-Knolls School. Research Monograph 32, Jewish Board of Guardians, New York, 1952.
Brakel, S. J., & Rock, R. S. *The mentally disabled and the law.* Chicago: University of Chicago Press, 1971.
Breed vs. Jones, 421, U.S. 519, 1978.
Carney, F. Inpatient treatment programs. In W. H. Reid (Ed.), *The psychopath.* New York: Brunner/Mazel, 1978.
Durham vs. United States, 214, F. 2nd, 862, D.C.C.R., 1954.
Ehrlich, I. The economic approach to crime. In S. Messinger and E. Bittner (Eds.), *Criminology review yearbook.* Beverly Hills: Sage, 1979.
English Homicide Act, 1957.
Finagrette, H. *The meaning of criminal insanity.* Berkeley: University of California Press, 1972.
Fisher, R. Factors influencing the prediction of dangerousness. Unpublished Ph.d. dissertation, University of Alabama, 1976.
Freedman, L. S. The use of multiple regression analysis to test for a deterrent effect of capital punishment. In S. Messinger and E. Bittner. *Criminology review yearbook.* Beverly Hills: Sage, 1979.
In re Gault, 387, U.S. 1, 1967.
Gendrau, P. & Ross, B. Effective correctional treatment: Bibliography for cynics. *Crime and Delinquency,* 1979 (Oct.) *25* (No. 4):197.
Glueck, S. *Crime and justice.* Cambridge, Mass.: Harvard University Press, 1945.
Glueck, S. & Glueck, E. *Predicting delinquency.* Cambridge, Mass.: Harvard University Press, 1969.
Goldstein, A. S. *The insanity defense.* New Haven: Yale University Press, 1970.
Hartung, F. E. *Crime, law and society.* Detroit: Wayne State University Press, 1966.
Kaufman, I. Juvenile justice: A plea for reform. *New York Times,* Oct., 1979.
Kozol, H., Broche, R., & Garafolo, R. Dangerousness: A reply to Monachesi. *Crime and Delinquency,* 1973, *19*:217–218.
Leiber, J. The American prison. *The New York Times Magazine,* March 5, 1981.
McCord, W. & McCord, A. *Power and equity.* New York: Praeger, 1977.
McDonald vs. United States, 314 F. 2nd., 847, 1962.
Monahan, J. *The clinical prediction of criminal behavior.* Rockville, Maryland: The National Institutes of Mental Health, 1981.
M'Naghten, 10, Clark and Finn, 200, 8, *Eng. Rep,* 78, 1843.
Newsweek, March 23, 1980.
Norbeck, E., Price-Williams, D., & McCord, W. *The study of personality.* New York: Holt, Rinehart and Winston, 1968.
Reiss, S. A critique of Thomas S. Szasz's The myth of mental illness. *American Journal of Psychiatry,* 1972 (March), *128:9.*

Rosenhan, D. L. On being sane in insane places. *Science*, 1973, *8:*218–223.

Rubin, H. T. Retain the juvenile court? *Crime and Delinquency*, 1979 (July) 25 (No. 3):31.

Sedgwick, P. Mental illness is *illness*. *Salmagundi*, 1972 (Summer–Fall) (No. 20).

Shaw, G. B. *The crime of imprisonment*. New York: Philosophical Library, 1946.

Shaw, S. Dangerousness. In *Perspectives in law and psychiatry*, New York: 1977.

Shetford Report, London: Govt. Printing Office, 1833.

Sosin, M. Perspective on the juvenile justice system. *Focus* (Institute for Research on Poverty) 1981 (Spring) *4* (No. 3).

Spiter, R. L. More on pseudoscience in science and the case for psychiatric diagnoses. *Archives of General Psychiatry*, 1976 (April), *3:*217–219.

State vs. Thompson, Wright's Ohio Report 617, 1834.

Szasz, T. S. *The myth of mental illness*. New York, Harper and Row, 1961.

Szasz, T. S. *The manufacture of madness*. New York: Harper and Row, 454, 1970.

Szasz, T. S. Criminal responsibility and psychiatry. In H. Toch (Ed.), *Legal and criminal psychiatry*. New York: Holt, Rinehart and Winston, 1961.

Tarasoff vs. Regents of the University of California, Sept. 131, Cap. Rptr., 14, 1976.

Taylor, S. Curbing civil liberties of the disturbed is no crime cure. *New York Times*, April 5, 1981, p. 4E.

Thompson, R. E. A validation of the Glueck prediction scale and proneness to delinquency. *Journal of Criminal Law, Criminology and Police Science*, 1952, *43:*431–470.

Tobias, J. J. *Crime and industrial society in the nineteenth century*. London: Pelican, 1972.

Ullman, J. *A judge takes the stand*. New York: Knopf, 1933.

United States vs Pollard, 17, Fed. Supp., 474, p. 481, 1964.

Wald, M. Children and the law. *Stanford Review*, 1980 (Winter).

In re Winship, 397, U.S. 358, 1970.

Washington vs. United States, 390, F. Ind., 444, D.C., 1967.

Subject Index